FAST AND CURIOUS

FAST AND CURIOUS

A History of Shortcuts in American Education

Robert L. Hampel

ROWMAN & LITTLEFIELD
Lanham • Boulder • New York • London

Published by Rowman & Littlefield
A wholly owned subsidiary of The Rowman & Littlefield Publishing Group, Inc.
4501 Forbes Boulevard, Suite 200, Lanham, Maryland 20706
www.rowman.com

Unit A, Whitacre Mews, 26-34 Stannary Street, London SE11 4AB

Copyright © 2017 by Robert L. Hampel

All rights reserved. No part of this book may be reproduced in any form or by any electronic or mechanical means, including information storage and retrieval systems, without written permission from the publisher, except by a reviewer who may quote passages in a review.

British Library Cataloguing in Publication Information Available

Library of Congress Cataloging-in-Publication Data

Names: Hampel, Robert L., author.
Title: Fast and curious : a history of shortcuts in American education / Robert L. Hampel.
Description: Lanham, Maryland : Rowman & Littlefield, 2018. | Includes bibliographical references and index.
Identifiers: LCCN 2017032035 (print) | LCCN 2017046154 (ebook) | ISBN 9781475836943 (electronic) | ISBN 9781475836929 (cloth : alk. paper) | ISBN 9781475836936 (pbk.)
Subjects: LCSH: Education—Experimental methods—United States—History. | Educational change—United States—History. | Educational innovations—United States—History.
Classification: LCC LB1027.3 (ebook) | LCC LB1027.3 .H363 2018 (print) | DDC 370.973—dc23
LC record available at https://lccn.loc.gov/2017032035

∞ ™ The paper used in this publication meets the minimum requirements of American National Standard for Information Sciences Permanence of Paper for Printed Library Materials, ANSI/NISO Z39.48-1992.

Printed in the United States of America

For my first mentors,
historians Michael F. Holt and Joel H. Silbey

✤ ✤ ✤

Before the gates of excellence the high gods have placed sweat; long is the road thereto, and rough and steep at first. But when the heights are reached, then there is ease, though grievously hard in the winning. —Hesiod

CONTENTS

Foreword ix
Acknowledgments xiii
Introduction xv

PART I: FASTER AND EASIER — 1
1. Shortcuts to Success: Correspondence Schools — 5
2. Shortcuts to Culture: From the Harvard Classics to Cliffs Notes — 45

PART II: FASTER AND HARDER — 73
3. Saving Time in Colleges and Universities — 77
4. The Zeal for Brevity: Simplified Spelling, Shorthand, and Speed-Reading — 125

Epilogue: The Enduring Appeal of Shortcuts — 153
Recommended Reading — 165
Index — 169
About the Author — 173

FOREWORD

In writing this book, Bob Hampel has accomplished a feat that I would have thought impossible. He has produced a wonderfully entertaining account of efforts by a series of entrepreneurs and scam artists—operating at the fringe of the massive American system of education—who tried to create quirky shortcuts for the laborious process of learning, and he has done so in a way that provides rich insight into the dynamics at the very core of this system. It turns out that the view from the periphery is remarkably revealing.

The cases he has assembled here run the gamut from correspondence schools and painting by numbers to speed-reading and shorthand and from the Harvard Five Foot Shelf and Classic Comics to abbreviated spelling and Trump University. But all of these widely divergent enterprises are responses to a single impulse: there must be a shortcut to learning, a way to work around the enormous time and effort required by traditional modes of education.

For this reason, the story Hampel tells is distinctively American. Where else in the world would so many people be looking so hard to find an easy way out of the learning process? This impulse has deep roots in the American psyche and has found broad expression in the American educational system. The reason for this is that we're a very practical people, more interested in making a living than in intellectual exploration. Toward this end, education is a means to an end rather than an end in itself. It's a necessary evil for everyone who wants to gain the social and economic benefits that schooling can provide: a good job, a reasonable income, and membership in the comfortable classes.

For that reason, we see education as a good investment. It's worth spending all of the time and money and effort required to get the credentials that will in turn open doors for opportunity and the good life. But wouldn't it be nice if there were an easier way to accomplish the same end? Why does it have to be so much work? Why do you have to spend 12 years in school and another four years or more in college, continually deferring your earning years long into the future while also accumulating debt? Wouldn't it be great if you could avoid suffering the endless series of teacher talk and assignments and tests and homework exercises that keep you from enjoying your time as a child and young adult? Wouldn't it be great if you could save yourself and your children from school-induced afflictions such as bullies, math anxiety, please-don't-call-on-me syndrome, writer's cramp, mean girls, burnouts, 11:15 lunch, and the inevitable paper cuts?

Americans tend to approach education the same way they approach buying a car. We want the most we can get for the money. We want the shiny car with all the bells and whistles, but we refuse to pay the full sticker price. That's for saps and suckers. Bargaining for a better deal is something that students learn early in their school careers. They learn to study strategically, focusing on the stuff that is most likely to be on the test and skipping the rest. They develop a canny ability to read the teacher, which then can save them from having to read the book. They focus their attention on the stuff about school that really matters—accumulating the grades and credits and degrees that can confer on them the extrinsic rewards the system has to offer. So shortcuts are built into American schooling.

This American preference for gaining the rewards of schooling without necessarily accumulating the learning that schools offer helps explain the wide array of efforts that various entrepreneurs have made to develop educational shortcuts. But it doesn't help explain why these efforts, for the most part, failed. If there was ever a promising market for shortcuts to learning, it would be the United States. Nearly all of the initiatives that Hampel presents in this book found a responsive audience and showed some of the elements of success. Harvard Classics and Cliffs Notes and Evelyn Wood's speed-reading classes and Famous Artists Schools found large numbers of customers who were willing to pay the freight.

The problem they faced was less a matter of willing customers than a matter of educational legitimacy. Educational credentials pay off only if everyone is willing to accept them as a proxy for learning. They need at least a modicum of credibility. And most of these efforts were hard to defend as serious educational enterprises. Cliffs Notes targeted like a laser on helping students pass the test without actually reading the book. The Famous Artists and Writers schools were hard pressed to demonstrate that anyone who took their courses would ever become a credible, much less famous, artist or writer. Correspondence schools, even the ones run by real universities, had trouble demonstrating that they were comparable to university courses taken for credit. You can read your way through the Harvard Classics, but that doesn't give you the equivalent of a bachelor's degree. You may be able to speed-read your way through the Bible in a single sitting, but it's hard to demonstrate that you really learned much from this process.

The problem that all of these enterprises confronted was the central premise of American higher education: universities give away knowledge, but they sell degrees. You can pick up all of the knowledge that university faculty generated by reading their publications, which are freely available at public libraries. However, if you want to attain formal certification that you have mastered this information, you will need to matriculate and pay to get a university degree.

Some of the problems faced by the entrepreneurs whom Hampel profiles came less from the illegitimacy of these enterprises than from their impracticality. One problem they faced was the classic barrier of sunk costs. Once you have gone through the laborious process of learning how to spell English words, why would you want to spend additional time learning Melvil Dewey's abbreviated spelling? A parallel issue is this: after learning to type using the QWERTY keyboard, why should you unlearn this in order to acquire skill at a more rationally designed keyboard? It's a lot easier to keep training students in this tradition than to require all former students to reeducate themselves. It takes people a long time to learn how to write English. Once you've mastered this task, why is it worth your while to invest a large amount of time in learning shorthand, whose promised long-term benefits come at the expense of a large up-front investment? If logical structure and ease of learning were such important values in the acquisition of language, then we would all be speaking Esperanto. Instead, we find that one of the world's languages with the quirkiest spelling and the most idioms, English, has become the global lingua franca. It's all about sunk costs.

We owe a debt of thanks to Bob Hampel for presenting all these issues to us so vividly and for using the perspective of shortcuts to reveal to us so much about the nature of the American system of education.

David F. Labaree
Lee L. Jacks Professor of Education
Stanford University

ACKNOWLEDGMENTS

No shortcut eliminates the need for historians to travel, so I thank the university archivists at Chicago, Columbia, Cornell, Harvard, Howard, Northwestern, Ohio State, Pennsylvania State, Princeton, Syracuse, Wisconsin, and Yale. Beyond the universities, Bard College at Simon's Rock let me use its small but excellent collection. My discussion of correspondence schools relied on the Distance Education and Training Council archives, the Hagley Museum, the National Museum of American History, the Normal Rockwell Museum, and the Smithsonian's Archives of American Art. The sections on shorthand, speed-reading, and Cliffs Notes would have been impossible without the materials in the New York Public Library, the Utah State Historical Society, and the Nebraska State Historical Society.

Browsing several other collections on my behalf, graduate students Rob Gross, Matt Kelly, Mario Perez, Sarah Schwebel, Kyle Steele, and Gail Wolfe sent detailed notes.

Special thanks to the people I interviewed. Austin Briggs Jr., Karl Decker, Randy Enos, Jak Kovatch, Charles Reid, and Warren Stadler recalled their years at the Famous Artists School, and David Apatoff shared stories about Albert Dorne, the founder of FAS. Robert Darling and I spoke twice about his work with Evelyn Wood. For the history of Cliffs Notes, I relied on Clifton Hillegass's daughter and son-in-law, Linda Hillegass and Jim McKee; former Cliffs Notes administrators Kelly Jo Hinrichs, Doug Lincoln, Rod Scher, and Richard Spellman; and former Cliffs Notes author Mary Ellen Snodgrass. The history of the doctor of arts degree benefited from conversations with historians Ted Fenton, John Modell, Tony Penna, and Joel Tarr.

The University of Delaware sustained me in many ways: sabbatical leaves, travel money, interlibrary loans, and remarkable students and colleagues in the School of Education.

Several friends sent advice on early drafts of this book. Norbert Elliot, Ken Finlayson, Ron Gallimore, Peter Haggerty, Ben Justice, Bill Lewis, Frank Murray, Bill Nemir, Scott Richardson, Steve Rodermel, and Jack Schneider convinced me to slow down. So did Arthur Powell, who read a later draft with painstaking care.

On the home front, Walter Cavers helped me step away from the desk to think about dinner, the garden, and the next episode of *House of Cards*. Every historian needs someone cherished who lives in the present but is willing to let the spouse dwell in the past. Thank you so much, Walter.

And from the distant past, I dedicate this book to the two men who believed in me when I took my first steps as an aspiring historian. "The Ohio Whig Party, 1848–1854" was my senior thesis at Yale, and it was my good fortune that Michael Holt was my adviser. Writing that paper convinced me I did not want to be a lawyer; I wanted to be like Professor Holt. At Cornell University, Joel Silbey made that possible. He pushed me to improve and expected me to revise, revise, and revise again. *Shortcut* was a word he never used.

INTRODUCTION

I began this book when a friend predicted that the invention of drugs would obliterate his field: educational psychology. No one would care about research on learning, he said, if a reputable pharmaceutical company figured out how to sharpen our minds. He was only half serious, but his joke sparked my interest in shortcuts. I started to explore the ways that Americans in the past tried to make education faster and easier.

For a long time, I read anything related to the topic rather than test a hypothesis or pick a few case studies. I roamed across the 19th and 20th centuries, and I also clipped articles from 21st-century newspapers and magazines. I included elementary and secondary schools along with colleges and universities, looking for shortcuts that saved hours as well as shortcuts that saved years. Cheating and fraud interested me; so did honest streamlining. I took notes on educational methods (how people learn) and educational outcomes (the results of learning regardless of the methods used). I even made a folder for pharmaceutical shortcuts. At times, it felt like the only place I hadn't looked was overseas—several people assured me that shortcuts were distinctly American, although one friend tempted me to keep searching when he said that Plato had argued that writing was a shortcut, a treacherous one that jeopardized the ability to memorize.

As I reread my notes to make sense of the accumulation, I was struck by how many shortcutters dissented from the late 19th- and early 20th-century consensus among American educators that longer was better.

Did all students have to be in residence or in class for so many years? Why not create a less rigid world where the pursuit of skills, knowledge, and credentials could happen on the students' terms? Why should professors and administrators dictate how, where, and when learning must take place? A new system had taken shape, and not everyone embraced it. Within that system, educators thought they offered a vast array of options, but I was seeing another perspective—many people wanted more choices, especially choices that would let them save time. Traditional schooling was criticized as unnecessarily cumbersome, out of step with an ingenious country proud of conveniences like instant coffee and overnight mail.

One type of time-saver claimed to be both faster and easier than the typical routes students were expected or required to take. The first part of this book looks at the evolution of two of those pathways: correspondence schools and shortcuts to culture. Their hyperbolic advocates promised many benefits; for instance, not only would their wares be fast and easy, but they would be fun, practical, and cheap. The caliber of what they offered varied enormously—was it truly education? genuine culture?—and many people gave up so quickly that the pathway took them nowhere. The shortcut that many people needed most was a keen skepticism of inflated and misleading appeals designed to get them to spend money.

A second type of time-saver offered speed for the price of hard work. These shortcuts would not be easier. For instance, finishing college in three years or learning shorthand took drive and discipline. Often promoted with much less hype than the faster-easier options, the faster-harder opportunities aroused less interest than their proponents expected. Only a small fraction of those eligible to accelerate chose to do so, and that is the story of the second half of this book.

And so the allegedly cumbersome educational system remained in place. With a few shortcuts available for the jackrabbits, most Americans accepted the traditional time lines. When students sought ways to save time, they usually did so within the customary structures—sign up for an easy course, borrow a friend's lecture notes, get the English translation of a French novel, or skim an assignment. Those little efficiencies were more attractive than skipping a year or learning by mail. Most students inside the lockstep had the freedom to decide how much effort to exert.

Because I eventually concentrated on the faster-easier and faster-harder types of shortcuts, I did not include many other shortcuts in these pages. I focused on those that emerged in reaction to the steady growth of higher education in the late 19th to mid-20th century, and thus I say very little about elementary or secondary schools; when I do discuss teenagers, it's usually around a shortcut that also appealed to many adults. Nor do I examine shortcuts that totally renounced effort, such as playing foreign language tapes while asleep or buying papers someone else wrote.

Experts in other fields could approach shortcuts in different ways, as psychologist Daniel Kahneman did in *Thinking, Fast and Slow*.[1] He studied snap judgments and gut feelings; people use many shortcuts that he called *heuristics*, simple procedures to answer difficult questions. Kahneman did not explore colleges, schools, or change over time; his remarkable laboratory work on the strengths and weaknesses of intuition looked at decisions made at work and at home. These pages, in contrast, go inside the enterprises in the past that tried to convince Americans that it was possible and desirable to pick up the pace of their education.

One of my own shortcuts will be obvious in each chapter: some of the examples are much shorter than others. The longer cases derive from previously overlooked archival sources. For instance, the Famous Artists correspondence schools get more space than Mortimer Adler, the *great books* cheerleader for whom there is a good biography in print. The sections with more detail are my reconnaissance of new territory, where I hope the specifics will bring to life the major themes for readers unfamiliar with the history of American education.

NOTE

1. Daniel Kahneman, *Thinking, Fast and Slow* (New York: Farrar, Straus and Giroux, 2011). For a recent biography of Kahneman and his collaborator Amos Tversky, see Michael Lewis, *The Undoing Project: A Friendship That Changed Our Minds* (New York: Norton, 2017).

Part I

Faster and Easier

From the 1890s on, several hundred companies and individuals, along with dozens of colleges and universities, offered instruction through the mail. Home study was particularly popular with young adults whose formal education ended in high school and later decided they wanted more. As one earnest student wrote, "Now our schooling may seem crude, we are daily conscious of small mistakes, frequently disobeying the laws of very finely discriminating grammarian[s], or now and then misspelling a word, our phraseology may not be smooth and fluent like a collegian's (and very likely devoid of his slang) yet the foundations are being laid for a substantial education."[1] By the mid-1920s, when home study enrollments per capita peaked, almost 500,000 people signed up each year. In comparison, the entire undergraduate college enrollment in 1925–1926 was just over 900,000.

Home study enthusiasts set forth enticing ways the new students would benefit. Not only would it be faster and easier (and cheaper) than going back to school or college, it might even be better. Useful secrets would be revealed—home study offered access to the tricks of the trade known only to the experts, and those experts who wrote the lessons and graded the assignments were men of experience, skillful practitioners rather than out-of-touch academics. Moreover, postal education would be more pleasant than life inside classrooms—less regimentation, simple textbooks, friendly teachers, and much higher grades.

The reward desired by most correspondence school students was in the job market. The vast majority of the courses were vocational. The largest schools attracted the men who wanted to learn the specific skills necessary for a promotion or self-employment. For blue-collar laborers, home study promised, as one ad put it, "better positions, high salaries, and more hopeful lives" for the "men with little schooling; men in 'dollar a day' positions; men with no hope of anything better."[2] Farmers could improve their productivity by virtue of books like *Horses, Cattle, Sheep, and Swine* or *Talks on Manure* or even a course about culture—as in fruit culture. For white-collar workers, $5,000 a year in the 1920s could grow to $10,000 even if they lacked a college degree. An aspiring artist or writer could earn freelance fees far beyond the tuition payments.

The largest 20th-century correspondence school, Famous Artists, connected its students with Norman Rockwell, the famous illustrator, and other eminent members of the guiding faculty. Created in 1948, the new school expanded rapidly and offered work in cartooning, photography, and writing, the most popular Famous option in the 1960s. What a thrill to think that the suave host of *The Twilight Zone*, Rod Serling, wrote several of your lessons and might even read your work. How exciting was it that Bennett Cerf, one of the panelists on television's *What's My Line?*, would be "at your shoulder," as one advertisement put it. The first chapter opens and closes with the rise and fall of the Famous Artists and Famous Writers, punctuated by comparisons to other proprietary schools as well as university home study departments at Columbia, Chicago, and Wisconsin.

Grand enticements also attracted men and women interested in another type of home study—acquiring on one's own what was known in the early 20th century as liberal culture. The equivalent of a college education could be acquired by reading the landmark classics of Western civilization, the *great books* chosen by well-known scholars. If those were too daunting, then simple summaries abounded in the 1920s, and by the 1940s, Classic Comics made the work even simpler.

Culture was so inviting because it had multiple meanings. For instance, my grandfather read the Harvard Classics to exercise a very good mind that never took a college course—his parents barely made ends meet let alone pay tuition for seven children. When my mother inherited those books, she put them on a hallway shelf where her friends could see these serious books that in her opinion were one more sign of her rise to the upper rungs of the middle class. From her reverential comments about those tattered old books, I got the point that culture was a Good Thing respected by the Right People. But as a child, I was interested in entertainment, so I thought I could make culture fun by getting a paint-by-numbers kit. Each section of each sheet was coded to show which color went where, and the set conveniently included premixed paints and several brushes. Why shouldn't I try it since President Eisenhower's staff had received paint-by-numbers kits as a Christmas gift several years earlier? By high school, I had another interest in culture—I saw it in terms of good grades. I wanted to earn enough As to get into selective colleges. As a sophomore pained by *The Iliad*, I bought the Cliffs Notes summary. I hid the small yellow pamphlet in my notebook; my teacher had said that the Notes were despicable, which had increased my desire to read them.

Culture as enlightenment for the partially educated, *culture* as status symbols for the upwardly mobile, *culture* as fun for the naive, *culture* as good grades—the word meant different things at different times to different people in the Hampel family. What each generation shared was the conviction that culture was desirable, whatever it was. Anyone credible who could assure us that it was within reach had our attention. Months and years of classroom instruction were not necessary, many advertisements claimed, to have a share of what the very well-educated possessed. Culture without endless effort: that is the topic of the second chapter.

Most vendors of home study and cultural uplift were aggressive salesmen, and at times these chapters might feel like a history of business, not education. Adroit advertising and savvy marketing played on the aspirations of men and women who wanted to improve their lot in life. The enticements often seemed 100 percent American—helping a nation of strivers eager to get ahead, expanding a democracy where no elites monopolized the better things in life—and they deftly echoed the exhortations of mainstream educators, who also urged their students to dream of a better life as a result of conscientious work.

But the shortcut pitches made extravagant and deceptive claims for their products and the dramatic results that would ensue. As they aroused hope, they also created unrealistic visions of what could be accomplished. *Buyer beware* should have been on the minds of everyone who opened a matchbook cover and saw an ad for an amazing new way to change their lives.

NOTES

1. Allen Chaplin to G. C. Watson, January 2, 1897, in Correspondence Courses in Agriculture, 1892–1908, Record Group 17, Pennsylvania State University Archives.
2. "STEP OUT of the Dinner-Pail Class" (1908) from the N. W. Ayer Collection, Box 77, National Museum of American History, Washington, D.C.

I

SHORTCUTS TO SUCCESS

Correspondence Schools

In the fall of 1950, Sydney Newbold in Richmond, Virginia, sent the nation's most famous illustrator a drawing of a girl holding a piece of bread. In return, Mr. Newbold received a one-page letter from Norman Rockwell. After two sentences praising the colors, Rockwell complained that no one who saw it would want to buy bread. "The picture of a pretty child holding a piece of bread does not make a bread advertisement." The girl should express either surprise or satisfaction; the ad should be clear and forceful. "Remember, no advertising illustration is successful unless it accomplishes its main purpose—that of *selling*."[1]

Why was Norman Rockwell reviewing the work of a stranger when he could have finished another *Saturday Evening Post* magazine cover or sketched his Boy Scout calendar, which usually sold 2 million copies? In 1948, he joined the new Institute of Commercial Art, a correspondence school in Westport, Connecticut, begun by illustrator Albert Dorne, an energetic man who loved women (four wives), luxury (custom-made British suits and Italian shoes), dark liquor ("white wine is for sissies"), and hard work (including prizefights at age 16 as he taught himself how to draw).[2] Students in the advanced courses could pick their instructors; when 90 percent chose Rockwell, the faculty recast the curriculum to balance the workload. For his participation, Rockwell received stock in the privately held company; he also split with the other 11 faculty 2 percent of the annual revenue. The institute grew so quickly that Rockwell and his 11 peers soon became the *guiding faculty* in the Famous Artists School, a new name that broadcast the prominence of the 12 artists who wrote the lessons, advised the officers, and came to Westport four times a year to coach the dozens of instructors hired to do the day-to-day work. Correspondence schools to teach art did not begin in the 1940s, but the link with eminent artists was a fresh and powerful strategy. Who could doubt the legitimacy of an enterprise sanctioned by well-known and well-respected creative giants? In the second year, almost 3,000 students enrolled.

Throughout the 1950s, the school expanded steadily. In only one year was the growth rate less than 20 percent. A new course in painting helped boost enrollment; so did a course in cartooning begun by Rube Goldberg (who in 1948 optimistically thought his annual stipend would exceed $90,000) and finished by the artist who drew Popeye and Olive Oyl.[3] The instructors respected Dorne, admired the textbooks, found time for their own creative pursuits, and thought that the daily workload—tissue overlay corrections and dictated letters—was reasonable.[4]

By 1960, the annual revenue, $7 million, was eight times the sales of 1950. Dorne bought a New York City duplex with a distant view of the tenement where his mother had scrubbed floors, and the $200 monthly check Rockwell received in 1950 quadrupled by 1960.[5]

"I see no reason why we shouldn't eventually have 2,000,000 students," Dorne said in 1961.[6] He recruited Richard Avedon, Alfred Eisenstadt, and other outstanding photographers to start the Famous Photographers School, but the more popular new option was the Famous Writers School, offering three-year courses in fiction, nonfiction, advertising, and business writing. Before the end of its first year, the director said that the school of 3,000 would "soon be bigger than Princeton."[7] He could have said "very soon and much bigger": within three years, the *enrollment counselors* for the Famous Writers School—full-time salesmen working on commission—had signed up 21,557 students (70 percent chose the fiction course) and the numbers kept rising throughout the 1960s.

The growth would not have been so rapid without extensive and enticing advertising. The for-profit schools, which had the lion's share of the home study market, did not wait for prospects to inquire; they created and heightened the demand for their wares. As a result, the money that Dorne spent each year on sales and marketing took approximately 40 percent of the annual revenues, at least twice the amount allocated for texts and teachers.[8]

The career of John Caples, one of the Famous Writers guiding faculty, illustrates the importance of savvy advertising for successful correspondence schools. Sell the product or sell its benefits to the buyer? By the 1920s, when Caples got started, more and more ads for all kinds of merchandise proclaimed the astonishing results from using the item instead of just describing its attributes, as most 19th-century ads had done. The object was now less important than the fulfillment it brought. The copy played on fears ("What Will *You* Do at 50?") but usually offered dreams ("Step Out of the Dinner-Pail Class").[9]

The visual layout of early 20th-century ads invited fantasies of happiness and success. Larger headlines, longer text, bolder colors, and lavish illustrations promised serenity and security in an allegedly bewildering and rapidly changing world. One historian who read 180,000 ads from the 1920s and 1930s called advertisers the "coach and confidante" of anxious people.[10]

John Caples was one of those coach–confidantes. In 1925, he joined an agency that specialized in mail-order accounts. One of its founders wrote patent medicine ads until most newspapers and magazines refused to print them, but the firm retained the same ailment–cure approach for its other accounts. Caples began with an ad for a home study course in "personal magnetism," then wrote one for dance lessons. He made his mark with two widely admired pieces for language and music lessons—"They Grinned When the Waiter Spoke to Me in French" and "They Laughed When I Sat Down at the Piano." Home study would end embarrassment and ridicule.

His mother wasn't so sure: "Can people really learn to play the piano by mail? Does this book really give people a magnetic personality? You better not let your father see this." But Caples agreed with his boss— "Most people are lazy. They want a quick, easy way to solve their problems." Assume that readers have the intelligence of a child, Caples wrote in 1931. As he later said, "Don't force the reader to think. Do his thinking for him."[11]

Caples carefully analyzed why some ads "pulled" and others did not. The legendary copywriter Bruce Barton wrote several ads for the Alexander Hamilton Institute, a large correspondence school in New York City. "The Years That the Locust Hath Eaten" impressed the institute's salesmen and officers, but few readers returned the coupon. Caples explained why. The headline offered nothing of value, and the image of a locust sitting on half a leaf was misplaced—"this picture belongs in an insecticide ad." The text was depressing rather than hopeful.

In contrast, another Alexander Hamilton ad Barton wrote did well. "A wonderful two years' trip at full pay—but only men with imagination can take it" had a fine headline—a reward along with a challenge. It was specific and cheerful, and unlike the locust ad, it addressed men, the market for Hamilton's business courses. Why did "To a $5,000 man who would like to be making $10,000" bring Alexander Hamilton four times as many coupons as "To men who want to work less and earn more?" It captured attention with a tangible benefit. "If the headline doesn't stop people, the copy might as well be written in Greek."[12]

Charles Revson once told his staff that they were not selling Revlon skin cream, lipstick, mascara, and other cosmetics—they were selling *hope*.[13] Dreams of a better life were also at the heart of the correspondence school ads, and Famous Artists was no exception. The school could have praised its courses as a good hobby—learn how to draw, paint, or write proficiently to make your spare time more enjoyable. That was not the message it emphasized. The courses promised to make middle-class men and women happier, and they also held out the prospect of making money. Those goals were certainly not unknown in traditional higher education, but the correspondence schools featured them much more prominently.

"It's a wonderful life. No commuter trains to catch, no office routine. Whether I'm at home, or abroad on assignment, I write from 8 a.m. to noon every day—no more, no less." That ad showed freelance writer Jack Ratcliff walking his dog in the woods, "where he conceives many of the articles" he will publish. In another ad, humor writer Max Shulman is also outdoors, sitting at his typewriter. Neither man wears a tie.

One Shulman ad considers the possibility of radical change— "Should your husband give up his job to become the writer he's always wanted to be?" Like other aspiring writers, he feels chained to "an ordinary job" and is thus like "a caged beast." But he has "responsibilities" alongside his "restless urge" to write, so the Famous Writers course offers a "middle way"—he can still be a dutiful husband, father, and employee while he learns to write in his spare time at home.

The message was subtle but unmistakable: many men are unfulfilled, they stifle the desire to write, and now they can let loose—without turning their backs on family and work to become beatniks, hippies, or other stereotypical forms of creativity that the Famous Writers School ads never mentioned. The writer was a free spirit but not a rebel.[14]

The same cautious jabs at conformity marked the ads that featured women. "It's a shame more women don't take up writing," according to Faith Baldwin. She raised four children while writing 80 books, but too many wives bury their talent "under a mountain of dishes" because they are "tied down" to the house. In another ad, a couple stares at a television set. They will "fritter away their lives" by spending 55 hours each month in front of the "boob tube" (where three of the guiding faculty—Bennett Cerf, Rod Serling, and Bergen Evans—had national TV shows). Years later, she will lean back and say to no one in particular, "I always wanted to write; I wonder why I never did."

A third ad reassured husbands: "Why are you so afraid of your wife becoming a writer?" If her days are "more fun, she's going to be happy. And when she's happy, you're happy, right?" She won't burn dinner or neglect the children. In fact, women with "fulfilling and productive outside interests are often *better* wives and mothers than those who regard themselves as housewives and nothing else," a point underscored by another ad reporting that the woman who sold three articles to *Reader's Digest* used the money to pay for her family's vacation. The booklet that was sent to prospective students offered additional reassurance in the picture of an immaculately dressed young woman sitting in front of a typewriter. On her tidy desk was a hallmark of conventional femininity—a silver coffeepot and creamer on a tray next to a saucer and a coffee cup.[15]

As the ads spoke to the widespread yearning to enliven but not abandon middle-class respectability in the prosperous 1950s and 1960s, they also reinforced traditional notions of success by celebrating money. Writing paid well. Famous Writers ads profiled current and former students who had sold their work, including how much they earned. The quarterly magazine that was sent to every student began with the pictures and short biographies of their peers who broke into print. *How to Turn Your Writing into Dollars* offered specific marketing tips (e.g., how to write a letter of inquiry to an editor) and also included 42 pages to incite dreams of what might be—copyright forms and sample contracts for books, television shows, and Hollywood agents.[16] After all, the "Your Future as a Writer" pamphlet claimed that "everything you need to know to be a successful writer is in your course," and so "you could become one of the famous writers of tomorrow."[17]

Future artists saw similar messages. "A Fascinating Money-Making Art Career Can Be Yours" promised one ad that featured Norman Rockwell. "They DREW their way from Rags to Riches—Now they're helping others do the same" depicted Rockwell and five other guiding faculty who came from modest backgrounds.

What would bring about the transformation from novice to expert? It wasn't a track record of previous accomplishments. The Famous Writers accepted approximately 90 percent of the people who took a short aptitude test—edit five verbose sentences, correct three errors of syntax, finish six similes, fill in the blanks from a short story, write 150 words about a memorable experience, and answer 23 questions to see if "you have a sincere desire to write and a willingness to learn, the two most important attributes for a student of writing."[18]

No transcripts, letters of recommendation, or standardized test scores were required. College or even high school graduation was not necessary, unlike many careers where the traditional credentials were required (especially as higher education expanded rapidly in the 1950s and 1960s). Short on ideas? Write about "your own unique experiences."[19] Unlike selective campuses where desire by itself was not enough to get in, the Famous schools claimed that nearly everyone who truly wanted to change their lives could do so.

But they should not try to do it alone. "Only successful artists can teach successful art"—that line was stamped on the faculty biographies in the salesmen's kit.[20] Only the successful knew the "tricks of the trade" and could share "the insider's knowledge of how the thing is done."[21] What the insiders knew, above all, were practical strategies. None of the instructors was ever called "doctor," very few had been professors, but all of them had what counted most: experience as writers. Throughout the materials from Famous Writers (and earlier correspondence schools) was a bias against theory. Eliminate whatever had no obvious bearing on immediate applications; focus instead on helpful pointers and useful tips. As a result, the curriculum was usually leaner than college fare. The Famous Writers students, for instance, needed only four books for their three-year course.

The lessons made another assumption: learning is linear. A student should make step-by-step progress, doing the assignments in the exact order and the precise manner stipulated by the correspondence school. Background knowledge and prior experience required no adjustments, nor did individual learning styles. The Famous schools (and their predecessors) rarely considered the possibility that the developing mind zigzags, with leaps of insight as well as bouts of confusion, rather than moves straight ahead. The guiding faculty acknowledged that their own careers had "fumbling and searching, false starts, delays [and] blind alley ventures," but the fortunate students would be spared what they had endured.[22]

And a third assumption pervaded the home study literature: students learn well without the company of other students. Classmates could be a distraction—who needs to listen to them talk about their writing?—or an obstacle if everyone had to wait for the slowpokes to catch up. It is striking how few correspondence schools ever tried what today is known as *hybrid* instruction—some sessions online, other sessions face-to-face. Several students suggested local clubs of Famous students; in response, the officers said that the quarterly magazine was the equivalent.[23] Several thousand students each year visited the Westport headquarters; they got a tour rather than a session with their instructors. If they had talked with the instructors, they might have sensed the value of learning alongside other artists. The younger teachers discussed their own projects at lunch, gathered for sketching sessions after work, received advice from the guiding faculty, took vacation days to show their work to art directors, and as a result benefited from the frequent give-and-take with peers and mentors.

Sold as a fast track to proficiency and success, the home study approach to learning—practical lessons, step-by-step progress, and solitary work—fell short for a majority of the students. Only a small fraction of the recruits completed the courses, and even fewer reaped what one ad called the "infinite possibilities" awaiting the graduates.[24] In one Famous Artists course, so rarely did students send a lesson in the teens or higher (there were 24 in all) that other instructors would walk across the room to see it.[25] Several estimates put the average graduation rates for all correspondence schools between 5 and 15 percent; the Famous schools said that their success was higher, around 25 percent, but that still made possible an instructor-to-student ratio of 1 to 700.

Attrition was a problem—home study was supposed to be faster and easier than life in classrooms—but attrition was also a blessing. All the dropouts were expected to pay for what they no longer wanted. Refunds were hard to get. Most of the students borrowed some or all of the fee (which was the equivalent of $4,000 today), and the Famous schools had them sign a legally binding contract to repay the entire loan, with interest, to a bank.[26]

Returning the books made no difference; one room of the Westport headquarters had a large bin for texts mailed back in the hope of escaping the contract.[27] Rather than a refund, the delinquents would get increasingly stern payment-due letters, some signed by lawyers, others sent from a collection agency. The profitability of correspondence schools hinged on the dropouts who paid for what they no longer wanted.

Even after deducting 10 to 12 percent of annual sales for unpaid accounts, the Famous Schools made money year after year. Sales and profits grew steadily, increasing by 20 to 30 percent annually in the early and mid-1960s. Dorne's salary exceeded $100,000, more than enough to supply the built-in bar in the backseat of his Mercedes. The stock began to trade publicly in 1961, and the price doubled by 1965, when the publishing firm Crowell Collier, owner of several correspondence schools, offered to buy one-sixth of the shares at a 25 percent premium.

"I am certainly not selling any of my stock," Norman Rockwell told Albert Dorne.[28] By 1965, his slice was worth $600,000, and his monthly stipend was $1,300. The stock kept rising. Rockwell wondered in 1966 if the company should merge with a large corporation—at age 72, "security is the biggest item" in life.[29] But he did not part with any of his 25,000 shares, and by late 1967 the market value of his stake was almost $1,800,000, the equivalent of $12,500,000 in 2017.

DISTINCTIONS BETWEEN THE WORTHY AND THE UNWORTHY

Before tracing the fate of the Rockwell fortune, the next two sections examine the rise of correspondence schools, the ethical lapses common by the 1920s, and the enduring ability of the proprietary schools, despite their unsavory reputation, to enroll far more students than the home study divisions of prominent colleges and universities. It is a story of the pursuit of wealth in a lightly regulated marketplace, an alluring opportunity for many correspondence schools to achieve the sort of success (and then some) that they assured their students would come their way.

Correspondence schooling in America began with a good reputation when it emerged in the 1870s. The pioneers were altruistic rather than mercenary. Home study rarely promised vocational rewards, and it attracted far more women than men.

The Society to Encourage Studies at Home was started in 1873 by Anna Ticknor, the daughter of a Harvard professor and cousin of Harvard's president. Inspired by a home study society in England, Ticknor recruited a small group of upper-class women to comment on the "memory notes"—recollections of the previous day's reading—from women across the country, women who paid $2 to undertake the equivalent of a liberal arts education, especially history, art, French and German literature, and natural science. The unpaid teachers offered encouragement and friendship rather than simply correcting errors. Affectionate letters suggest that the society bolstered self-confidence in an age when higher education for women was sparse. Earning marketable credentials was not the goal.[30]

Another way for women to connect with other women was through a Chautauqua Literary and Scientific Circle. Chautauqua began in the 1870s as a combination of summer vacation, religious retreat, and academic institute. For several weeks in western New York, families could play, pray, and study. All forms of knowledge were sacred, and education would *awaken, elevate, quicken,* and *inspire* the heart and the mind, according to a Methodist bishop who cofounded Chautauqua.[31]

As it grew, one of Chautauqua's most popular offshoots was the reading group, the circle, to discuss the books and submit papers in a four-year course emphasizing literature and history. During the circle meetings, the members would summarize the assignment, define difficult words, read short essays they wrote, hold a debate, discuss contemporary topics, and occasionally sing.[32] Although some women (approximately 85 percent of the circle Chautauquans were female) used what they learned to qualify as schoolteachers, vocational benefits attracted fewer members than the chance to take the equivalent of the liberal arts education offered by most high schools and colleges.[33] Like Ticknor's society, the work was especially popular in small villages and isolated areas, where educational opportunities were meager.

Chautauqua demonstrated the popularity of home study—it attracted several hundred thousand students over 20 years—and it also established its legitimacy. Although some critics said that the circles superficially covered too much too quickly (including controversial public policy issues best left to the men), no one argued that Chautauqua was a fraud.

In the 1890s, vocational training for men began to overshadow the general education of women through home study. Finding a better job and earning more money were the reasons most people bought a course. In the shifting workforce of a rapidly industrializing and (after the mid-1890s depression) vibrant economy, good new jobs attracted the attention of employed adults who could not quit working to acquire the skills needed to get ahead.

The International Correspondence Schools (ICS) dominated the field by promising bright futures, including salaried desk jobs, for unskilled and semiskilled laborers.[34] As its founder told his advertising manager, "We are not selling education. We are selling the better job and the better pay that special training will bring."[35] The headlines on the ICS ads were not bashful: "Boys—Get the Fat Pay Envelope," "The Trained Man Wins," "We're Going to Raise Your Salary," "On Which Side of the Desk Are YOU?," "Here Is a List of Good Positions—Which Do YOU Want?," and other words of encouragement for Americans, especially white American men, to aspire far beyond their current stations.[36]

No wonder the ICS student magazine was titled *Ambition*. It was a time when the avenues of upward mobility expanded—and gave the appearance of expanding even more than they actually did.[37] As high school and college enrollments surged from the 1890s on, even those who did not graduate could seek second chances. The prosperity of late

19th- and early 20th-century America encouraged millions to have high aspirations, including the desire to reshape leisure in the direction of middle-class norms. Courses could be purchased in foreign languages, social skills, fashion, music, and so on. For instance, the popular Arthur Murray dance studios began as correspondence courses, and an Institute of Charm helped young women make small talk at parties.

By the 1920s, annual enrollment in the several hundred correspondence schools exceeded the number of freshmen on college campuses.[38] By then, home study was no longer dominated by women meeting in small groups to pursue liberal education—men who took vocational courses independently of one another had become the mainstay.

With few restrictions on who could sell courses, the number of unscrupulous and unethical vendors increased rapidly. "An appallingly large proportion of the schools are little better than frauds," according to John Noffsinger's 1926 book.[39] The reputable schools felt that unless their unsavory counterparts reformed or closed, the public would distrust every correspondence school.

Eleven schools in 1926 created the National Home Study Council (NHSC), the first trade association for proprietary correspondence schools. The organization tried to draw a sharper line between the honorable and the dishonorable. "I very much hope that some appropriate distinction can be made between the worthy and the unworthy institutions," an officer of LaSalle Extension told Frederick Keppel, the president of the Carnegie Corporation, when that philanthropy coordinated the formation of NHSC.[40]

John Noffsinger, whose book Carnegie commissioned, was Keppel's choice for executive secretary, although he was stunned to learn that in October 1925, Noffsinger, his wife, and three partners had opened the University of Washington in the District of Columbia, offering both residential and correspondence work in history, psychology, sociology, pedagogy, philosophy, education, and "the various arts and sciences." Noffsinger stayed in Keppel's good graces when he reluctantly agreed to abandon the venture. "Prospects were in sight, at a conservative estimate, of from $10,000 to $15,000 for the first year. What the future might have been one can only conjecture . . . [now I have] an empty purse and a clear conscience."[41]

Noffsinger and the founding members of NHSC helped the Federal Trade Commission (FTC) write 26 rules of ethical conduct in 1927. The first four rules targeted the heart of the schools' marketing: the financial gains awaiting graduates. Exaggerating the number of vacancies in a field, inflating the average salaries in an occupation, promising promotions or pay raises, and misrepresenting the schools' employment services were all forbidden. Deceptive inducements to enroll were also prohibited—bogus tuition discounts, false limited-time offers, specious scholarships, misuse of the word *free*, placing ads in newspapers' help-wanted columns, and money-back guarantees omitting the terms of the refund.

Misleading assertions about the school included names ("a correspondence school is not a plant, factory, association, laboratory, or shop"), pictures (shots of buildings in which the school occupied little or no space), and collection letters designed as court documents. Moreover, the curriculum could not be distorted ("a wonderful new method that teaches [music] in half the time"), and the same was true for the instructors (false pledges of personal attention from the head or founder were unacceptable). The scope of the 26 rules was far reaching, and every magazine that published home study ads received a copy.[42]

By the start of World War II, the FTC sanctioned 15 of the council schools for code violations. As part of the 194 correspondence schools punished by the FTC in those years, 15 was a small number, but the 15 offenders constituted 23 percent of the 64 schools that belonged to the NHSC at one time or another in those years.[43]

Hyperbolic ads triggered most of the FTC's cease-and-desist orders, including three for the largest NHSC schools. "We can make you superintendent" was unacceptable, even if it was relatively tame compared with ICS ads earlier in the century that dangled cash ("double, triple, and quadruple" salaries from training that "ensures you more money now") in return for minimal effort ("all that is required of you is the ability to read and write" to understand "the surest, quickest, and easiest way in the world" to become an "expert"). LaSalle Extension was told to stop claiming that it ran a university (it had some evening classes in Chicago), and the American School had to abandon promises of promotions and 50 percent salary increases. Noffsinger compiled and published the cease-and-desist orders with the names of each offender, and he warned the members that what they might consider harmless *puffing* could be interpreted as lies.[44]

Another form of marketing tarnished the reputations of schools within the NHSC, where 60 percent of the members employed salesmen. ICS had demonstrated the benefits of a sales force in the late 1890s. Enrollment of 6,530 in 1896 soared to 71,885 in 1899 after hiring agents in the second half of 1897.[45] In many schools, zealous salesmen did whatever they felt was necessary to generate commissions. Prospects who were too young, too poor, and too uneducated were assured that they qualified for a course. The career opportunities and average wages for graduates were often inflated or invented; some brash salesmen even promised good jobs with a particular company on completion. When civil service correspondence schools burgeoned as President Franklin Roosevelt's New Deal expanded federal employment, salesmen of those schools occasionally posed as government workers.[46]

Aside from the hard sell by brazen ads and agents, what else hurt the reputation of the schools within and outside the NHSC? Prying money from the dropouts cast many schools as heartless, especially when the economy withered in the 1930s.

Most schools required students who lacked the full fee to sign a legally binding contract obligating them to pay even if they stopped sending lessons or returned the books. Installment sales for automobiles, furniture, record players, and household appliances pervaded America by the 1920s, and most correspondence students enrolled that way.[47] To collect what they were owed, the schools relied on three strategies: persuasion through letters, pressure from collection departments (or outside agencies), and coercion by lawsuits.

Convincing the debtors to pay was a form of instruction by mail that the schools tried to perfect. Delinquents received letter after letter, beginning with friendly reminders of the wonderful results of home study. Sterner warnings ensued if the initial efforts failed, and the pressure came from several directions. At LaSalle Extension, the second-largest school in the 1930s, the head of collections often wrote to the employers of students who had not paid, including excerpts of letters sent by the students to LaSalle. LaSalle also sent letters from attorneys, sometimes offering to settle the account for partial payment, sometimes threatening to invoke state law to garnish wages.

But severity was not a surefire tactic. LaSalle set aside almost two-fifths of its new sales each year as a reserve against unpaid fees.[48] Moreover, the firm suffered a setback when the Nebraska Supreme Court in 1934 affirmed lower-court rulings that fined LaSalle $500 for the mental anguish caused by 40 letters over almost two years to James Fogarty as well as two notes to his neighbors besmirching his integrity. Several grim letters to Fogarty arrived in bright red envelopes emblazoned with bolts of lightning.[49]

Lawsuits were another option. The schools preferred to threaten legal action rather than carry it out, but they felt it was useful to sue now and then to establish the fact that it could happen. Usually the defendant would plead poverty, change of employment, misrepresentation by the salesman, or other plausible reasons to stop, and his friends and relatives would then see the school, not the student, as the wrongdoer. The accounts that were referred to lawyers yielded a small fraction of the unpaid fees, not enough to offset the bad publicity from cases where the student should never have been enrolled in NHSC schools in the first place: a boy in grade school (who died after several lessons—his father had to pay the full tuition plus interest and court costs), a mother of five whose husband earned $54 a month (she gave birth and stopped payments), a 17-year-old Italian boy with one-half year of night school (his illiterate mother cosigned the contract), and a girl who was told to sign a paper to get more information (she signed a contract and lost the court case).[50]

In short, misleading advertising, aggressive selling, and relentless collecting afflicted a wide range of correspondence schools. Seeing quick and easy profits in this mail-order business, hundreds of shameless pied pipers lured the naive and cheated the trustful. Deceitful schools hurt the reputation of all schools, but even the older and largest schools periodically fell short of the standards they said they honored.

For students interested in taking a shortcut, who will guarantee the legitimacy of what they buy? Where is the line between truth and illusion, fact and fantasy? For instance, did good health actually require Charles Atlas's regimen of nude sunbaths, milk every hour, occasional enemas, and a cold, wet cloth on the genitals each morning?[51] If Lawrence Welk learned to play the accordion thanks to the U.S. School of Music, could anyone "play by note the instrument he likes best and become an accomplished and welcome member of any society."[52]

When education is bought and sold in the marketplace, what type of regulation is possible when the educators' peer review falters?

Caveat emptor (let the buyer beware) was the answer to those questions. There wasn't much oversight of home study. The consumers had to rely on their own judgment. Unlike shoppers for appliances, cars, food, clothing, and other household goods, home study prospects lacked the equivalent of the Consumers' Research bulletins that evaluated a wide range of products. A local Better Business Bureau could investigate and possibly alert the post office to a case of mail fraud, but by then the damage had been done. State laws offered some protection—often they required the proprietary schools to submit lessons, ads, contracts, and other evidence of legitimacy—but enforcement was sporadic. The main effect of state laws stiffened the requirements for licensure in many occupations—for instance, accounting attracted thousands of home study students in the early 20th century, but by the 1930s most states required two or four years of college, not just success on an examination previously open to anyone.

Entering a field with a long history of questionable practices, a legitimate new home study school at mid-century would want to establish its integrity and set itself apart as completely ethical. That is what the Famous Artists School tried to do. The founder, Albert Dorne, compared the school to its major rival: Art Instruction (where "Peanuts" cartoonist Charles Schulz was an instructor from 1946 to 1950).[53] Dorne disliked their "Win a Free Scholarship" contests, followed by calls from salesmen claiming that the contestant almost won and should therefore become an artist. He would not copy their habit of placing ads in pulp magazines, and he was furious that their salesmen sometimes said that Norman Rockwell had studied there. Unlike Art Instruction, the Famous Artists salesmen would show prospective students parts of each lesson, and on the enrollment form they would see at the top of the page "PLEASE READ THIS CAREFULLY" before signing a binding contract to pay nearly $300.[54]

Several years later, an advertisement for Dorne's new Famous Painters school said that 10 eminent artists will "conduct" the school, where they will "guide your personal development." One of the 10 was not happy. Ben Shahn considered the ad a misrepresentation of the work of the guiding faculty, and he told Dorne that the ad distressed him.[55] Dorne had heard no objections from anyone else, and he reminded

Shahn that they had changed "directing faculty" to "guiding faculty" to be accurate. As always, not everyone agreed on what was fair and unfair, true and false, in the world of correspondence schooling. Dorne was sure that *conduct* was a suitable verb, and for proof he sent Shahn a page from the dictionary.[56]

WHY DIDN'T THE COLLEGES AND UNIVERSITIES CORNER THE MARKET?

The brick-and-mortar campuses offering home study were not as self-assured as the for-profit vendors. They hesitated to make the same bold claims on behalf of home study. Several dozen universities decided to offer correspondence courses, but their commitments to face-to-face education constrained what they said. As a result, the private correspondence schools gathered nearly 90 percent of the annual enrollments even though the universities that offered home study were more prestigious, charged less, and often awarded course credits. Why did that happen?

Chicago, Columbia, and Wisconsin—those three superb research universities had the largest home study enrollments in the early 20th century. At each campus, there were various *extension* activities for nonmatriculated students—summer sessions, evening classes, itinerant lectures, traveling libraries, and other programs that would provide "service for mankind wherever mankind is," in the words of William Rainey Harper, the first president (1891–1906) of the University of Chicago.[57] He had a vision of the American university broader than its older counterparts in Germany; the citadels of research would not only require original scholarship but also disseminate knowledge beyond the campus (the typical American college of the time did neither).

That combination of research and service had been the core of his career. A prolific scholar of sacred literature and a popular Chautauqua lecturer, Harper, in his mid-20s, had created a well-respected correspondence school for the study of Hebrew, Greek, Arabic, Assyrian, and the Bible. When he joined the Yale faculty in 1886, Harper rented a house in New Haven for his instructors, stenographers, clerk, and business manager. He drew a small salary for his correspondence work, but the school was constantly in debt; Harper covered the shortfall.[58] In his opinion, extension work was the secular counterpart of itinerant preaching—"the whole movement is primarily a missionary work . . . to make people long for improvement."[59]

In defense of correspondence work, Harper at first was intrepid. After he acknowledged eight disadvantages of home study, he refuted each one and then enumerated seven advantages, including the assertion that students who wrote their examinations acquired "a more thorough knowledge of the subject" than those who recited orally. Near the end, he backtracked—only students who cannot attend traditional schools should sign up for postal education. Then in the conclusion, he reasserted the value of correspondence work: "The student who has prepared a certain number of lessons in the correspondence-school knows more of the subject treated in those lessons, and knows it better, than the student who has covered the same ground in the class-room." In the final paragraph, he predicted that "the day is coming" when "the students who shall recite by correspondence will far outnumber those who make oral recitations."[60]

To Harper's dismay, several private schools quoted him on the relative merits of home study. The American Correspondence School for Nurses included his name in its advertisements, and as a result many people thought it was part of the University of Chicago.[61] To the Home Correspondence School in Massachusetts, Harper explained that the comments referred only to *his* students, most of whom were well-educated and highly motivated ministers. "I beg you, therefore, to cease using my name in any connection" with your school.[62] One father asked Harper about the ICS ad, quoting his praise of "more thorough instruction" in home study. "I have a son that I want to educate and if the correspondence course is better than the classroom I can save considerable [*sic*] by giving him the former. Have you been correctly quoted?"[63]

Harper knew that many of his professors were dubious about home study, so he muted his enthusiasm for the enterprise. He never forced or assigned anyone to do the work (although he did scold philosopher John Dewey for giving off-campus lectures without the imprimatur of the extension division).[64] He refused a request by the director of home study to require every freshman and sophomore to take several home study courses.[65] To allay fears of cheapening the diploma, Harper required that home study students who wanted college credits must be admitted to the university, take the course exam on campus, and finish the rest of the degree requirements at Chicago.

Those conditions proved attractive. Of the 2,952 students who took home study courses from July 1892 to July 1902, 58 percent matriculated (which was 11 percent of the total undergraduate enrollment in those 10 years).[66] The recruitment of new correspondence students (from 124 in 1893–1894 to 799 in 1901–1902, climbing thereafter to 2,164 in 1910–1911 and peaking in the late 1920s at just over 5,000) happened without extensive advertising, a sales force, or installment payment plans, the three foundations of the proprietary schools. But the slow increase lagged far behind the spectacular growth of two large Chicago correspondence schools: American and LaSalle. The University of Chicago had tiptoed into the field in contrast with its assertive proprietary neighbors.

Unlike Chicago, home study at Columbia borrowed the tactics of the for-profit schools. The sluggish growth of the first five years accelerated as soon as Columbia hired salesmen in 1925, when enrollments jumped from 827 to 1,854 and more than doubled in 1926. By early 1929, Columbia had the largest university home study division in the country, with nearly 10,000 recruits, 13 percent of the entire home study enrollment in American universities. To avoid the mischief widespread in proprietary schools, no one could enroll without the permission of an officer in the Department of Admissions. Furthermore, nearly half of the 65 salesmen were former ministers. Two were former college presidents, all but four had college degrees, and everyone received a week of training.[67]

Columbia also ran frequent newspaper and magazine ads, and they were more subdued than the hyperbole from the private schools. Most of the space featured a large photograph of the library, the name of the university in boldface letters, and a long list of courses. The text occasionally made sweeping generalizations, assurances along the lines of "everyone can reap great benefit from continued study" and "to be happy and successful to one's capacity one must continue study throughout life."

But often the global claims were qualified, as the italics in the following phrases indicate: "These courses offer *opportunity for* increased business efficiency," "*many of* the advantages which a resident academic course would have given you," and "the instruction that can *help so much* in bringing inherent ability into competent expression."[68] The frequent references to "genuine Columbia courses" were a stretch in the case of secretarial studies, Boy Scouting, and interior decorating, but each course had to be approved by a Columbia department and then taught by an instructor in or endorsed by that department.

There were occasional allusions to the tangible rewards a student might reap—"greater business or professional effectiveness"—but no specific figures were ever mentioned, and no testimonials were ever published, two familiar features of the private schools' relentless emphasis on money. And the catalog of English courses, which attracted the most registrations, bluntly said that "no promises of practical results can be made. . . . Students, particularly young ones and those lacking a sound background of education, are therefore frankly warned against expecting extravagant results for any of these courses."[69]

Columbia's president was not happy about the ads—they gave the impression that his university groveled for money—nor was he pleased that home study used another tactic of proprietary schools: installment payment contracts. Four-fifths of Columbia's students took that option. President Butler was upset to learn in 1927 that the annual budget counted unpaid "receivables" as cash in hand when in fact the debt exceeded $200,000. Butler criticized the partial fee arrangement as endangering the university's financial stability and its good name. He preferred the semiannual payments required of campus students, but he let installment sales continue as home study revenues finally exceeded expenses in 1928.[70]

Unlike the for-profit firms, Columbia did not refer delinquent accounts to collection departments or agencies, nor did it file (or threaten) lawsuits to recover the unpaid balances. Coercion "would lead us straight into the worst vices that have in the past earned the distrust of the public" for correspondence work.[71] Columbia's contracts committed its dropouts to a fraction of the total tuition plus a prorated sum for the lessons submitted. During the worst months of the Depression, the university relented from that provision, canceling the contracts of students who were unemployed or destitute.

That unwillingness to hound students hurt financially—the division lost so much money that the ad budget and all the field advisers were eliminated in 1933. President Butler insisted that home study sustain itself even though the profits from other extension activities could have covered its losses; by 1936, he said it was time to stop.

In his final report, James Richards, director of home study since 1930, offered his explanation for the dwindling enrollments.[72] Columbia had held back from truly competing in the marketplace. Rather than striving too hard to sell its courses, it had been stymied in two ways. On the one hand, the courses had to resemble the comparable fare offered on campus but without the benefit of college credits. Approximately 80 percent of the other universities offering correspondence work (including Chicago) made it possible to earn some course credits, but Columbia refused to do so.

On the other hand, Columbia never offered the full range of vocational courses available at ICS and elsewhere. Many prospects wanted to learn the skills necessary for a promotion or self-employment in fields where university course work was sparse. The result was that Columbia suffered more than it gained from its cautious adoption of proprietary tactics. It had come close enough to unsavory methods to mar its reputation but not close enough to reap all the benefits. It had been accused of operating a business. Richards probably thought to himself, *If only we had been a business*.

At the University of Wisconsin, the staff attracted thousands of home study students with very few ads, no salesmen, and no contracts. To summarize a long story told elsewhere, Wisconsin took pains to avoid the appearance of doing what the private schools did. Circulars in place of ads, salaried *field agents* in place of salesmen on commission, and installment sales only for hardships—Wisconsin home study cast itself as a public service from a land grant university devoted to helping state residents. It also distanced itself from the for-profit schools by compiling and sharing evidence of fraud and deception; anyone with a question about a private school could contact the staff for information or get advice on breaking a contract after enrolling.[73]

At all three universities, the unwillingness to adopt the full range of aggressive tactics used by the for-profit schools more than offset their greater prestige and lower fees. The service mission that justified collegiate home study was no match for the businessmen who lured hundreds of thousands of students with beguiling promises of speed and ease.

LET US NOW APPRAISE FAMOUS WRITERS

The cigars, scotch, and rich food caught up with Albert Dorne in 1965. The founder of Famous Artists died that fall at age 61. His heart attack did not halt the rapid expansion of his school. The growth he had envisioned early on—"Art School for Everyone Everywhere"—continued. One woman was so eager to get started that she financed her enrollment by selling her burial plot.[74] A course for teenagers did well; 17,000 signed up in the first two years.

European sales rose so quickly that the company made plans for a 14-story headquarters in Amsterdam. "We will soon have an empire on which the sun never sets," the head of Famous Writers boasted in April 1967, and two years later, with strong sales in Australia and Japan, his confidence seemed warranted. At home, Norman Rockwell helped out by displaying students' paintings in Senator Edward Kennedy's office and during guest appearances on the popular Joey Bishop and Johnny Carson television shows.[75]

The company's new leaders were businessmen, not artists, and they decided to grow by moving beyond the Famous schools. "We intend to diversify and expand into every viable sector of the education industry," the president declared in March 1967.[76] The major acquisitions included correspondence schools for accounting and foreign languages, the Evelyn Wood speed-reading program, and, defining education very broadly, the most expensive acquisition, Welcome Wagon, a company with 6,000 *hostesses* who greeted new neighbors in their town or city and bestowed coupons from local stores. FAS International (the new name for the firm) also bought vocational home study schools in France and created an advisory board to find more European acquisitions. To create goodwill in the tiny country of Monte Carlo, Norman Rockwell contributed a charcoal drawing of the Prince and Princess. Shortcuts to wealth were everywhere.[77]

The Famous Schools were not alone in bulking up. Anything related to students and education was a target for takeover in the 1960s, a decade when high school and college enrollments soared. Huge conglomerates acquired publishers (RCA bought Random House, and CBS acquired Saunders and Holt Rinehart), and General Electric, Time, and Westinghouse also bought small firms. Small companies could become conglomerates. The National Student Marketing Corporation, for instance, began by selling posters and handing out free samples on college campuses and soon owned telephone directories, bus companies, Frommer's travel guides, and much more. The company went public in April 1968, and its stock spiked from 6 to 14 on the first day of trading and hit 82 later that year. The 33-year-old president purchased a yacht and a jet.[78]

For proprietary schools, the issue was whether to buy or be bought. ICS rebuffed seven suitors in 1961; ICS wanted to buy. At the end of the decade, ICS owned three vocational schools, a book jobber to libraries, an audiovisual company, a training program for overseas corporations, and five niche publishers. Annual sales surged 160 percent from 1961 to 1973. But profits peaked in 1967, declined for three years, and became losses in the early 1970s. Some of the acquisitions were unprofitable, yet all of them had increased the company's debt.[79]

The largest ICS shareholder was the former governor of Pennsylvania, William Scranton. He urged the president to cut the debt and pare the international operations.[80] On one annual report where the president boasted that "we implemented a plan to create a growth and diversified company within the broad educational—or knowledge—field," Scranton wrote, "Baloney."[81] ICS barely survived the acquisition binge—the stock fell from 32 in 1969 to a low of 1 in 1974. Anyone who owned ICS shares had a roller-coaster ride quite unlike the economic security that its home study advertisements promised.

FAS seemed to be on the same trajectory as ICS. By 1967, when FAS sales rose 40 percent, the stock commanded a price–earnings ratio above that of the overall market. Rather than use stock to make acquisitions, FAS usually borrowed the money. To close the deals, FAS paid a premium for several acquisitions. Sales continued to rise in 1968 and 1969, but earnings per share began to decline thanks to interest payments and the cost of running so many far-flung initiatives—for instance, the New York City administrative offices took two entire floors of a Madison Avenue building. When the bull market wobbled in the summer of 1969 and slumped in 1970, the price of FAS fell from $36 to $10 by May 1970.

One investment firm said that $10 was too low for a company with 169,000 students, including the blonde cheerleader on Norman Rockwell's October 28, 1938, *Saturday Evening Post* cover.[82] The company remained profitable, and annual sales in 1970 would exceed $80 million, more than 11 times the comparable figure for 1960. The guiding faculty were still well paid—Rockwell's monthly check was close to $2,000, and his Famous Writers counterparts received almost $1,500. But like ICS, the company's balance sheet was stretched, and the economic downturn of the early 1970s would have been a serious challenge even without Jessica Mitford's *Atlantic Monthly* article on Famous Writers.

Mitford's article, "Let Us Now Appraise Famous Writers," laid out some embarrassing facts: the dropout rate was at least two-thirds and possibly as high as 90 percent (the head of the school wasn't sure), there were 800 full-time "field representatives" (salesmen on commission) compared to 55 full-time instructors, six of the seven testimonials in a recent *New York Times* ad were five years old, and a few universities offered comparable courses for one-fifteenth of the $780 the school charged.[83] Several examples of indefensible enrollments were described at length. Mitford quoted from the befuddled essay in the successful aptitude test from Louella Mae Burns: "a flock of people who started merging along the sidewalk . . . when out of the blue came a honking and cars and motorcycles and policemen. It was really something! Everybody started shouting and waving and we finally essayed to see the reason of all this. In a sleek black limousine we saw real close Mr. Calvin Coolidge, the President Himself!"

Mitford also heard a two-hour sales pitch with half a dozen lies when she coaxed a neighbor to apply. She saw for herself what illustrator Robert Fawcett had told Norman Rockwell in 1967: "It is just as well that some of us are not around to listen to our salesmen sign up prospects. I have talked to a few of them, and they make magazine salesmen, with one foot in the door as they tell you they represent wounded veterans, seem like pikers. It is a far cry from the scrupulous integrity with which some of us paint our pictures."[84]

The most astonishing material in her article were the quotes from her interviews with five of the guiding faculty, especially the comments from Bennett Cerf, the avuncular panelist on the *What's My Line?* television show and head of Random House publishers. Cerf tried his best to charm Mitford: "The suavity, the sophistication of it all! Oh, he was very nice—so confidential—there we were, two old pros, two clever people above any storm," Mitford later recalled.[85] Cerf blithely said he did not follow the day-to-day operations of the school: "I know *nothing* about the business and selling end and I care *less*." How many Famous Writers had published books with Random House? Mitford asked. "Oh, come on, you must be pulling my leg—no person of any sophistication, whose book we'd publish, would have to take a mail-order course to learn to write."

And then the clincher: when he talked about mail-order tactics, Cerf said, "The crux of it is a very hard sales pitch, an appeal to the gullible." When he saw Mitford taking notes, he asked her not to quote him. "You'll have all the mail-order houses in the country down on my neck!" She let him rephrase—"I don't like the hard sell, but it's the basis of all American business"—but Mitford said that wasn't a paraphrase. She would have to use both statements.

For the Famous Writers students who read that interview, there were several lessons. First, it was Cerf who was gullible. Jessica Mitford was a very famous writer, an investigative journalist whose best-selling *The American Way of Death* (1963) had excoriated the funeral industry. Her specialty was unmasking exaggeration, misrepresentation, and overcharging. As her husband later said, "She could be ruthless, even savage, when she was on the warpath."[86] Why was Cerf so unguarded with the woman who said when he asked if he could call her Jessica, "I don't see why not. *Mortuary Management* always does"?

Furthermore, the guiding faculty came across as far less involved in the school than the marketing let on. As one letter to the editor put it, "Bennett Cerf's association with the project is enormously reprehensible because the ads do suggest—and the salesmen vow—that he or his equivalent is right there at your shoulder every minute."[87] Not only were the guiding faculty distant from the school, but their own self-interest required that some students give up. As poet Phyllis McGinley told Mitford, "We couldn't make any money if all the students finished."[88]

Another lesson about fame came from the information Mitford drew from *Writing Rackets*, a book published by the not-famous Robert Byrne in 1969. There was enough information in his book to dissuade anyone from taking a home study course in writing in order to make money. The market for freelancers had shrunk, not grown, since the 1940s. A survey of 26 magazines reported that 560 of 182,505 fiction manuscripts were accepted. The *Atlantic Monthly* received 27,000 submissions each year, and Norman Rockwell's *Saturday Evening Post* had stopped reading any unsolicited work. The only decent freelance market was for hard-core pornography.[89]

"Having Fun with Famous Writers," Byrne's 20-page chapter on the school, was as critical as what Mitford wrote. It was Byrne's wife who applied as Louella Mae Burns and sent the stilted essay that Mitford quoted. What Byrne lacked was a Mitford-size reputation to interview the guiding faculty or find a top-tier publisher. He sent the book to Doubleday, but an editor there told him, "It's too negative. People want to keep their dreams, they don't mind paying for them." Even after publication, he was scared he would be sued. Mitford said that was "*ridiculous*, the last thing these people want is that sort of publicity; what they hope is that his book will die a natural death."[90]

Her article did not die a natural death. Letters to the editor two months later heightened the disenchantment. One former instructor revealed that each "personal" letter of criticism included prewritten or canned paragraphs—the instructor jotted down the numbers for a typist to access. Two former students said that the salesmen told them that their publications would recoup the entire tuition within the first year. And several editors called Famous Writers' manuscripts "dreary and dull" and mocked the authors who boasted of their graduation—the credential they cherished had the opposite effect on the editors: it was a reliable warning sign of inept work.

Mitford herself answered several hundred letters, urging the dissatisfied to stop paying "and tell the school I advised this" (her article revealed that the Famous schools never sued to enforce the contracts).[91] Larger numbers were reached by an article in *Time* magazine and by Mitford's appearance on the *Merv Griffin Show*, where she said that funeral directors and Famous Writers resembled one another: "Both of them promise a measure of immortality, over-charge for it and then don't come through."[92]

Soon, the state and federal governments began to investigate. Officials in Indiana and Washington sent reprints of the article to every high school counselor and principal. Iowa suspended sales there, and New York's attorney general sought revisions in the ads. Consumer advocate and former Miss America Bess Myerson quoted Mitford in a radio address on unscrupulous correspondence schools. A congressman entered the entire *Atlantic Monthly* article into the *Congressional Record* and convinced the FTC to follow up.[93] Four of the guiding faculty were subpoenaed by the FTC in early 1971.

Rod Serling, the host of the popular science fiction TV show *The Twilight Zone* (1959–1964) and winner of six Emmy awards, told the FTC that he hated the phrase *guiding faculty*. It implied that they were in Westport, "on the scene," when "contributing editor" or "founding member" would be more accurate. "We spent hours and hours wondering what the hell we would call ourselves, this was one of the arbitrary things that came out by virtue of its, you know, the beautiful alliteration of it, rather than, you know, any judgment as to whether or not it specifically fitted our real roles."[94]

Serling had concentrated his attention on the textbooks rather than teaching. He knew the names of only two instructors, was unaware of how much time the instructors devoted to each assignment, and didn't know the attrition rate. The last time he saw a sample of student work was six or seven years ago. He stayed in touch with Famous Writers staff by telephone and an occasional trip east. When asked if his contract stipulated four visits each year, he admitted that he had never read it.

He had mixed feelings about the advertisements. Before the deposition, he told an FAS officer that his "deep concern" with the ads was "a matter of record over the years," and he told one disgruntled student that Mitford's criticisms of the ads were "valid and altogether on target."[95] Serling said that he never wrote the copy in the ads, although they were sent to him for his approval.

Several of his ads focused on financial gain: "What every creative person should know about writing for money" and "Here are interesting facts about full-time and part-time careers in writing." He told the FTC that he believed that opportunities for new writers were "almost wide open," including the rookies whose work he occasionally bought for *The Twilight Zone*. On the other hand, he did not like the Famous Writers ad that showed him sitting next to a swimming pool. "I didn't want a suggestion of affluence being an integral part of the results of our school."

The FTC did not indict Famous Writers after the attorney general in New York negotiated revisions of the advertisements. The company was ready to make other changes. The guiding faculty would review and evaluate the sales, advertising, and admissions practices. New students were called soon after enrollment to be sure the salesmen did not misrepresent the course. Several guiding faculty suggested a booklet on "how to start small. Too many try to sell Reader's Digest right away" along with a new emphasis on "writing in your career" rather than "your career in writing."[96] No one questioned the need to modify the exuberant ads and curb misleading salesmanship—as one painter said, "I don't give a damn how good the teaching and the art courses are, or if Jesus Christ himself was on the faculty of the photography course and doing crits. If the sales department stinks we might just as well make like the Arabs and fold our tents."[97]

But there was no all-out rebuttal of Jessica Mitford's article. At the meeting of the guiding faculty a week after the article appeared, they agreed with John Caples not to broadcast it by replying. In his diary, Caples wrote, "Circ[ulation] of Atlantic only 325,000. Not important."[98] The head of the school sent a letter to the *Atlantic Monthly* pointing out several errors and omissions, but there were no ad campaigns to refute Mitford or announce new policies, no flyers to current and former students, and no chance to deflect the "Unlikely Events of 1971" *National Lampoon* parody of Bennett Cerf staying up all night to grade aptitude tests.

In a school that had relied for two decades on the persuasive power of famous artists and writers, there was surprisingly little awareness that other famous people and their allies could destroy what eminent people had built. Four months before her article appeared, Mitford urged her British agent to short the stock.[99] That was good advice. Although the price of FAS stock did not plunge after Mitford's article appeared—from May to December it dropped only from 10 to 9—a series of dismal earnings reports soon revealed the damage that her article caused. For July through December, the company posted a small loss and predicted more losses in 1971. The president and treasurer resigned in May 1971, but the bleeding continued.

Enrollments fell throughout 1971, and overdue accounts rose—dropouts were less willing to pay the balance of what they owed, and the accountants insisted that FAS stop recording as revenue the full value of new enrollment contracts. The Securities and Exchange Commission suspended trading in FAS stock for almost six months as the company calculated the damage and tried unsuccessfully to convince its creditors to exchange debt for common and preferred stock. When the stock reopened for trading just before Thanksgiving, buyers offered 50 cents a share. Three months later, FAS filed for bankruptcy.[100]

When Norman Rockwell's banker looked at the 1971 annual report from FAS, he thought that the corporate assets were at least $20 million less than the liabilities. The best outcome, the banker advised Rockwell, would be a deduction on his income tax for the worthless shares. He could also take a loss on the $23,000 of deferred compensation he had set aside from 1958 to 1965.[101]

Ben Stahl thought that Rockwell could have turned the tide. As one of the original guiding faculty of the Famous Artists school, Stahl did not like the new name adopted in 1973: Art Skills. "Sounds like some kind of a place little old ladies make corny jewelry and knit doilies." He wanted to return to the past. "How management can disregard the gimmicks that made the school famous and prosperous is beyond me. If Al Dorne were alive he would throw the whole bunch out." In his opinion, "The school is finished. For Christ's sake why didn't they give Norman a big cut and call it the Norman Rockwell School of Art. Then they would have had something."[102]

Norman Rockwell was 79 years old in 1973. He wanted to step aside. "You may use my name as a founder," but that would be the extent of the association. The company told Rockwell that he would not have to do anything if he remained. But that, his attorney pointed out, would be fraud.[103]

INNOCENT EXAGGERATION

"A little hyperbole never hurts. People want to believe that something is the biggest and the greatest and the most spectacular. I play to people's fantasies."[104] President Donald Trump's faith in "truthful hyperbole" marked his controversial Trump University enterprise. Many of the same tactics used by correspondence schools resurfaced in the for-profit venture he launched in 2005. A famous American once again promised that everyone could now learn his secrets—"I can turn anyone into a successful real estate investor."[105] Aggressive sales, misleading advertisements, illegal use of the word *university*, distortions of Trump's involvement, and other mischief sparked more and more criticism, including government investigations and a class-action lawsuit that Trump eventually settled out of court for $25 million.

What Trump defended as "innocent exaggeration" can be especially expensive for the students who pay for the slim chance to transform their lives. The loss is not just time and money. Throughout the 20th century, millions of correspondence school students were enticed by promises that spare-time study would lead to remarkable benefits. Testimonials from the fortunate few who leapt ahead reinforced the American faith in education as the path to a better life. But the vast majority who sought a better future through home study did not get it, and their disappointment could be more painful than their financial loss. As one Famous Writers student asked after reading Jessica Mitford's expose, "What shall we do now with our ambition or, if we have any, talent? What used to seem like a hopeful adventure toward an eventual accomplishment now has abruptly become a disturbing question."[106] Her question will remain timely as long as Americans believe that they can buy shortcuts to education.

LINKS

Famous Artists advertisements: http://www.infomarkingblog.com/images/Like_To_Draw.jpg
Jessica Mitford's critique of FAS: http://www.theatlantic.com/magazine/archive/1970/07/let-us-now-appraise-famous-writers/305319
Pictures of the Famous Artists: http://www.nrm.org/2013/11/ryan-mitten/
Profile and picture of Albert Dorne: http://www.americanartarchives.com/dorne.htm
Sketch of Jessica Mitford: http://www.newyorker.com/magazine/2006/10/16/red-sheep

NOTES

1. Norman Rockwell to Sydney Newbold, Box 37, 1950 folder, Norman Rockwell Business Papers, 1918–1978, Norman Rockwell Museum, Stockbridge, MA.

2. David Apatoff, *Albert Dorne: Master Illustrator* (San Francisco: Auad Publishing, 2012), 13–18.

3. Goldberg owned 49 percent of the cartoon course, a partnership not created for any other artist. He projected a profit of $50 per student annually and was told that 5,000 students "is not too extravagant." After paying his five guiding faculty 12.5 percent each, he would keep 37.5 percent. The course took forever to finish (February 1956), enrollments lagged other Famous

courses (women and middle-aged men were not interested), expenses were higher than he anticipated, and Goldberg decided to exchange his shares for Famous Artists stock in 1958. Rube Goldberg to Milton Caniff, June 5, 1948, and April 26, 1958, in Institute of Commercial Art folder, Milton Caniff Papers, Ohio State University Archives.

4. The former instructors I interviewed warmly recalled their time at FAS. The starting salary ($4,000) in the mid-1950s was modest, but in the highly competitive art world a secure full-time job was attractive. The "den mothers" who oversaw the instructors were friendly rather than stern, and there was nonstop bantering and teasing among the all-male staff. The formation of a union in 1961 brought higher salaries, but it eroded the old come-and-go-as you-please freedoms when Dorne (who was upset—he thought of the school as a big family) required instructors to punch in and out on a time clock. Telephone interviews of Randy Enos (August 5, 2015), Jak Kovatch (December 13, 2014), Charles Reid (August 24, 2016), and Warren Stadler (September 12, 2015). For similar comradery at the Art Instruction correspondence school in Minneapolis (where "Peanuts" cartoonist Charles Schulz worked from 1946 to 1950), see David Michaelis, *Schulz and Peanuts: A Biography* (New York: HarperCollins, 2007), 179–85.

5. Statistics compiled from the 1950–1960 folders, Box 37, Rockwell Business Papers; telephone interview of Austin Briggs Jr. (September 4, 2016) regarding Dorne's duplex (and a private table at the Oak Room in the Plaza Hotel).

6. Granville Hicks, "Mail-Order Creativity," *Saturday Review*, April 29, 1961. Hicks had serious misgivings about Famous Writers. The literary critic was dismayed by ads implying that professional success awaited the graduates, and he thought that novice writers should be around other writers. His short article did not "go viral" as we say today, and several Famous students who wrote him said they realized that perseverance was essential. Sybil L. Deering to Granville Hicks, April 26, 1961, and the letters from L. Weatherwax (June 6, 1961) and Dr. Martin J. Kaplan (April 26, 1961), Granville Hicks Papers, Syracuse University Archives.

7. Gordon Carroll to Bergen Evans, October 3, 1961, Box 21, folder 1, Bergen Evans Papers, Northwestern University Archives.

8. The 40 percent figure is an average computed from the Famous Artists annual reports in the Rockwell Business Papers. A summer of 1964 report revealed more salesmen (306) than instructors (123). "Facts, Figures and Percentages as of July 31, 1964," Box 21, folder 1, Bergen Evans Papers. The fame of the guiding faculty also yielded valuable free publicity. For instance, seven artists appeared on the *Ed Sullivan Show* in 1956. They sat in the front row, drew caricatures of the host, and then made Sullivan an honorary student.

Famous Artists Magazine 4, no. 3 (Spring 1956): 4. And the fame of several students (actors Tony Curtis and Henry Fonda and singers Dinah Shore, Pat Boone, and Jose Ferrer) provided valuable public relations, so much so that when actress Marilyn Monroe inquired about enrolling, the school immediately offered to waive her tuition (http://www.julienslive.com/view%e2%80%94auctions/catalog/id/180/lot/83402).

9. Ads from 1907 and 1908 for the International Correspondence Schools, Box 77, N. W. Ayer Collection, National Museum of American History, Washington, DC.

10. Roland Marchand, *Advertising the American Dream: Making Way for Modernity, 1920–1940* (Berkeley: University of California Press, 1985). For the earlier years, see Stephen Fox, *The Mirror Makers: A History of American Advertising and Its Creators* (New York: William Morrow, 1984), chaps. 1–3; Charles F. McGovern, *Sold American: Consumption and Citizenship, 1890–1945* (Chapel Hill: University of North Carolina Press, 2006), chaps. 1–6; and Daniel Pope, *The Making of Modern Advertising* (New York: Basic Books, 1983). For a case study of one coach–confidante ("You can do it, and I can help"), see Susan Marks, *Finding Betty Crocker: The Secret Life of America's First Lady of Food* (New York: Simon & Schuster, 2005). *Fortune* magazine said that she was the second-best-known woman in America in the 1940s (even though there never was a cook named Betty Crocker; General Mills hired various women to appear as Betty Crocker).

11. John Caples, *Making Ads Pay* (New York: Harper and Brothers, 1957), 171, 14; Marchand, *Advertising the American Dream*, 379, n. 47; Caples, *Making Ads Pay*, 83.

12. Caples, *Making Ads Pay*, 66–70, 89; Gordon White, *John Caples: AD-MAN* (Chicago: Crain Books, 1977), 51. In 1962, a list of 100 outstanding headlines in 20th-century ads included eight for correspondence schools. Maxwell Sackheim, *My First Sixty Years in Advertising* (Englewood Cliffs, NJ: Prentice Hall, 1970), 195.

13. Michael Schudson, *Advertising: The Uneasy Persuasion* (New York: Basic Books, 1986), 129.

14. The undated advertisements are from the Bergen Evans Papers, the John Caples Papers (National Museum of American History), the Rockwell Business Papers, the Phyllis McGinley Papers (Syracuse University), and the (now very small) Famous Writers School in Wilton, CT.

15. In 1964, 52 percent of the Famous Writers students were female. The commercial art (60 percent) and cartooning (95 percent) courses had more males than females, unlike the painting course, which was 65 percent female. The average age of Famous Writers students was 42. "Facts, Figures and Percentages as of July 31, 1964," Box 21, folder 1, Bergen Evans Papers. On

the front and back covers of the 1964 annual report, four of the 70 students were black, which is the only information I found on the racial composition of the school. The ads often claimed that gender, age, geographical location, or part-time exertion would not handicap the aspiring writers and artists, but there were no references to race, religion, or disabilities in the ads.

16. *How to Turn Your Writing into Dollars* (Westport, CT: Famous Writers Schools Inc., 1960).

17. "Your Future as a Writer," 13, Famous Writers School offices, Wilton, CT.

18. "Famous Writers Aptitude Test," Box 21, folder 2, Bergen Evans Papers.

19. From a letter to a prospective student who requested but did not return the Aptitude Test after 60 days. Box 9, "F W S 1970" folder, McGinley Papers.

20. Copy in the Famous Writers School, Wilton, CT.

21. From p. 13 of "Famous Writers School" (1962), a 48-page illustrated brochure, printed on heavy bond paper. The layout of this large (8- by 14-inch) flyer matched one message inside: this is a solidly middle-class enterprise. For instance, pictures of instructors in private offices contrast with the photos earlier in the century from correspondence schools where dozens of teachers sat in rows of desks in cavernous rooms. Furthermore, the brochure praised the school's location, Westport, as "well-kept, active, wealthy." Those words (and the proud display of the school's "coveted certificate" of completion) were probably too earnest, too middle class, for the upper-middle-class preference for understatement. From the John Caples Papers, Box 35, folder 2.

22. *The Famous Artists Course in Commercial Art* [1948?], 5, "Institute of Commercial Art, 1948–1956" folder, Milton Caniff Papers, Ohio State University.

23. *Famous Artists Magazine* 1, no. 1 (Autumn 1952): 4.

24. When Al Dorne read those words in the ad, he said that they *understated* the rewards of artistic creation. Telephone interview of David Apatoff, August 22, 2016.

25. Telephone interview of Jak Kovatch (FAS instructor, 1957–1959), December 13, 2014.

26. The banks bought the loans for 85 to 90 percent of face value, setting aside the other 10 to 15 percent as a reserve against defaults. If unpaid debt exceeded the reserves, the bank kept the interest it had charged but returned the lapsed contracts to the Famous Schools, which then tried to collect by using four different letterheads, including that of the Guaranteed Collections Bureau, which in fact was a division of the Famous schools. "Famous Artists School" (October 1961 research report from Carter, Berlind, Potoma and Weill, investment bankers), "Famous Artists School, 1960–61" folder, Milton

Caniff Papers; telephone interview of Warren Stadler (FAS instructor, 1958–1963), September 12, 2015.

27. Because each student's name was stenciled on the book covers, they could not be reused.

28. Norman Rockwell to Albert Dorne, August 3, 1965, 1965 folder, Rockwell Business Papers.

29. Norman Rockwell to Fred Ludekens, June 7, 1966, 1966 folder.

30. Harriett F. Bergman, "The Silent University: The Society to Encourage Studies at Home, 1873–1897," *The New England Quarterly*, September 2001, 447–77; Anne Bruder, "Outside the Classroom Walls: Alternative Pedagogies in American Literature and Culture, 1868–1910" (unpublished dissertation, University of North Carolina, 2009), 99–152. Bergman and Bruder agree that the death of the founder was the key reason for the end of the society in 1897, which in 24 years reached 7,086 women.

31. John H. Vincent, *The Chautauqua Movement* (Boston: Chautauqua Press, 1886); Joseph F. Kett, *The Pursuit of Knowledge under Difficulties: From Self-Improvement to Adult Education* (Palo Alto, CA: Stanford University Press, 1994), 156–70; Richard K. Bonnell, "The Chautauqua University: Pioneer University without Walls 1883–1898" (unpublished dissertation, Kent State University, 1988).

32. Similar methods characterized the thousands of *women's study clubs* in late nineteenth-century America. Unaffiliated with Chautauqua, small groups of middle-class, middle-aged women met in each other's homes to "quicken their minds, foster a sense of independent achievement, and lessen their isolation from the social and intellectual mainstream of American life." Theodora Penny Martin, *The Sound of Our Own Voices: Women's Study Clubs, 1860–1910* (Boston: Beacon Press, 1987), 38.

33. From 1882 to 1893, almost as many women graduated from the Chautauqua Literary and Scientific Circle (27,141) as finished college (32,684), according to Andrew C. Rieser, *The Chautauqua Movement: Protestants, Progressives, and the Culture of Modern Liberalism* (New York: Columbia University Press, 2003), 167.

34. James D. Watkinson, "Education for Success: The International Correspondence Schools of Scranton, Pennsylvania," *The Pennsylvania Magazine of History and Biography*, October 1996, 343–69.

35. G. Lynn Sumner, *How I Learned the Secrets of Success in Advertising* (New York: Prentice Hall, 1952), 49.

36. From the N. W. Ayer Collection, Box 76–Box 78, National Museum of American History, Washington, DC. One ad was so alluring that Adlai Stevenson quoted it during the 1952 presidential campaign (unaware of its origins)—"On the plains of hesitation bleach the bones of countless millions who, at the

Dawn of Victory, sat down to wait." J. M. Flagler, "How Wilson Hunt Lost His Overalls," *New Yorker*, April 14, 1956.

37. For white-collar workers, business mail-order courses abounded, especially in accounting, sales, shorthand, and even law. Schoolteachers in districts where exams influenced hiring were another sizable market. Nearly any academic subject could be studied, although the vocational options were more popular. The surging economy is carefully described by Robert J. Gordon, *The Rise and Fall of American Growth* (Princeton, NJ: Princeton University Press, 2016), chaps. 2–9.

38. David O. Levine, *The American College and the Culture of Aspiration* (Ithaca, NY: Cornell University Press, 1986), 39. Even prisoners in San Quentin created "letter box" courses for each other, and some took correspondence classes from the University of California. Benjamin Justice, "A College of Morals: Education Reform at San Quentin Prison, 1880–1920," *History of Education Quarterly*, Autumn 2000, 298.

39. John S. Noffsinger, *Correspondence Schools, Lyceums, and Chautauquas* (New York: Macmillan, 1926), 33–34.

40. William Bethke to Frederick Keppel, December 14, 1925, Box 2, folder 16, Carnegie Corporation Papers, Columbia University. I analyzed the early years of the organization in Robert L. Hampel, "The National Home Study Council, 1926–1942," *American Journal of Distance Education*, 2009, 4–19.

41. John Noffsinger to Frederick Keppel and Morris Cartwright, January 18, 1926, Box 253, folder 4, Carnegie Corporation Papers.

42. John Noffsinger to Morris Cartwright, February 1, 1927, Box 253, folder 4, Carnegie Corporation Papers; "For Release in the Morning Newspapers of Thursday, July 21, 1927," Distance Education and Training Council (DETC) archives (Washington, DC).

43. John S. Noffsinger, comp., *Orders and Stipulations Issued to Home Study Schools by the Federal Trade Commission, 1925–1938* (Washington, DC: National Home Study Council, 1938). The FTC also worked with the federal Post Office Department to prosecute cases of mail-order fraud. By 1939, 71 home study employees were in prison, on probation, or indicted. "Proceedings of Annual Conference, 1939," 90. Verbatim transcripts of the annual meetings of the National Home Study Council from 1929 to 1932 and 1934 to 1942 are in the DETC archives.

44. "Proceedings of Annual Conference, 1940," 145, DETC archives. For a widely read spoof of outlandish correspondence school advertisements, see Sinclair Lewis, *Babbitt* (New York: Harcourt, Brace and World, 1922), 77–85.

45. J. J. Clark, "The Correspondence School—Its Relation to Technical Education and Some of Its Results," *Science*, September 14, 1906, 328.

46. "Bulletin of the Better Business Bureau of Philadelphia," N. 494, 1933, BBB Office, Philadelphia): "Money paid for civil service coaching courses at this time might almost as well be thrown to the four winds." The federal Civil Service Commission put signs in post offices and made radio broadcasts warning the public of fraudulent schools. They had received thousands of complaints, often from students who were "positively illiterate," requesting an "animal report" rather than annual report, addressing the "Silver Service Commission," and signing off with "Urs," "Proceedings of Annual Conference, 1936," 58–95.

47. In the 1920s, a majority of washing machines, radios, and even vacuum cleaners were sold on installment, according to Walter A. Friedman, *Birth of a Salesman: The Transformation of Selling in America* (Cambridge, MA: Harvard University Press, 2004), 196–97. The schools without salesmen usually charged for each lesson or set of lessons rather than rely on contracts signed by students they had never seen.

48. The reserves were 36.2 percent (1931), 42.5 percent (1936), and 37.8 percent (1938) of sales. "LaSalle Extension University, 1913–1944" folder, DETC archives.

49. *LaSalle Extension University v. Fogarty*, 126 Neb. 457, 253 North Western Reporter, 425 (1936). The resentment caused by lawsuits had convinced the Pennsylvania Railroad's Western Regional Division in 1926 to withhold an endorsement of LaSalle's courses for training station agents, courses the railroad considered valuable. Box 1081, Pennsylvania Railroad Papers, Hagley Museum, Greenville, DE. Even the teenagers who signed up for the Charles Atlas bodybuilding lessons received threats that the overdue account would soon go "to the Attorney for immediate court action." Box 5, "Debt Collection" folder, Charles Atlas Papers, National Museum of American History.

50. "Proceedings of Annual Conference, 1938," 106–11.

51. Elizabeth Toon and Janet Golden, "Live Clean, Think Clean, and Don't Go to Burlesque Shows: Charles Atlas as Health Advisor," *Journal of the History of Medicine* 57(2002), 39–60.

52. From David Kemp, "Music for the Millions" (unpublished autobiography, 1956, in the possession of his granddaughter, Ann LaSalle), 183, 123. I describe Kemp in more detail in my article "The National Home Study Council, 1926–1942."

53. Michaelis, *Schulz and Peanuts*, 164–89, 281–83, for Schulz's years at Art Instruction.

54. "Minutes of Faculty Meeting, June 9, 1951" and Dorne to Rockwell, December 18, 1951, 1951 folder, Rockwell Business Papers.

55. Ben Shahn to Al [Dorne], January 23, 1954, Box 10, folder 16, Shahn Papers, Archives of American Art, Smithsonian Institution, Washington, DC.

56. Al Dorne to Ben Shahn, February 3, 1954, Box 10, folder 16, Ben Shahn Papers.

57. Maureen Anne Fay, "Origins and Early Development of the University of Chicago Extension Division, 1892–1911" (unpublished dissertation, University of Chicago, 1976), 65.

58. Kenneth N. Beck, "The American Institute of Sacred Literature" (unpublished dissertation, University of Chicago, 1968), 40–60.

59. Richard J. Storr, *Harper's University: The Beginnings* (Chicago: University of Chicago Press, 1966), 196.

60. "On Teaching by Correspondence," reprinted in C. Hartley Grattan, ed., *American Ideas about Adult Education, 1710–1951* (New York: Bureau of Publications, Teachers College, Columbia University, 1959), 75–83.

61. F. W. Shepardson to Mr. Stewart, October 28, 1902, Office of the President, Harper, Judson and Burton Administrations, Box 36, folder 12, Special Collections Research Center, University of Chicago.

62. William Rainey Harper to Home Correspondence School, December 3, 1901, Box 36, folder 12, Special Collections, University of Chicago.

63. C. L. Moore to William Rainey Harper, July 9, 1900, Box 36, folder 12, Special Collections, University of Chicago.

64. Maureen Fay, "Origins and Early Development," 142; William Rainey Harper, *The President's Report: July 1892–July 1902* (Chicago: University of Chicago Press, 1903), 334.

65. Storr, *Harper's University*, 203.

66. Harper, *The President's Report*, 314.

67. For a longer analysis of home study at Columbia, see Robert L. Hampel, "The Business of Education: Home Study at Columbia University and the University of Wisconsin in the 1920s and 1930s," *Teachers College Record*, September 2010, 2496–517.

68. I added the italics in each phrase.

69. *Home Study Courses: English* (New York: Columbia University Press, 1931), 17. A harsher account of how Columbia "befuddles the public and lowers its own dignity by offering extension courses to misguided people" is in Abraham Flexner, *Universities: American, English, German* (New York: Oxford University Press, 1930), 133–45. Flexner also scolded Chicago and Wisconsin for "absurd" courses that "bamboozle well-meaning but untrained persons with the notion that they can thus receive a high school or a college education" (147). Flexner had a high standard of academic excellence—he thought that the creation of the business school at Harvard was a terrible mistake. In his opinion, many vocational majors, such as journalism, education,

and business, relied on pseudoscientific "hocus-pocus" and trivial "tiddledewinks" rather than trusting common sense and on-the-job experience to give students what they needed. Abraham Flexner to Paul Hanus, November 1, 1930, container 9, "Paul Hanus" folder, Abraham Flexner Papers, Library of Congress, Washington, DC.

70. Nicholas Murray Butler to James Egbert, June 1, June 3, 1927, folder 8, James Egbert Papers, Columbia University Archives.

71. *Annual Report of the President and Treasurer, 1930–1931* (New York: Columbia University Press, 1931), 334.

72. *Annual Report of the President and Treasurer, 1936–1937*, 330.

73. Hampel, "The Business of Education," 2507–11.

74. Telephone interview, Charles Reid (FAS instructor, 1963–1973), August 24, 2016.

75. "The You-Too-Can-Write-a-Best-Seller-Row," *Sunday Times* (London), February 15, 1970, Box 11, "Robert Byrne" folder, Granville Hicks Papers; Gordon Carroll to Phyllis McGinley, April 7, 1967, Box 9, "Famous Writers School, 1967–1969" folder, McGinley Papers; *20th Annual Report*, 5, 34, Box 9, "Famous Writers School, 1968–1975" folder, McGinley Papers.

76. *Wall Street Journal*, March 10, 1967, 17. One of the guiding faculty for painting later called the president "a wild man" who "felt that they could expand forever." Kitty Gelhorn interview of Will Barnet, Columbia University Oral History Collection, 315–16.

77. FAS 1969 Annual Report; "Report to New York Society of Security Analysts," May 13, 1969, 1969 folder, Rockwell Business Papers. FAS also tried to buy the Barnes & Noble bookstores, and the company hired Alvin Eurich, the former head of the State University of New York, to plan an accredited "university for independent study" on the assumption that rising college enrollments would soon swamp face-to-face education.

78. John Brooks, *The Go-Go Years* (New York: Weybright and Talley, 1973), 281–82.

79. "InText Position Report," October 20, 1969 (ICS renamed itself InText as it expanded), Box 85, folder 3, William Scranton Papers, Pennsylvania State University Archives; InText 1973 Annual Report, Box 85, folder 11, Scranton Papers.

80. William W. Scranton to Richard Kislik, August 23, 1973, Box 85, folder 12, Scranton Papers.

81. InText 1968 Annual Report, Box 85, folder 11, Scranton Papers. In 1970, Scranton owned 6 percent of the 1,430,921 shares of InText. He was the vice president for legal affairs at ICS from 1949 to 1954. It is possible that he inherited some of his shares from his father, who was on the board of directors when his son joined ICS.

82. Rex Taylor to Norman Rockwell, April 28, 1969, 1969 folder, Rockwell Business Papers; The Forbes Investor, May 25, 1970, 1970 folder, Rockwell Business Papers.

83. Jessica Mitford, "Let Us Now Appraise Famous Writers," *Atlantic*, July 1970, 45–54.

84. Robert Fawcett to Norman Rockwell, n.d., 1967 folder, Rockwell Business Papers.

85. Handwritten notes in Box 100, folder 2, Jessica Mitford Papers.

86. August 20, 1998, C-Span 2/Book TV tributes to Jessica Mitford. He did not mention her sly tactic of telling the officers and guiding faculty that she was only interested in writing a review of Byrne's book. John T. Lawrence to Phyllis McGinley, January 15, 1970, Box 9, "Famous Writers School, 1970" folder, McGinley Papers.

87. *Atlantic*, September 1970, 44.

88. Ibid., 50.

89. Robert Byrne, *Writing Rackets* (New York: Lyle Stuart, 1969), chap. 2. "I made it deliberately negative in an effort to offset the thousands of inspirational books that have been written about writers and writing," Byrne told Granville Hicks (January 7, 1970), Box 11, "Robert Byrne" folder, Hicks Papers, Syracuse University.

90. Peter Y. Sussman, ed., *DECCA: The Letters of Jessica Mitford* (New York: Knopf, 2006), 409.

91. Jessica Mitford, *Poison Penmanship: The Gentle Art of Muckraking* (New York: Knopf, 1979), 177. From the Mitford Papers, it is clear that she was eager for a lawsuit. She thought that the revelation of "canned paragraphs" in the instructors' letters was evidence of fraud, and she sent one student the address of a lawyer she thought might take the case. She hoped that Miles Copeland would sue because the school mentioned his best seller in several advertisements (he had dropped out). She considered suing the school when it circulated a letter alleging 23 errors in her story (she acknowledged only two). Alternatively, she hoped that the school would sue her, which a lawyer for the *Atlantic Monthly* predicted would happen but never did.

92. Transcript in the Bergen Evans Papers, Box 21, folder 3.

93. Mitford, *Poison Penmanship*, 177–78; John T. Lawrence to FWS Guiding Faculty, December 15, 1970, Box 9, "Famous Writers School 1970" folder, Phyllis McGinley Papers.

94. March 30, 1971, deposition (transcript), Box 10, folder 9, Rod Serling Papers, Wisconsin Historical Society.

95. Rod Serling to John Lawrence, December 16, 1970; Rod Serling to Sara Sendelbach, September 18, 1970, Box 10, folder 9, Serling Papers.

96. Diary entries of June 22, 1970; November 11, 1970; January 21, 1971 ("Should we add new members—younger? A woman? A black man—James Baldwin? Vance Packard?"), and April 22, 1971, Box 7, folder 5, John Caples Papers.

97. Ben Stahl to Fritz Henning, January 11, 1972; Ben Stahl, folder in FAS Papers, Norman Rockwell Museum.

98. June 22, 1970, diary entry, Box 7, folder 5, Caples Papers.

99. Sussman, *DECCA*, 415.

100. For the woes of 1971 and 1972, I relied on articles in the *Wall Street Journal* as well as entries in John Caples's diary. The company emerged from bankruptcy in 1974, when the annual sales for all FAS schools was only $1.2 million and freelance staff replaced all the full-time instructors. Both the chairman and the president were investment bankers; they used the huge tax loss to borrow enough to buy a much larger company, a distributor of pipes, and thus avoid paying taxes until 1979. Cortina Learning, a correspondence school started in New York City in the 1890s by a Spanish count, bought the home study remnants of FAS in 1981. *26th Annual Report*, Box 9, "Famous Writers School, 1968–1975" folder, McGinley Papers; Fritz Henning to Will Barnet, July 2, 1975, Box 3, folder 42, Will Barnet Papers, Archives of American Art, Smithsonian Institution, Washington, DC.

101. Earle Robbins to Norman Rockwell, August 28, 1972; Leonard Shine and Paul Kurmay to Guiding Faculty of Famous Artists School, 1971/72 folder, Rockwell Business Papers.

102. Ben Stahl to Fritz Henning, March 1973; Ben Stahl folder, FAS Papers, Norman Rockwell Museum.

103. Arthur F. Abelman to Norman Rockwell, October 10, 1973, 1973 Folder, Rockwell Business Papers.

104. Donald Trump, *Trump: The Art of the Deal* (New York: Random House, 1987), 40.

105. William D. Cohan, "Big Hair on Campus," *Vanity Fair*, December 3, 2013.

106. Ruth L. Smith to Jessica Mitford, August 13, 1970, Box 101, folder 6, Jessica Mitford Papers.

2

SHORTCUTS TO CULTURE

From the Harvard Classics to Cliffs Notes

In the wilderness of all the books which have been written, the perplexed reader must always be grateful for friendly and competent guidance.[1]—Harvard Classics (1909)

Today, a whole generation of English teachers has grown up on Cliffs Notes. Teachers often ask their students to read sections of the Notes before they actually begin to teach the assigned work itself.[2]—Clifton K. Hillegass, chairman and founder of Cliffs Notes (1985)

Most Americans today want education to lead to a good job. Years of hard work should pay off. Whether the graduates use their hands or their heads usually matters less than the financial security from earning a diploma or degree. Most policy makers share that point of view. They justify the billions spent on schools and colleges by linking education with economic strength. *America's ability to compete* and *workforce readiness* are allegedly at risk if students drop out or graduate without useful skills.

So we often forget that *liberal culture* was once a cherished outcome of prolonged study. Knowing the masterpieces of literature, philosophy, art, and music was part of liberal culture, as was the ability to read Latin and Greek. Beyond the appreciation of specific subjects was a certain temperament. Words like *polish*, *taste*, and *discernment* suggest the traits of liberal culture, and the word *liberal* meant liberating, not a political position—the well-educated graduate was free of ignorance, error, and superstition. For Princeton's Woodrow Wilson, liberal culture required "the intimate and sensitive appreciation of moral, intellectual, and aesthetic values."[3] The enemies were greed, anti-intellectualism, and overspecialization.

Despite the fear of graduating prigs and snobs unprepared to make a living, most people in the late 19th and early 20th centuries felt that liberal culture enhanced rather than diminished the character and the careers of the young.[4] The mind would acquire *power* (a widely used word at the time) that transferred across fields. For instance, landscape design impressed Harvard's president as a good way to "open the eyes to natural beauty and the mind to the principles of harmony, contrast, and proportion."[5]

If the acquisition of culture required immersion in books in addition to (or in place of) the right friends and family, then the ambitious reader need not return to school or college or pay for a correspondence course. The pursuit of knowledge could happen independently. Anyone could buy inexpensive books from publishers who reprinted the works of eminent writers. Cost was not an obstacle; publishers often undercut each other with lower and lower prices.[6] To get started, a novice could ask friends, copy what the local schools assigned, or buy a book to find out what to read. The self-educated rarely went at it entirely alone. As one advertisement asked, "How can a busy man or woman know what is the best literature? How can you single out the books that will entertain and benefit you most when the smallest public library contains enough volumes to keep you reading for fifty lifetimes?"[7]

Trust the president of Harvard University: that was one way to know what to read to be cultured. When Charles W. Eliot retired in 1909 after 40 years in office, Harvard was the nation's premier university. Linking Eliot's prestige with any publication was sure to impress readers in search of dependable advice. When the Harvard overseers agreed to let the books he chose be called the Harvard Classics even though a commercial publisher, Colliers, would sell them, the appeal of the enterprise was guaranteed. Approximately 20,000 sets sold each year while Eliot was alive.[8]

Working with a professor of English, Eliot assembled 50 books soon known as the "five-foot shelf." Their choices included science and politics, not just the humanities. As one clerk wrote to Colliers, "I did not put these books in my library—they are my library."[9] Some of the wide-ranging selections were creative—a book of prefaces, a volume of American historical documents, and five compilations of essays. Other choices were quirky—nothing by Aristotle, Marx, or Freud; only two works of 19th-century literature; and little space for Rousseau because Eliot deplored his desertion of his children.[10]

Eliot thought that "partially educated" Americans would be the main market (although the publisher sent flyers to Harvard alumni).[11] He reassured them that they could decide how to proceed. Going in chronological order was fine; so was focusing on a particular subject. Comparing and contrasting different authors was a third option. Reader's Guides offered introductory essays and recommended authors on particular topics and eras, and dozens of Harvard faculty contributed to *Lectures on the Harvard Classics*, a book of 60 snapshots of 12 subjects.

Eliot acknowledged that it would not be quick or easy. Although he said that 15 minutes a day would let a conscientious reader make progress, the Harvard Classics "require attention and a resolute spirit." He hoped that the outcome would be a lifelong "taste for serious reading of highest quality."[12]

Exertion for the intrinsic reward of cultivation—Eliot's goal—was rarely what the advertisements stressed. Self-education would be "pleasant" and even "thrilling." The Readers Guides became "easy reading courses" for the volumes that "compressed all the really important things ever written." The free pamphlet describing the five-foot shelf was titled "15 Minutes a Day," a phrase repeated in many headlines.

Moreover, the ads often promised that any exertion would be repaid in financial and social success. Reading the books marked "the difference between the plodding clerk and the clear-thinking executive" because "the time has passed when the untutored man can reach the heights of success." In an ad that could have glorified soap or shampoo, one woman "is seldom invited to go out; she is lonely all day long," while the fortunate one who "has learned the secret of Fifteen Minutes a Day" had "a calendar that is crowded with interesting, delightful engagements."[13] The ads set a precedent for later claims for similar wares—the pursuit of culture would be painless, and the results of that pursuit would be profitable.

Eliot disliked the breezy advertisements for clouding his message—everyone can and should read the classics, but it will take hard work—a message that reappeared in the writing of another famous champion of the great books: the philosopher Mortimer Adler. A professor at the University of Chicago from 1930 to 1952, Adler made the headlines by virtue of his close collaborations with Robert Hutchins, the Chicago president who shared Adler's enthusiasm for Plato, Aquinas, Locke, and other heavyweights. Adler oversaw the publication of The Great Books of the Western World, a 54-volume, 32,000-page compilation of 443 works by 74 authors.

Like the Harvard Classics, this massive series offered assistance to the reader. The entries were indexed to 102 "great ideas" that encompassed nearly 3,000 topics. A separate "author to author" index let readers see when particular men (and they were all men) took up the ideas of their predecessors and contemporaries. The "author to idea" index tallied how many great ideas each writer covered (Aristotle and Aquinas touched all 102; Kant missed one, and Plato missed two). Adler himself wrote 102 essays for the 102 great ideas, devoting every day for more than two years to that exhausting job.

Encyclopedia Britannica published the books for $250 in 1952 (the equivalent of $2,000 in 2016), and with the help of eager door-to-door salesmen (twice sanctioned by the Federal Trade Commission for misrepresentations) and extensive advertising (including testimonials from boxer Gene Tunney), nearly 1 million copies were sold by the late 1970s. Like the combination of Eliot, Harvard, and Colliers, the alliance of a famous educator, prominent university, and savvy publisher let Adler, Chicago, and Britannica accomplish their goals.[14]

Even more than Eliot, Adler insisted that serious reading was hard work. Unlike the entertainment and information conveyed by radio shows, thinking was difficult, more rocks than roses, as he put it.[15] Reading quickly made sense only for getting the gist of a book; truly important books required slow reading several times. Adler devoted six months in one University of Chicago class to dissecting Plato's Meno, and for another course he agreed to the students' request to repeat it so that they could reread everything. The best books are "always over my head," he wrote in his autobiography, and he made his 32,000-page Great Books behemoth harder by not including notes on arcane language, technical terminology, or historical context.[16]

Yet like Eliot's 15-minutes-a-day claim, Adler also implied that the daunting job of understanding Western civilization could be done by ordinary men and women. He encouraged millions with peppy articles in *Good Housekeeping, Ladies Home Journal, Reader's Digest,* and *Playboy.* Adler wrote one book in the form of an outline (he was disappointed that readers did not find it as simple as he thought they would), and another book had the alluring title *Aristotle for Everybody: Difficult Thought Made Easy.* For those unable or unwilling to buy 54 volumes, he published a 10-volume *Gateway to the Great Books* as well as a one-volume book of quotations. His syndicated newspaper column "Great Ideas from the Great Books" offered bite-size lessons.

Even with assistance and encouragement, most readers found the great books difficult. One of Adler's advisers predicted that the prospect of grappling with the masterpieces would "terrify many potential buyers who would perhaps fail to buy if they thought they were supposed to read them," so he suggested an index to the index to provide suitable topics for polite conversation at Thanksgiving and Christmas dinners. As Hutchins reminded Adler, "Most of my friends are interested in money, fame, power, and sex—I don't see those in the 102 ideas."[17] The most impenetrable authors were the early modern scientists, like Kepler and Copernicus; Columbia Professor John Erskine agreed with Adler on most issues, but he thought it was "ridiculous if not criminal" to include technical treatises that had been superseded by later investigations.[18] The supplemental aids—the introductory essays, indices, and suggested order of reading—required more time without making the selections much easier to comprehend. Often, the great books stayed on the owner's shelves, unread yet prominently displayed as conspicuous evidence of noble aspirations.[19]

CULTURE CAN BE FUN

At one point in the selection of Adler's great books, Robert Hutchins praised the novel *Tristam Shandy.* "It's a very funny book, and I thought the set was a little deficient along those lines."[20] Hutchins had a sharp wit—he could not resist calling Adler the "great bookie"—and his endorsement of *Tristam Shandy* spoke to the possibility that the pursuit of culture could be fun. What if the "partially educated" read, for pleasure, less strenuous fare derived from the great works? The satisfaction of tracing complicated arguments and interpreting unfamiliar prose might not gratify readers who could be attracted by less austere language and less intricate ideas.

In the 1920s, several authors eager to make culture enjoyable reached far more people than ever opened the Harvard Classics or The Great Books of the Western World. Books that sketched the *outline* of a vast field or that told its *story* sold very well. "Give the reader a break" was the motto of one publisher, and the outline books certainly did that.[21] Simple diction, short paragraphs, brief chapters, second-person comments to the reader, rhetorical questions, frequent illustrations: those strategies gave the readers many breaks. To ease the burden even more, the outlines usually omitted footnotes, overlooked disagreements among scholars, and included short biographies to show the ordinary trials and tribulations of extraordinary people.

"The cream of the world's knowledge for quick and easy self-improvement!" one outline ad announced—a 700-page "equivalent of a College education" for the person enrolled so far in "the College of Hard Knocks." What might have been complex and dry became clear, interesting, and entertaining.[22] In a decade when college enrollments rose more rapidly than ever before (doubling from 1920 to 1930), the assurance that the readers could keep pace with the well educated was a shrewd marketing strategy.[23] Furthermore, the popularizers enlivened their books with material unlikely to appear in scholarly work. For instance, philosopher Will Durant would periodically offer a platitude—"nothing is as terrible as solitude"—or an unsubstantiated assertion—"those who have suffered much become very bitter or very gentle."[24] Historian Hendrik van Loon spiced his books with occasional fabrications—a letter from a soldier who had supposedly talked to witnesses of Christ's crucifixion or Marie Antoinette on the scaffold recalling an opera by Rossini, who, at the time of the Queen's execution, was one year old.[25]

Van Loon and Durant, both of whom earned PhDs, criticized scholars as boring. To keep his students alert, van Loon used crayons to draw people and places when he lectured at Cornell for a few years; colleagues there thought he belonged in vaudeville, and one son later called him a clown. Van Loon in turn felt that "the professors may rave and I bid them go jump in the lake for I merely took their unpalatable product and fixed it up in such a way that the average man and woman began to suspect that history was not completely a waste of time."[26] Van

Loon's cheerfulness enlivened a stream of letters to Eleanor and Franklin Roosevelt, sending political advice, postage stamps for FDR's collection, and even food—"the papers are so full of unpleasant news that I thought the President might find solace in a fresh Edam cheese."[27]

Unlike van Loon, Durant would occasionally use Latin phrases and refer to authors he had not yet discussed. Those infrequent pirouettes reminded the readers of what Durant spared them—he was sure that his books sold well because they were easy to read. When criticized as too simple, he defended himself by dismissing the specialists as tedious and incomprehensible. "Dullness is by sacred tradition the necessary mark of the scholar; and if a man cannot make himself understood, he must be profound."[28] Durant assumed that most people did not share the notion of fun held by David Denby, a film critic who returned to Columbia University, 26 years after his graduation, to take two courses in literature and philosophy. What he meant by excitement, happy, and pleasure was far from what Durant or van Loon had in mind. Denby wanted the assigned books to be arduous—"the more difficulty the better." The violence of the metaphors he used conveyed the intensity of the year—"tumbled around like a sneaker thrown into the dryer," "a bumpy ride," and "turned upside down." He found Hegel "excruciatingly difficult," and Kant was "exhausting." Rather than feeling depressed or confused, Denby relished the chance to try to understand minds more powerful than his own.[29]

Compared to Eliot and Adler, Durant and van Loon were irreverent. They were intellectuals who were willing to mock other intellectuals and also flout conventional norms—Durant had been a socialist, and van Loon had a lifelong obsession with women's feet. All four were seen by most readers as authorities and experts, trustworthy allies to help the uninitiated. But Durant and van Loon were friendlier, less remote, and more amusing than Eliot and Adler, who provided only advice and guidance rather than transform culture into lively summaries and simple overviews. The alliance that sustained the Harvard Classics and The Great Books—famous scholar, prestigious university, and savvy publisher—shifted whenever writers like Durant and van Loon lacked university affiliations and became famous after, not before, their popularizations sold well. The publisher was therefore even more crucial as the pipeline to a vast audience—skillful marketing was essential. Without faculty appointments and scholarly achievements, the purveyors of culture drew sharper criticism than Eliot or Adler incurred, but they also reached more Americans.

To the skeptics, the engaging outline and story books trivialized culture. "You cannot bring Kant down to the level of the casual reader," literary critic Howard Mumford Jones insisted; "the casual reader must labor up to Kant." Durant crossed the line between simplification and oversimplification; he caused harm "by leading naïve readers to suppose that this is the way to unlock the gates of wisdom. Here it all is—so simple, so clear, so predigested. Why go further?"[30] The most scathing review he ever received compared his gigantic history of civilization to cheese spread: "good color, little taste, easy to use, boring in bulk, and infinitely remote from the true product." Durant ignored recent scholarship, overemphasized the importance of individual people, and saw progress as inevitable. "This book is unworthy of the traditions of American scholarship. It is also dangerous for it is so facile that the unwary will be first ensnared and then misled."[31]

To optimistic outliners and storytellers, the ensnared would eventually read original work by philosophers, academic historians, and other serious authors. Popular accounts would ease reluctant and skeptical readers into a wide range of good books, they claimed. As historian Rhys Isaac said, "Writers of popular histories are frequently sneered at, but I wonder how often their work has encouraged young beginners like me."[32] *The Story of Philosophy* could be a transition to harder fare. Durant proudly reported the unprecedented demand at public libraries for the authors he had discussed in that book.[33]

But the readers could also run the other way in the 1920s, as the history of the popular "little blue books" indicated. Newspaper editor Emanuel Haldeman-Julius (who, unlike Durant and van Loon, was not a PhD) sold reprints of the classics for a dime each and did so well that he lowered the cost to a nickel and expanded the list to include many subjects. He soon stopped using the word *classics* in his advertisements. "People would rather read something they know will interest them, instead of gambling with something merely on a reputation fostered largely, they think, by old fogy college professors and bespectacled students of literature."[34]

His tiny booklets (usually 18 square inches and 32 or 64 pages) on romance, psychology, health, sports, crime, religion, and humor outsold the landmarks of Western civilization. *The Physiology of Sex Life*, *The*

Art of Kissing, Catholicism and Sex, Facts about Venereal Diseases, Prostitution in the Modern World, and other racy fare were among the dozens of little books in the most popular category: sex and love. In contrast, poetry, plays, and fiction were hard to sell; so were speeches, essays, and literary criticism. He saw that "the reading public wants books that are not too esoteric, not too high-hat, not too refined and highbrow," even though he continued to call his list a "University in Print."[35]

To keep the hats from looking too high, Haldeman-Julius changed the title if a book did not sell well. "Who on earth cares to read a story about a ball of tarrow?" Guy de Maupassant's *The Tarrow Ball* became *A French Prostitute's Sacrifice*, and sales tripled. Francis Bacon's *Apothegms* survived as *Terse Truths about the Riddle of Life*; Oscar Wilde's *Pen, Pencil and Poison* reappeared as *The Story of a Notorious Criminal*; and sales quadrupled by adding "lustful" to Victor Hugo's *The King Enjoys Himself*. A Guide to Rabelais didn't do as well as *How to Understand Rabelais*, but *How to Enjoy the Humor of Rabelais* did even better. *How to Get a Liberal Education* and *Facts You Should Know about the Classics* sold 15,000 and 25,000 copies, respectively, in 1927, enough to stay in print but far behind the best sellers, like *What Married Men Should Know* (97,500), *How to Improve Your Conversation* (77,000), *Care of Skin and Hair* (52,000), *Best Jokes of 1926* (50,500), and *Facts about Fortune-Telling* (44,000).

Durant, van Loon, and Haldeman-Julius simplified but never abandoned the printed page; what if a gateway to culture relied on illustrations rather than words in order to give the readers a break? One company tried to interest the young in great literature by selling them comics. For a dime, 64-page condensations of *The Three Musketeers, Ivanhoe, The Count of Monte Cristo, The Last of the Mohicans, Moby Dick*, and other novels offered adventure, fights, and heroism, the main themes of the Superman, Flash Gordon, Dick Tracy, Wonder Woman, and Batman titles that made comics so popular in the late 1930s and beyond.[36]

Early in the boom, subjects other than science fiction or superhuman crusaders appeared. True Comics covered contemporary and historical topics, the focus of Picture Stories from American History.[37] They did not fare nearly as well as Classic Comics, which featured tales of daring and danger rarely found in the Harvard Classics or Adler's

Great Books. Jules Verne was chosen most often, followed by Alexandre Dumas, James Fenimore Cooper, and Robert Louis Stevenson (none of them impressed Eliot or Adler). Millions of free copies were sent to servicemen in World War II. Total sales in the first decade topped 200 million, helped in part by the parents who found Classic Comics more wholesome than the violent crime and horror stories that pervaded other comics in the late 1940s and early 1950s.

The popularity did not derive from the imprimatur of famous scholars or top-tier universities. The founder of the company was a salesman, a high school dropout who hired freelance artists and writers, not scholars, to create each comic. But the Classics seemed more aligned with schooling than did other comics. Each issue included a short biography of the author, literary quizzes, synopses of great operas, or profiles of sports legends, scientists, explorers, and inventors. The name changed in 1947 to Classics Illustrated to highlight the educational aspirations, and issues began to carry this line: "Now that you have read the Classics Illustrated edition, don't miss the added enjoyment of reading the original."[38]

No one knows how many Classics Illustrated readers eventually read unabridged fiction, but we do know that teachers rarely used the comics. The company developed a nonfiction Picture Progress series specifically for schools, with titles in history (*Paul Revere's Ride*), science (*The Story of Flight*), current events (*Around the World with the UN*), and so on. The line folded after two years. The swashbuckling in Classics Illustrated was more popular than the didactic Picture Progress comics. In the wake of early 1950s congressional investigations of the gore, sadism, and sexuality in many comics, educators were unwilling to welcome a type of publication that aroused so much concern. It might be fine to get a taste of great literature, but all comic books had been tainted by the severed heads and murdered parents on sale for a dime.[39]

Not everyone thought the Classics Illustrated were harmless. The changes to the original often altered the distinctive style and voice of the writers; for instance, "Call me Ishmael" at the start of *Moby Dick* became "Out of the bleak December dusk, walks the lone figure of Ishmael, looking for a night's lodging" (perhaps wondering why there was a comma after *dusk*). The 222 words in Hamlet's famous "to be or not to be" speech turned into "Life is sad. If death is like sleep, it might be better to die." The characters in *Wuthering Heights* were attired in the fashions of the next century.

A well-known writer, Delmore Schwartz, mocked the changes. The absence of the heroine from *Crime and Punishment* made Dostoyevsky's novel "a trite detective story," and the captions in *A Midsummer Night's Dream* were entirely prose rather than poetry (on the other hand, *Julius Caesar* retained many short lines from the original and kept big words like *vouchsafe, entreat,* and *prostrate*).[40]

Schwartz might have been happier if he had known how one English teacher in Philadelphia shrewdly used *Ivanhoe*. He told everyone to buy the Classics Illustrated (many students already had it, hidden in their larger history textbook). They read several pages together in class. At one point, he told the group that it was good, although it did not describe one character as fully as the original. A girl took the bait and asked him to read that section to them. The class then decided to make their own comic book, devoting three weeks to writing and illustrating it on large brown paper hung on the walls and shared with another English class. The best testimonial to the project came when one boy said, "Gee, you really have to know what a book's about when you're writing it."[41]

In art education, a popular fad in the early 1950s raised the same question as the comics: would a quick and painless introduction to creative work convince the novices to try it on their own? Aspiring artists could read Winston Churchill's *Painting as a Pastime* (1950) for encouragement to take up the hobby, or they could follow the advice of Grandma Moses, who began painting at age 78 when she decided it would be easier than baking a cake for the mailman: "Anybody that's got two eyes can paint."[42]

To be sure that the initiation succeeded on the first try, millions of Americans bought inexpensive kits with a canvas covered by tiny numbered sections to be filled in with the oil paints supplied by the manufacturer. The paint-by-numbers advertisements promised that everyone could do it successfully because it was "easy as 1-2-3."[43] "If you can count, you can paint. No bother, no work—just fun." The largest company, Palmer Paint, sponsored demonstrations in department stores where one sign read, "Anyone can do it: the lady painting this picture is not a painter."[44]

The hardest decision for the consumer was selecting from the dozens of options created by the companies' artists, who were not famous and were not affiliated with universities. The most popular choices were landscapes, seascapes, animals, flowers, foreign scenes, and religion; abstract art didn't do well, and only a few vendors offered a nude (from the waist up).[45] Tiles, trays, and magazine racks could be adorned in the same foolproof way. For $20, anyone could send a black-and-white photograph of a relative or friend and receive a numbered board with supplies so that the buyer could then paint the oil portrait. Former President Herbert Hoover, FBI Director J. Edgar Hoover, Governor Nelson Rockefeller, UN Ambassador Henry Cabot Lodge, Attorney General Herbert Brownell, and a few other officials did not have to pay anything for their sets because they were a Christmas gift from President Eisenhower, who was a decent painter in his own right.[46]

When the National Museum of American History in Washington, D.C., had a paint-by-numbers exhibition in 2001, several visitors mentioned that the kits sparked their interest in taking classes and making art their career. For the vast majority, it had been enjoyable in childhood (although many adults also bought the sets, and the ads usually showed wide-eyed young women joyously displaying what they had created). Fun on a rainy day, relief when sick in bed, pride at framing the canvas to hang on the wall, happy that the parents who gave the kits as gifts liked the results, glad to help decorate a house without other art: for various reasons, painting by numbers had been pleasurable.[47]

The visitors' recollections expressed several themes that also mark the array of shortcuts to culture. Each shortcut offered a bridge to a deeper immersion, but they could be satisfying without going farther, especially when the shortcut sold itself as an enjoyable pursuit that made culture fun rather than an ordeal. And the enjoyment could be widely shared. All the shortcuts sketched so far were remarkably democratic. Everyone was invited to partake regardless of social class, gender, or previous education, with the assurance that everyone in their spare time could succeed.

Another parallel was the energetic promotion of the shortcuts in the marketplace. The fast track to culture was for sale rather than distributed for free. Adroit advertising extolled and exaggerated the benefits not just from faith in the merit of what was offered; there was also a quest to make money and ward off rivals who wanted a piece of the action.

And that fueled a final parallel: critics often deplored the packaging of elite culture as an alluring purchase rather than a disposition apart from and elevated above commerce. In their opinion, whatever benefits could be readily bought lacked the enduring distinctions earned by the small band who took the longer and harder paths. Genuine culture was not a commodity in the lives of the truly cultured.[48]

Each well-known shortcut therefore evoked criticism, ridicule, and lamentations about the slothfulness and gullibility of the masses. Selling quick and easy paths to culture had misrepresented *how* a person became cultured and distorted *what* constituted culture. But for millions of Americans, there was no shame in seeing culture—its pursuit as well as its possession—as fast, easy, fun, cheap, and useful. They far outnumbered the skeptics who thought that shortcuts bamboozled the naive and revealed their lack of culture.

"THESE NOTES ARE NOT A SUBSTITUTE FOR THE TEXT"

The "anyone can do it" spirit of paint by numbers captivated artist Andy Warhol, who, in 1962, made five do-it-yourself paintings modeled on the popular kits. He left the numbers on each painting, and only one of the five had each section finished. He claimed that he just got bored, but the work is more powerful partially done. If someone else could finish a painting, who is the artist? What is originality? Does "real" art have to be difficult? When two things look alike, why is one considered art and the other not?[49]

Warhol's provocations were one sign of changing notions of culture by the 1960s. Fewer Americans accepted the old idea that a small set of masterworks defined culture. Creative work of many kinds, including popular music, abstract art, and avant-garde fiction, seemed to be admirable. To be cultured came to signify an open-mindedness to a wide range of books, art, and other forms of expression. Scorning mass and popular culture, as highbrows had done, began to seem silly rather than wise. An omnivorous approach to the world, a cosmopolitan curiosity, was now the mark of distinction. "Jaws and Beowulf are both cultural artifacts to be played with," as one sociologist observed.[50]

With less urgency to find shortcuts to culture because culture can be everywhere for the person who is open to variety, the shortcut of choice for many students is practical and specific: earning a decent grade for the least possible expenditure of time and effort. That attitude became more widespread as late 20th- and early 21st-century Americans increasingly saw learning in utilitarian terms—the market value of the credential mattered more than the other benefits of education. Liberal arts enrollments declined, and goals like "developing a meaningful philosophy of life" became much less important to college freshmen. Books like *Excellent Sheep* accused even the very best students of turning the Ivy League into vocational training.[51]

In the past 50 years, the options expanded for the student in search of a road map through the classics assigned in school or college, where many older landmarks of culture stayed on the course syllabi. Classics Illustrated had provided a thumbnail sketch of a play or book, but tests and papers usually required considerably more.[52] Encyclopedias, book reviews, commentaries, anthologies, and abridgements had been around for centuries, but they were rarely written with high school or college students in mind—snippets like *Beauties of Shakespeare*, *Wit and Wisdom of George Eliot*, or the Thomas Hardy calendar with a quote for each day of the year were designed for adults.[53] The rise of written tests in the late 19th century did spur the publication of *pocket manuals*, *question books*, *quiz compends*, and other reviews, but they typically printed hundreds of question-and-answer items rather than paraphrases of canonical works.[54] What if someone published an inexpensive study guide for students offering more summary and commentary than an article but less than a monograph?

When Clifton Hillegass received the first of his four honorary doctorates, the graduating seniors at Nebraska Wesleyan University stood and cheered as he walked across the stage. For 30 years, his company had been their friend.[55] Cliffs Notes began in 1958 as $1 reprints of Canadian study guides for 16 plays by Shakespeare. At that time, Hillegass worked in Lincoln, Nebraska, for a major distributor of college textbooks. As the director of the wholesale department, he knew hundreds of campus bookstore managers across the country. Those close relationships (he had a good memory for the names of wives and children) gave him the first outlets for the Notes. As one manager said,

"Well, they'll never sell, but since Cliff's putting them out, we gotta give them a shot. Order ten of each."

Operating from his basement until 1965, Hillegass and his wife (who did the day-to-day work, with envelope stuffing and post office runs by the children) offered several incentives for his colleagues to sell the Notes—toll-free phone orders, same-day shipments, free display racks, advertisements in the campus newspaper, and no time limits on returns. As the business grew in the 1960s—sales reached 1 million copies in 1964—the bookstores also received posters, drawstring bags to give away, and little "Ask clerk for Cliffs Notes on this title" stickers to put underneath other books. The display racks became larger—of the 10 designs in 1969, the largest could hold 1,000 Notes.

To reach beyond college campuses, copies of the yellow and black pamphlets appeared in drugstores, department stores (which at that time often sold books), national chains like B. Dalton, and even unusual but very successful spots like O'Hare airport in Chicago and a liquor store across from a California high school. Hillegass knew the book business, and his dozen full-time salesmen worked hard in the mid- to late 1960s to offer prompt and reliable service. Success did not require affiliation with a premier university or the recruitment of famous scholars to write or endorse the Notes—most of the authors taught at small colleges, many lacked PhDs, and over time more and more high school teachers did the revisions.[56]

National advertising also helped. Hillegass took out a loan for more than the value of his family's house to buy space in regional editions of magazines like *Seventeen, Time, Sports Illustrated, Playboy*, and so on. Most of the messages were playfully empathetic—Dickens got you down? Pained by Twain? Mangled by Melville? Take the murder out of *MacBeth*. Another theme was obvious in the ads that announced, "Better grades start here," "108 ways to make better grades," and "How busy people earn better grades," where a football player swipes a Cliffs Notes from the back pocket of a teammate. As college, graduate, and professional school admissions became more competitive in the 1960s (and the military draft took the dropouts, sometimes to Vietnam), the references to grades spoke directly to the younger generation's ambitions and anxieties. Several ads in *McCall's* and *Family Circle* even coaxed mothers to buy the "study aid" for their teenagers.[57]

An ad in a Shakespeare newsletter promoted another product, the Complete Study Guides, with the full original text in the center, a glossary on the left, commentary on the right, and occasional sketches and illustrations throughout. Hillegass thought that those paperbacks would soon outsell the Notes, and to encourage their use he gave away thousands of copies at the annual meetings of the National Council of Teachers of English. They never did. Although the company kept them in print, the line had only 12 titles by the 1990s with annual sales only 3% percent of what the Notes brought in.[58]

The Cliffs Notes company grew by creating more study aids rather than finding mainstream respectability with the Complete Study Guides. Course outlines; "keynote reviews" to prepare for exams; audio-cassettes of the Notes; coaching for high-stakes standardized tests like the SAT, ACT, GRE, and GMAT; a Coif series for law school courses; and Advanced Placement overviews eventually contributed half of the company's annual revenues.

The short Bluffer's Guide books—80-page humorous overviews of football, wine, computers, sex, and 20 other topics—could have been a blockbuster. They had sold well in England, so the company bought the rights to sell them in the United States. The title worried the sales force—the Notes had tried for decades to overcome the perception that they were a way to bluff—and the new line was overshadowed by other vendors' longer, cleverly titled, and more fact-filled Complete Idiots and For Dummies guides.[59] Had Hillegass positioned Bluffers just a bit differently—more self-deprecatory titles and more useful content—he might have dominated the vast market captured by those rivals, who sold over 100 million copies in their first 10 years.

Even so, the company's overall sales grew steadily, helped by expansion overseas and the occasional distribution of other publishers' books. The company was always profitable, and rivals like Monarch Notes never took more than a fraction of the market. In 1988, Hillegass said he had 20 offers to buy the company.[60] Occasionally, a Note would appear on the *New York Times* best-seller list until the newspaper refused to include them.[61] Annual revenue peaked in the mid-1990s at $20 million and then declined as Internet study aids proliferated; even so, the company was sold for $14.2 million in 1998 to IDG Books, a publisher of travel guides, cookbooks, and the Dummies series of how-to manuals.

By that time, the phrase Cliffs Notes was a shortcut, a readily understood term for any type of brief explanation. For instance, the quiz show *Jeopardy!* once had a Cliffs Notes: Drama category, with short clues like "Laura: You broke my unicorn! Gentleman caller: Whoops." One corporate leader knew that even the phrase "Bob's Notes" on a bright yellow page with the familiar black diagonal stripes would be understood by the readers of his annual report.[62] The trademark cover was so familiar that the company sued the publisher of *Spy Notes*, a parody that spoofed rather than summarized various novels and also poked fun at Cliffs Notes by offering a "Novel-O-Matic Fiction-Writing Device" to let an author create 16,765,056 different plots.[63]

More than 200 different Notes helped several generations of high school and college students throughout the country make sense of what their English teachers told them to read.[64] For some students, *make sense* meant reading Cliffs Notes instead of the assignment, ignoring Hillegass's capitalized warning inside the front cover: THESE NOTES ARE NOT A SUBSTITUTE FOR THE TEXT ITSELF OR FOR THE CLASSROOM DISCUSSION OF THE TEXT.[65] The scene-by-scene, chapter-by-chapter summaries provided straightforward overviews of plot, characters, symbols, and other aspects of the text. The factual bits and pieces let many students pass high school exams with true-or-false, matching, fill-in-the-blanks, and short-answer questions, almost a necessity for teachers with 120 to 150 students. The Cliffs Notes were closer than the landmark literature to what the overburdened teachers expected students to know. Deeper understanding was usually optional, not required.

But for some students, the Notes supplied more than factual scraps. As one literary critic said, "The producers of Cliff Notes know what educators often ignore, which is that most students need special help to produce a kind of literary-critical talk that is rarely spoken outside the literature class or the book review pages."[66] Reading the text does not reveal how to write about the text, which is usually required of college students, who bought 30 percent of the Notes.[67]

Students have to learn two types of language—the words in the assigned pages and the words to discuss those pages. The commentaries, character analyses, historical background, and other guidance modeled how to think, speak, and write (which meant that a diligent student who used Cliffs Notes in addition to the assigned pages would spend more, not less, time; the Notes, in other words, did not have to be a faster-easier shortcut). One popular set of study guides created in 1999, Spark Notes, included a section titled "How to Write a Literary Analysis" along with a sample essay, and Pink Monkey, born in 1997, offered a 24-lesson "Study Smart" course for students as well as advice for parents.

Teachers could also enhance their skills by using the Notes. Hillegass told a reporter that 45 percent of classroom teachers approved of the Notes,[68] and he paid one Notes author to write a Cliffs Notes in the Classroom. She offered 64 different ways to use the Notes, including several activities where students critiqued them (disagree with and then revise a section), others that expanded what was there (write more study questions), a few that could be done without buying the Notes (what if Huck Finn had been a girl?), and one that recast them as references—in her own ninth-grade classroom she had good results from tacking a copy to the bulletin board for students to use when they felt lost.[69] "I did whatever was necessary to get the points across."[70]

The coaching is usually more concise than the assistance extended in the scholarly editions of major literary masterpieces. For instance, many reprints of a relatively simple play like *Julius Caesar* include historical context, biographical details, definitions, footnotes, suggestions for further reading, and commentary. The Oxford Shakespeare offers 83 pages from the editor, the Signet edition has seven critical essays, and Norton provides 68 pages of analysis from 11 scholars, 34 introductory pages from the editor, and 70 pages on the play's sources, leaving the play itself (82 pages) less than half the length of the supplemental sections. Help is available in many forms; everyone needs and deserves assistance. One older edition of Shakespeare's work even offered two sets of notes: one for the "average reader" and another for the "critical student or scholar."[71] However, some tools are more accessible than others. Not only are the Cliffs Notes and Spark Notes shorter, but they are also easier to find, slightly cheaper (or free—several online vendors earn money only from advertisements), and thin enough to tuck inside a notebook or read on a smartphone.

And they are far worse than the original, according to the skeptics. Faulkner's widow sued Cliffs Notes for copyright infringement of *The Sound and the Fury*,[72] but it is the lack of the author's words that irritated many writers and teachers. To Arthur Miller, "Notes are notes, the play's the play, never the twain shall meet."[73] Notes strip a work of its distinctive style, leaving the equivalent of a vitamin rather than a meal, one teacher complained. A teacher at St. Paul's, one of the very best boarding schools, was appalled that many students used online summaries—"*Knowing* Beowulf was enough; it did not matter *how* you knew it or whether you knew it with any depth. In fact, learning it yourself was seen as an almost foolish way to master the material."[74]

In some schools, teachers fought back, devising tests and assigning papers they knew could not be passed without reading the assignment. Frank McCourt, the author of the best-selling *Angela's Ashes*, wrote quizzes at Stuyvesant High School in New York City that he said caught anyone who relied on the Notes.[75]

"Throw them out. Right now."[76] The Folger Shakespeare Library in Washington, D.C., abhors study guides. The Folger staff believes that everyone can connect with early 17th-century language. Students of all ages can engage the plays if they go beyond silent reading. Learn Shakespeare by doing Shakespeare. Actors can cut some lines, but the original words should never be changed. Listen to tapes. Watch performances. Speak the words while walking—try again by emphasizing nouns one time, verbs another time, and pronouns the third time. Scrutinize individual scenes—one lesson plan focuses on the word *two* and examples of pairs in the short prologue to Romeo and Juliet.[77] Instruction along those lines can educate in ways that are impossible if a student reads a modern English translation (available for $4.95 from the No Fear Shakespeare series of Spark Notes) or visits http://www.abbreviatedshakespeare.com, where simplified, abbreviated, condensed, and minimized versions range from six to 17 paragraphs.

If students did throw away their Cliffs Notes and close their computers, they faced temptation elsewhere and could turn to other books for assistance. *A Brief Guide to Shakespeare without the Boring Bits* includes synopses of all the plays as well as character sketches, source notes, and famous passages. *How to Read Shakespeare* offers a handful of excerpts followed by painstaking analyses. Those titles reflect the widespread demand for succinct overviews of many different complicated subjects; it is not just bewildered students who want brevity and clarity.

In recent years, there are more and more books that are longer than the traditional scholarly article (of 20 to 25 pages) and shorter than the monograph (of 200 pages or more). The 90 Minutes series from one publisher offers snapshots of fewer than 100 pages of the "world's greatest thinkers, deciphering philosophical thought in entertaining and accessible fashion." The Philosophy in Your Pocket series gives "brief biographies and basic tenets" of the same pantheon. Elsewhere, *Introducing Foucault* is longer, but it is a comic, whereas *Foucault for Beginners* is an illustrated overview with comic strip balloons throughout.

For topics beyond literature and philosophy, many first-rate publishers use the same strategy: survey big issues in short books with alluring titles. Oxford publishes "very short introduction" books of approximately 150 pages on huge subjects like modern China or the U.S. Congress. Yale University Press's "little history" books sprint across vast fields (*A Little History of the World*), and Stanford Briefs examines controversial issues like health care and climate change. Individual books not in a series often receive the same treatment, even when the book is not very slender. *A Very Short, Fairly Interesting and Reasonably Cheap Book about Qualitative Research* is 168 pages. Stephen Hawking's best-selling (and very difficult) *A Brief History of Time* takes 198 pages. *A Brief History of Nakedness* covers 286 pages, and the subtitle of the 755-page *Literary Criticism: A Short History* winks at how much more William Wimsatt and Cleanth Brooks could have written. And the rise of the Internet brought e-books that resemble short stories more than books, with names that signal their brevity: Read Petite, Nook Snaps, Snack Reads, and Kindle Singles.

If all those options are still too long, then there are the laminated reference guides of Bar Charts, which contain six or fewer pages conveying the key points of anatomy, chemistry, English composition, and 227 other subjects.[78] Everything can fit on one large page if the student decides to buy a Bar Chart poster. And by turning the computer back on, students in 2015 could download a three-minute "Cram Cast" about a book and its author from Houghton Mifflin, the current owner of Cliffs Notes.

Fast and easy, cheap and useful. The study aids offer all those benefits. And fun? Until recently, the vendors put humor in their ads but not in the products. Since 2008, Shmoop (Yiddish for "move ahead" or "nudge forward") made everything lighthearted. "Learning shouldn't feel like a root canal," and therefore the materials used colloquial expressions like "bent out of shape," "throw you under the bus," or "total drama queen" along with little "WTF" balloons ("why's this funny," not the cruder meaning of those three letters) to click in case the slang was unfamiliar. "We speak student," the Shmoop website proclaim, convinced that the best path to great literature is through playful language that is miles away from the words of the authors. "Nothing but fun with Shakespeare 101."

And for students in search of hip-hop humor, there are the five-minute Thug Notes, illustrated online plot summaries by Sparky Sweets, PhD, played by comedian Greg Edwards. Brutus claims to act not for the republic but *for the good of the hood*. With the help of Friar Lawrence's drug, Juliet takes a *long ass nap*. Benvolio asks, *Rosaline won't put out?* and Romeo answers, *Word. Ain't that some shit?* The large marketplace for shortcuts shows no signs of shrinking, with Shmoop selling its wares to school districts that need to raise standardized test scores to meet state and federal requirements. The Folger Library can *stir up a beef*, as Iago did in *Othello*, but millions of students want an enjoyable version of the classics. If it's fun, it will be faster and easier. The prospect of what one literary critic praised as the *difficult pleasure* of reading was not what most people want to feel when they open a book.[79]

LINKS

Andy Warhol: https://news.artnet.com/exhibitions/andy-warhol-paint-by-numbers-do-it-your self-sailboat-museum-497072
Harvard Classics: http://www.harvardmagazine.com/2001/11/the-five-foot-shelf-reco.html
Paint by Numbers: http://www.americanhistory.si.edu/paint/introduction.html

NOTES

1. "The Publishers Statement. December, 1909," Box 405, "Harvard Classics, 1909–1910" folder, Charles Eliot Papers, Harvard University Archives.

2. Cliff Hillegass, *Cliff Notes, Inc: Quality of Product . . . Service . . . Policy* (New York: The Newcomen Society of the United States, 1985), 23.

3. Laurence R. Veysey, "The Academic Mind of Woodrow Wilson," *Mississippi Valley Historical Review*, March 1963, 632. See also Veysey's influential *The Emergence of the American University* (Chicago: University of Chicago Press, 1965), chap. 4, and Caroline Winterer, *The Culture of Classicism: An-*

cient Greece and Rome in American Intellectual Life, 1780–1910 (Baltimore: Johns Hopkins University Press, 2002), 142–44.

4. For the erosion of the old concern that liberal culture undermined rather than fortified middle-class masculinity, see Daniel A. Clark, *Creating the College Man: American Mass Magazines and Middle-Class Manhood* (Madison: University of Wisconsin Press, 2010).

5. Hugh Hawkins, *Between Harvard and America: The Educational Leadership of Charles W. Eliot* (New York: Oxford University Press, 1972), 104.

6. Richard D. Altick, "From Aldine to Everyman: Cheap Reprint Series of the English Classics, 1830–1906" in *Writers, Readers, and Occasions: Selected Essays on Victorian Literature and Life* (Columbus: Ohio State University Press, 1989), 180–84; Jonathan Rose, *The Intellectual Life of the British Working Class* (New Haven, CT: Yale University Press, 2001), 129–31; Jay Satterfield, *The World's Best Books: Taste, Culture, and the Modern Library* (Amherst: University of Massachusetts Press, 2002), 24–26.

7. *Forum*, February 1930, 19.

8. Hawkins, *Between Harvard and America*, 292–96; *New York Times*, August 25, 1926, obituary for Eliot, reporting the sales from 1910 to 1926.

9. Fred West to P. F. Collier, November 5, 1911, in *Fifteen Minutes a Day* (New York: P. F. Collier and Son, 1917), 37.

10. "Interview with W. A. Nielson. Harvard Club, August 22, 1927," Box 405, "Harvard Classics, 1909–1910" folder, Harvard University Archives.

11. Charles W. Eliot to John Jay Chapman, August 24, 1910; "The Harvard Classics" [flyer to Harvard alumni] in "Harvard Classics, 1909–1910" folder, Harvard University Archives. For Chapman, "Collier's is in control. The name of Harvard is an asset worth thousands of dollars. Eliot and Harvard have become mere trade-marks. . . . A little bad taste in the advertising will carry his name and his books where good taste will not carry them." *Science*, October 1, 1909, 441.

12. *The Editor's Introduction, Reader's Guide, and Index* (New York: P. F. Collier, 1910), 6, 8.

13. The advertisements quoted in this paragraph ran in the *New York Times* between 1925 and 1929.

14. Mortimer J. Adler, *The Great Conversation: A Reader's Guide to the Great Books of the Western World* (Chicago: Encyclopedia Britannica, 1990). Alex Beam's *A Great Idea at the Time: The Rise, Fall, and Curious Afterlife of the Great Books* (New York: Public Affairs, 2008) is a lively overview; for a less jaunty but more scholarly account, see Tim Lacy, *The Dream of a Democratic Culture: Mortimer J. Adler and the Great Books Idea* (New York: Palgrave Macmillan, 2013). Adler's close friendship with Robert Hutchins is described

thoroughly in Mary Ann Dzuback, *Robert M. Hutchins: Portrait of an Educator* (Chicago: University of Chicago Press, 1991), esp. chaps. 5, 6, and 11.

15. Mortimer Adler, *How to Read a Book* (New York: Simon & Schuster, 1940), 61.

16. Mortimer Adler, *Philosopher at Large: An Intellectual Autobiography* (New York: Macmillan, 1977), 141, 155, 234. His own first drafts could be dense. "Tone a little insulting," "Don't be so fucking moral," and "Please throw out all cute Latin or French phrases" was the advice from Clifton Fadiman in regard to *How to Read a Book*, a volume designed to reach a wide audience (and it did). Lacy, *The Dream of a Democratic Culture*, 29.

17. Beam, *A Great Idea at the Time*, 89.

18. Lacy, *The Dream of a Democratic Culture*, 54; Dwight McDonald, "The Book-of-the-Millennium Club," *New Yorker*, November 29, 1952.

19. The set looked "official, approved, not so much enshrined as embalmed . . . [they] invited worship rather than discussion," Michael Dirda recalled. Although he repeatedly read Adler's "How to Mark a Book," he would not make notes in the Great Books. *Coming of Age in the Heartland* (New York: Norton, 2003), 195–99. "Domestic bookaflage"—book bindings as interior decoration—in the 1920s could be inexpensive (the 30-volume "little leather library" cost $2.98) or costly ("fine editions" of elegantly printed books could be $15 or more; one owner said, "I do read a few, but mostly I just look or take them down and stroke them from time to time"). Megan L. Benton, *Beauty and the Book: Fine Editions and Cultural Distinctions in America* (New Haven, CT: Yale University Press, 2000), 179, 290.

20. Beam, *A Great Idea at the Time*, 88. Part of the fun in the novel was Walter Shandy's claim that auxiliary verbs were a "North-West passage to the intellectual world."

21. Joan Shelley Rubin, *The Making of Middlebrow Culture* (Chapel Hill: University of North Carolina Press, 1992), 249.

22. Rubin, *The Making of Middlebrow Culture*, chap. 5 (and elsewhere in her superb book); James S. Smith, "The Day of the Popularizers: The 1920s," *South Atlantic Quarterly*, Spring 1963, 297–309. The February 1930 ad ran in *Forum* magazine.

23. David O. Levine, *The American College and the Culture of Aspiration, 1915–1940* (Ithaca, NY: Cornell University Press, 1986), 38–42. The immensely popular *Reader's Digest* magazine began in the 1920s (and flourished during the Great Depression); its 64 pages also promised "a broad understanding of the world—a liberal education—in a pleasurable way." Most of the two-page articles—condensations of articles originally published elsewhere—had nothing to do with culture, but the tone sounded like the outline books: entertain-

ing, optimistic, and clear. James P. Wood, *Of Lasting Interest: The Story of Reader's Digest* (Westport, CT: Greenwood, 1958), 27, 261–62.

24. Will Durant, *The Story of Philosophy* (New York: Simon & Schuster, 1926), 170, 171.

25. Richard O. Boyer, "The Story of Everything," *New Yorker*, March 20, 1943, 25, and April 3, 1943, 24.

26. Quoted in Cornelis A. van Minnen, *Van Loon: Popular Historian, Journalist, and FDR Confidant* (New York: Palgrave Macmillan, 2005), 239.

27. Van Loon to Eleanor Roosevelt, January 20, 1938, Box 16, folder 10, Van Loon Papers, Cornell University Rare Book and Manuscript Collections. Van Loon met FDR after he wrote several campaign essays for Roosevelt's reelection.

28. Will Durant, "In Defense of Outlines: *Apologia pro Libro Suo*," *Forum*, January 1930, 13.

29. David Denby, *Great Books: My Adventures with Homer, Rousseau, Woolf and Other Indestructible Writers of the Western World* (New York: Simon & Schuster, 1996), 226, 363, 184, 310, 261.

30. Howard Mumford Jones, "Are the Cultural ABCs Softening Our Brains?," *Forum*, January 1930, 7, 6.

31. J. H. Plumb, "Some Personalities on the Paths of History," *New York Times Book Review*, September 15, 1963, 3, 44. Durant used small type for the "dull" and "difficult" parts of his mammoth 11 volumes.

32. In James M. Banner Jr. and John R. Gillis, eds., *Becoming Historians* (Chicago: University of Chicago Press, 2009), 2.

33. Will and Ariel Durant, *A Dual Autobiography* (New York: Simon & Schuster, 1977), 103.

34. E. Haldeman-Julius, *The First Hundred Million* (New York: Simon & Schuster, 1928), 120.

35. Ibid., 194, 198. Haldeman-Julius thought that universities were pointless unless each department had a question-and-answer bureau so that anyone who wrote could get a quick reply. Andrew N. Cothran, "The Little Blue Book Man and the Big American Parade" (unpublished dissertation, University of Maryland, 1966), 183.

36. Bradford W. Wright, *Comic Book Nation: The Transformation of Youth Culture in America* (Baltimore: Johns Hopkins University Press, 2001), chaps. 1–4.

37. David Hajdu, *The Ten-Cent Plague: The Great Comic Book Scare and How It Changed America* (New York: Farrar, Straus and Giroux, 2008), 89.

38. William B. Jones Jr., *Classics Illustrated: A Cultural History* (Jefferson, NC: McFarland, 2002), 91.

39. In the wake of the investigations, Classics Illustrated edited 10 comics and changed four covers to make them less violent. Jed Rasula, "Nietzsche in the Nursery: Naïve Classics and Surrogate Parents in Postwar American Cultural Debates," *Representations*, Winter 1990, 61–62.

40. Delmore Schwartz, "Masterpieces as Cartoons," *Partisan Review*, July–August, 1952, 461–71.

41. R. Baird Shuman, "Classical Comics: SIC AUT NON?," *The English Journal*, January 1954, 37–38.

42. Karal Ann Marling, *Designs on the Heart: The Homemade Art of Grandma Moses* (Cambridge, MA: Harvard University Press, 2006), 242. Jon Gnagy's *You Are an Artist* television show (1946–1971) offered similar assurance. Michele H. Bogart, *Advertising, Artists, and the Borders of Art* (Chicago: University of Chicago Press, 1995), 296.

43. Dozens of ads are in Box 2, folder 4, Paint by Numbers Collection, National Museum of American History, Washington, DC.

44. William L. Bird Jr., *Paint by Number* (New York: Princeton Architectural Press, 2001), 64.

45. Dan Robbins, *Whatever Happened to Paint-by-Numbers?* (Delavan, WI: Possum Hill Press, 1997), 23, 115, 162.

46. Bird, *Paint by Number*, 75–77; Karal Ann Marling, *As Seen on TV: The Visual Culture of Everyday Life in the 1950s* (Cambridge, MA: Harvard University Press, 1994), 65.

47. From the "Post a Reminiscence" Web page (http://americanhistory.si.edu/paint/reminiscence). The nation's largest retailer of supplies for hobbies estimated that 10 percent of people who bought paint by numbers later purchased traditional art supplies. Bird, *Paint by Number*, 69.

48. For insightful reflections on the intersection of culture and commerce, see Michael G. Kammen, *American Culture, American Taste: Social Change and the 20th Century* (New York: Knopf, 1999), chaps. 2–6; Lawrence W. Levine, *Highbrow/Lowbrow: The Emergence of Cultural Hierarchy in America* (Cambridge, MA: Harvard University Press, 1988), 206–33; and Janice A. Radway, *A Feeling for Books: The Book-of-the-Month Club, Literary Taste, and Middle-Class Desire* (Chapel Hill: University of North Carolina Press, 1997), pt. II.

49. Arthur C. Danto, *Andy Warhol* (New Haven, CT: Yale University Press, 2009), 23, 57, 62; for his quip "whoever buys them can fill in the rest," see Kenneth Goldsmith, ed., *I'll Be Your Mirror: The Selected Andy Warhol Interviews* (New York: Carroll & Graf, 2004), 8. Throughout his life, Warhol admired repetition and reproduction; his do-it-yourself paintings are not necessarily a satire or parody. For instance, he was thrilled that every can of Coke tasted the same.

50. Shamus R. Khan, *Privilege: The Making of an Adolescent Elite at St. Paul's School* (Princeton, NJ: Princeton University Press, 2011), 191. The complicated changes sketched in this paragraph are explored at length in Kammen, *American Culture, American Taste*, esp. chap. 5, "Blurring the Boundaries between Taste Levels."

51. William Deresiewicz, *Excellent Sheep: The Miseducation of the American Elite and the Way to a Meaningful Life* (New York: Free Press, 2014).

52. A profile of one student who wrote book reports on the basis of comics was part of an indictment of American education in the *Life* magazine issue (March 24, 1958) that compared Stephen's slothfulness with Alexis's diligence in Russia (33).

53. Ann Blair, *Too Much to Know: Managing Scholarly Information before the Modern Age* (New Haven, CT: Yale University Press, 2010), chaps. 1, 3–5; Leah Price, *The Anthology and the Rise of the Novel* (Cambridge: Cambridge University Press, 2000), 80, 113, 150.

54. William J. Reese, *Testing Wars in the Public Schools* (Cambridge, MA: Harvard University Press, 2013), 205–8.

55. This paragraph relies on interviews with Linda Hillegass (October 8, 2014), former advertising and sales manager Jim McKee (November 5, 2014), and Richard Spellman, president of Cliffs Notes from 1985 to 1995 (November 13, 2014, and December 18, 2014). For Clifton Hillegass's recollections, see his *Cliff Notes, Inc.*

56. The best-known Cliffs scholar, Northwestern University's Professor Bergen Evans, was on an advisory committee. Although the company distributed one of his books, it rarely used Evans in advertising or marketing the Notes. The one well-known author, novelist John Gardner, wrote two Notes before he prospered. There were no partnerships with the nearby University of Nebraska, where one longstanding consulting editor taught English (and Hillegass, at age 80, endowed a chair).

57. The ads from 1965 to 1970 are in Box 1, folders 1–6, and Box 2, unsorted items, Cliff Notes Collection, Nebraska State Historical Society, Lincoln.

58. "Quarterly Income Statement for the Nine Periods Ended March 31, 1997," copy courtesy of Jim McKee.

59. Interview of Doug Lincoln, August 10, 2015; "How to Sell How-To Books," *Wall Street Journal*, March 14, 2001, B1, B4.

60. *Forbes*, October 30, 1989. Hillegass wanted the company to stay connected with the people and businesses of Lincoln, Nebraska. Each year, he donated 10 percent of the pretax profits to local charities and civic organizations (which, on his death, received half of his entire estate). Most employees

who received generous bonuses and benefits were lifetime Lincoln residents, and his local printer had the company's business for 40 years "on a handshake" instead of a formal contract. Interview of Rod Scher, August 6, 2015.

61. Interview of Doug Lincoln, August 10, 2015.

62. *Barron's*, October 14, 2002, 32.

63. The court of appeals overturned a lower-court injunction. Even with a yellow cover and black stripes, Spy Notes "raises only a slight risk of consumer confusion that is outweighed by the public interest in free expression." U.S. Court of Appeals, 2nd Cir., 886 F. 2d 490.

64. Approximately 70 percent of the buyers were high school students, with juniors (26 percent) ahead of sophomores and seniors (19 percent each). *U.S. News & World Report*, August 21, 1989.

65. One market research report (the only one in the archives) indicated that most students bought Cliffs Notes after they started the assignment. It was either harder than they imagined (50 percent) or a useful way to prepare for a test (36 percent). Carroll Novicki, "Project 70 Research," Box 1, Cliff Notes First Aid Kit binder, Cliff Notes Collection, Nebraska State Historical Society. For a television depiction of (and warning against) using "Cleland Notes" after trying to listen to a recording of *MacBeth*, see episode 15, season 2, of *The Cosby Show* (on YouTube). The boys loved the Notes—"Can you believe we're done and it's only 9 o'clock! I think I'll watch some TV"—and didn't mind earning a C on the test, but the parents forced them to read the play and seek better grades.

66. Gerald Graff, *Beyond the Culture Wars: How Teaching the Conflicts Can Revitalize American Education* (New York: Norton, 1992), 76. See also his *Clueless in Academe: How Schooling Obscures the Life of the Mind* (New Haven, CT: Yale University Press, 2003), chap. 2.

67. *U.S. News & World Report*, August 21, 1989.

68. *Omaha Sunday World Herald*, November 20, 1988. In 1985, the director of the National Council of Teachers of English said that "they have a good reputation among most teachers." *Chicago Tribune*, December 24, 1985.

69. Mary Ellen Snodgrass, *Cliffs Notes in the Classroom* (Lincoln, NE: Cliffs Notes, 1990).

70. Telephone interview of Mary Ellen Snodgrass, August 10, 2015. She also oversaw the creation of Cliffs Teaching Portfolio, a series of manuals for teachers that included some of the background and summary in a Note but featured classroom activities, tests, worksheets, and other instructional tools. These tools for teachers never attracted the attention or the criticism directed at the Notes.

71. Levine, *Highbrow/Lowbrow*, 72.

72. *New York Times*, July 12, 1967, 46. The case was settled out of court with an agreement to quote less extensively from the original. Hillegass later said it was a blessing—the Notes thereafter would include more analysis and less summary, reinforcing their claim to supplement rather than supplant the text. Norman Atkins, "Fast Food for Thought," *Rolling Stone*, March 26, 1987, 160.

73. *New York Times*, August 4, 2002, 7 (Education Life section). For an old but still useful elaboration of that point of view, see Cleanth Brooks, "The Heresy of Paraphrase," in *The Well Wrought Urn* (New York: Harcourt Brace Jovanovich, 1947), chap. 11.

74. Khan, *Privilege*, 181. For a witty defense of skimming books, see Pierre Bayard, *How to Talk about Books You Haven't Read* (New York: Bloomsbury, 2007). What Bayard advocates is for advanced readers: "Being cultivated is a matter not of having read any book in particular, but of being able to find your bearings" in the relationships among many books, and so "connections and correlations should be the focus of the cultivated individual. . . . It is this that allows those unintimidated by culture to speak without trouble on any subject" even if they only read bits and pieces of a particular book (10, 11). In Khan's book, the St. Paul students stumbled when they tried to do that.

75. *New York Times*, June 19, 2002, A-17.

76. "Folger's Philosophy of Teaching and Learning," http://www.folger.edu.

77. Folger Shakespeare Library, *Shakespeare Set Free: Teaching Romeo and Juliet, MacBeth, and A Midsummer Night's Dream* (New York: Simon & Schuster, 1993).

78. "History of the U.S. Civil War, 560 Words," *Wall Street Journal*, July 5, 2000.

79. Harold Bloom, *How to Read and Why* (New York: Scribner's, 2000), 29.

Part II

Faster and Harder

Onstage, comedian Don Novello appeared as Guido Sarducci, inventor of the five-minute university. He knew how to simplify the curriculum. "In five minutes you learn what the average college graduate remembers five years after he or she is out of school." Everything likely to be forgotten is dropped. Two years of Spanish becomes *como esta usted* and *muy bien*. "Economics? Supply and demand. That's it! Business? You buy something and you sell it for more." Theology was also simple. "What you have to learn in theology is the answer to the question, Where is God?" Not only is the five-minute university fast, it is also fun—20 seconds under a sunlamp in place of a trip to Fort Lauderdale—and very cheap—just $20, "and that's tuition, cap and gown rental, graduation pictures, snacks, everything, everything included."

Onstage of another kind, President Obama in 2014 wondered if course work in law school could take two years rather than three. His comments continued an old tradition: asking whether educators required too much time in classrooms. Why not encourage talented undergraduates to finish in three years or leave whenever they could demonstrate the competencies the faculty had established for graduation? Could the marathons required to become a physician or a scholar be shortened? Did all new teachers have to take a raft of education courses? Five minutes would be absurdly fast, and the "One Day University" sponsored by the *New York Times* ("No grades. No tests. No homework. No stress.") is just a clever name for a set of lectures, but maybe the essential knowledge and the enduring skills in many fields could be grasped more quickly.

Throughout the 19th century, there was a conviction that shorter was weaker. Schools that let students finish in a few years were usually third-rate, grubbing for higher enrollments by setting low standards. The lines between secondary and higher education were often blurry, especially hard to see at the shakier schools. In the late 19th and early 20th centuries, the stronger colleges and their allies made the case that longer was better. They argued that there was more to learn thanks to the rapid growth of the social sciences and breakthroughs in the hard sciences. The nonacademic benefits of college were also celebrated as intercollegiate sports, extracurricular activities, and social clubs proliferated. Why rush when there was so much to know and so many ways to mature?

That point of view took hold, as we will see in the next chapter, but not everyone was persuaded. Harvard President Charles Eliot proposed a three-year bachelor's degree, and the argument he advanced arose again and again as other educators called for brevity: many students arrived well prepared, and after they left they would continue learning. If the talented and motivated youth already excelled and would keep shining later, then maybe a year or even two could be saved. That reasoning marked later proposals on other campuses to shorten medical training, offer a six-year BA/PhD, or create a new doctoral degree for outstanding college teachers.

Most of those innovations faltered; when they survived, they were an option exercised by a small percentage of the eligible. The customary time spans proved remarkably durable, and the capstone *residency* in America's most prestigious profession, medicine, became longer rather than shorter from the 1930s on. Only the emergency of World War II sparked widespread acceleration. Competency-based education might have done so, but that has remained rare. What the University of Chicago did in the 1930s and 1940s—graduation on the basis of comprehensive exams—was so well known because it was so unusual.

For the students who truly want to save time, they can find the express lanes, but they will have to make the move. Colleges and universities rarely promote the fast track. And the eager few will find that the vast majority of their classmates have no interest in picking up the pace. More than half of the Harvard freshmen today could finish in three years or earn a master's in four; approximately 3 percent do.

Whether in school or out of school, everyone can save time if they use language more efficiently. Is spelling as economical as it could be if it were phonetic? Is writing wasteful when we could use shorthand abbreviations? Do most of us read too slowly? No one doubts the value of calculators in making mathematical computations easier, but when a shortcut requires an initial investment of dozens of hours to learn the quicker method, odds are that the number of recruits will be modest. The advocates of using language more adroitly made impressive claims for their reforms. They had no doubts that their arguments were airtight and thus failed to understand why anyone would question the wisdom of doing exactly what they proposed. Simplified spelling, shorthand, and speed-reading attracted zealous champions—as we will see in chapter 4, their energy kept each crusade alive without mobilizing the broad support they had envisioned. As with saving time in college, the opportunity to take a faster but not easier path through the English language remained an option rather than an expectation or a requirement.

LINK

Guido Sarducci: http://www.youtube.com/watch?v=kO8x8eoU3L4

3

SAVING TIME IN COLLEGES AND UNIVERSITIES

As tuition kept rising in the late 20th and early 21st centuries, more and more colleges told incoming students that they could finish in three years. The number of courses and credits required for the degree rarely changed, but good Advanced Placement (AP) scores, community college credits earned in high school, summer projects, winter sessions, or a heavy schedule let the ambitious slice a full year from the customary four. A few bold colleges set aside credit hours and let undergraduates leave whenever they could demonstrate the competencies and skills stipulated for a diploma. Those options would not necessarily be easier—they usually required hard work—but they could be faster and cheaper.

Yet when asked how long they expected to take, 84 percent of the freshmen in 2014 said four years. Fewer of them expected to finish in three years (2.1 percent) than anticipated staying for five years (9.4 percent) or six years (2.2 percent).[1] Choosing double majors or multiple minors is more popular than graduating early, and for the one-third who switch majors, it is hard to finish quickly. And in a way, four years is a shortcut. Only 40 percent of the incoming freshmen will graduate within four years rather than stay longer or drop out.

Why four? For centuries, that has been standard, a tradition usually taken for granted rather than explained and justified. During the colonial period, the nine colleges here copied the English precedent of four years. Only Harvard and Pennsylvania started with three years, but they soon moved to four years. As more colleges opened after the American Revolution, several began with only one year of work, but in each case they added more years when they could attract students and afford more faculty. An early 19th-century college without a four-year curriculum was usually a weak college.

On some 19th-century campuses, the shorter path was an option alongside the customary four-year route. Most of the coeducational colleges offered a three-year "ladies" or "English" course that usually minimized or eliminated Latin and Greek. In many colleges, the study of chemistry, engineering, agriculture, and other sciences yielded a degree after three years, often earned apart from other students. For instance, Yale's Sheffield Scientific School was a semi-independent affiliate, required to pay its faculty, balance its budget, and find its own accommodations, thus the name Sheffield in recognition of the land, the building, and the $50,000 donated by a New Haven railroad tycoon whose son-in-law was on the faculty.[2] The more prestigious choice at Yale and elsewhere was the traditional four-year diet of ancient languages, logic, rhetoric, moral philosophy, and a few scoops of math and science.

Two years of college? Long before junior colleges opened in the early 20th century, a two-year commitment in a quasi college was possible. Elementary school teachers in the 19th century did not need a college degree. The main hurdle to clear was the local school board. Most trustees could hire anyone they wanted. An aspiring teacher might have an edge over other candidates if she had been in a public high school or a private academy (many of them offered teacher training). Or she could attend a normal school. Modeled on teacher education in Prussia and adopting the French phrase *École normale*, the first normal school in the United States opened in 1839. After a slow start, those schools spread quickly after the Civil War, offering from one to four years of course work.

Few normal school students stayed more than two years. Those who were least prepared took academic courses akin to what a high school freshman or sophomore faced and spent the rest of the day on classroom management, instructional methods, practice teaching, and the history and philosophy of education. Students with stronger backgrounds could take various academic courses (some comparable to high schools, others to college) as well as pedagogical work.[3]

Another path for the fleet of foot was the private commercial school. As the economy prospered in the 1880s, these schools expanded rapidly, from 162 institutions with 27,000 students in 1880 to 263 schools with almost 79,000 students in 1890, which was more than the entire enrollment in American colleges that year. The curriculum focused on the practical skills needed for entry-level jobs—bookkeeping, math, and even penmanship—and as clerical work became women's work, courses in typing and shorthand abounded. Most of the commercial schools claimed to equip their students for managerial jobs, an inflated promise bolstered when President Garfield said, "These business colleges furnish their graduates with better education for practical purposes than either Princeton, Harvard, or Yale."[4] Most students were unwilling or unable to devote the time needed to learn economics, law, accounting, and other disciplines that started (by World War I) to fill the curriculum of a strong four-year undergraduate major in business. Often, the students stayed in a commercial school for six months to one year. As one educator said, "The question with a very large proportion of our students is not, 'How much learning can I get?' but 'How little can I get along with?'"[5]

So with a shadow over the two- and three-year options, could a student go elsewhere to receive a diploma from a good four-year college without spending the full four years in residence? Before the late 19th century, the typical college curriculum had very few electives, usually reserved for upperclassmen. A student aspiring to, say, Princeton not only knew what subjects all freshmen took but also could find the specific books they had to read. Mastering those assignments on his own (the AP program didn't start until the 1950s) could mean admission as a sophomore or even a junior, which was the case for future architect Louis Sullivan at the Massachusetts Institute of Technology (MIT) in 1872.[6] The savings were substantial—the cost of room and board exceeded tuition, scholarships were scarce, and several hundred dollars for college in 1850 (the equivalent of at least $6,000 now) was a stretch for many parents.

Youth in a hurry had another option: they might not lessen their time in college, but they could start in their early or mid-teens and thus reduce the total number of years spent inside classrooms. Before the late 19th century, colleges did not require graduation from a high school or academy. Admission hinged on passing several entrance exams. Grades, class rank, and scores on national tests like today's SAT or ACT: none of that evidence was requested. Nor did colleges want to see the extracurricular activities, athletic feats, and summer service that today can be enhanced by staying in high school. Instead, everything depended on whether the entrance exams went well. Whenever the candidates were ready to take the exams in Latin, Greek, mathematics, English, and history (created and graded by the college faculty), they could do so.

Because the colleges indicated what books to read and often published the previous year's exams, students knew how to prepare even if their schoolteachers assigned other texts. They could read on their own, or they could be tutored (the private eight-week Princeton Summer School, for instance, coached 40 to 60 boys for the September exams—"only the *essentials* of each subject are studied, and all *unnecessary* matter is omitted" as they scrutinized recent Princeton exams and devoted the last two weeks to taking practice tests).[7] For older students who had worked to save enough money to attend college, the exams were the same as they were for everyone else. Virgil's *Aeneid*, Cicero's orations, the commentaries of Caesar, and a grammar book: that quartet would equip the 15- and the 25-year-olds for the Harvard entrance exam in Latin in the 1870s.[8] And if the candidates failed one or more exams, they could still be admitted with *conditions* and have a year or more to make up the deficits. Often one-fourth to one-half of the incoming class were conditioned.

Even so, 19th-century colleges rarely had enough fully qualified applicants to fill the empty seats. The number of colleges in America had soared from nine in 1775 to approximately 800 by 1880. Supply outstripped demand. Most of the places were poor and small, and many barely survived—the largest college in Delaware, for instance, closed from 1859 to 1870. Hundreds of colleges made ends meet by opening *preparatory departments* on campus to attract younger students who might or might not take the entrance exams.[9] In short, no 19th-century college called the students *customers* (as is common now), but it was definitely a buyer's market: if American youth wanted to start college before age 18, they could easily do so.

Mediocre colleges were the most accessible. They called themselves colleges, but as the president of Pennsylvania State observed in 1892, "All sorts of institutions assume the name of college."[10] In Tennessee in

1885, for instance, there were four public high schools and 35 colleges and *seminaries* (a term sometimes used for academies and for colleges for women), with higher education often doing the work that could have been done in secondary schools.[11] In one southern town, six parents withdrew their children from a local college when the high school added a senior year (throughout the late 19th- and early 20th-century South, many districts only offered 11 years of elementary and secondary schooling).[12] In Atlanta, Clark College renamed itself a university in 1877, but for several decades thereafter it "consisted chiefly of a grammar school and a high school."[13] The same overlapping arose outside the South, if not as frequently. Agricultural colleges, for instance, often expected no more than an elementary school education of its incoming students.[14] Why not start early at those colleges when part of the curriculum was not college fare and there were no better options close to home?

To put the point another way: schools and colleges were not a system in the 18th and 19th centuries. The different institutions emerged at different times rather than arising together as a part of a coherent plan. They were not harnessed by federal mandates, and state oversight was modest. Because the schools responded to local needs, their scope varied from place to place. Reformers might refer to schools as a pyramid, but the metaphor was misleading. When only a small fraction proceeded beyond today's equivalent of elementary school, there was not much urgency to clarify the boundaries of each place. They were all higher education, and how much of it the young wanted to consume and at what period of their lives was their choice.

In the 18th century, there was no consensus on when higher education should begin, nor did most parents worry that early college would jeopardize their sons' psychological and spiritual growth. Approximately 40 percent of the first-year students at Harvard and Yale were 16 or younger.[15] Most boys not in school were at work by then. Historians report somewhat different expectations by the middle of the 19th century—prolong childhood, cherish the innocence of the young, and protect the vulnerable from the perils of a rapidly changing world.[16] Within higher education, parents knew that colleges were not as safe as they had been. Riots and protests disrupted many early 19th-century campuses, more and more students lived off campus, and the faculty disciplinarians' strictness often provoked more uproar.[17] Furthermore, the gradually rising enrollments in 19th-century private academies and public high schools kept more and more youth in school after they finished the common or elementary school.

And so the fraction of very young college students steadily declined in the 19th century; for instance, just under 20 percent of the Harvard freshmen were 16 or younger by the 1850s. But it was still possible to leap into college, and each family had to consider what future Yale President Timothy Dwight heard in 1844 when he planned to take the Yale entrance exams at age 15. Dwight excelled at the Hopkins Grammar School in New Haven, but the principal came to see his parents to urge them to have their son wait. "I want those years to do all for him that is within their possibility, and for this end he is not yet as fully prepared as he ought to be."[18] When Dwight entered Yale at 16, he was several years younger than the average freshman.

Twenty-five years later, Lyman Bagg, the author of an encyclopedic 713-page account of undergraduate life at Yale, wondered why anyone would want to enter his alma mater at that age. A freshman who is 15 or 16 "knows nothing of the world"—he would probably struggle in class, and, even worse, his social skills would be inept. The youngsters rarely won the respect of their peers. And why seek advanced standing by virtue of exceptional entrance exams? That misfit "never gets fully in the sympathy of the new class which he joins. Unless a man spends the whole four years in connection with a single class, it seems to me that he can never really experience the full glory of student life at Yale." The "full glory" came not from the hours devoted to course work but rather from friends, clubs, and sports.[19]

Yale freshmen in the 1860s got to know each other very well. They took the same courses; the 120 new students were divided into four divisions, but the classes and the instructors were the same for each division. Every morning, the freshmen sat together in the chapel; so did the sophomores, juniors, and seniors. Nearly everyone joined a freshman society in the first week of the fall term. Sophomores hazed and pestered the freshman, forbidding them to carry *bangers* (canes) or wear beaver hats. Sophomores helped themselves to the contents of unlocked freshmen rooms, told them to stay off the fence around the oldest buildings, and in other ways heightened the solidarity of the harassed freshmen.

Juniors had their own rituals. In addition to several clubs, the students competed with each other in contests open only to members of their class. Some of those honors were academic, but they were not based on outstanding grades. It was more prestigious to win an oratory or essay contest than to rank at the top of the class (the instructors didn't even tell the students their grades). Becoming an editor of the *Yale Literary Magazine* was another desirable prize. The highest honor was election to one of the senior societies where the anointed met each Thursday evening.

For Lyman Bagg, all those customs were entirely admirable. Students knew each other's strengths and weaknesses better than the faculty, and the quest for distinction outside the classroom promoted the formation of gentlemen, which for Bagg was the central purpose of college.[20] As one Yale president put it, "A boy goes to college not primarily nor wholly for the sake of pursuing certain studies, but for the sake of breathing a certain atmosphere, of competing for certain traditional rewards of undergraduate life, of entering certain societies that his father had known and meeting certain men or the successors of certain men whom his father had met."[21]

Not everyone enjoyed the Yale life fondly recounted by Bagg. Norman Cary entered when he was 17, and he learned that his youth was a disadvantage. "I found out sophomore year that one as young as myself could not be successful in his class unless he was a smart fellow, dressed always neatly in style, was a perfect gentleman, was guarded in his speech, especially avoiding freshness." The freshmen had formed *crowds*, and when Norman offered to join others on a walk, "I am received but the conversation is entirely among themselves." He had failed three times to join a boarding club where he could escape the vulgar conversations at the table where he dined. He had acquaintances but no close friends. The only one who welcomed him "chews, smokes, drinks, is profane, and I fear worse," an unattractive companion for a future minister.[22]

If he had been born 25 years later, Norman Cary would have been able to attend many other colleges. Rather than focus his Phillips Academy years on gearing up for Yale's unique entrance exams, he could have gone to any college that offered Phillips graduates *admission by certificate*. Dozens of colleges began to accept without examination the graduates of the high schools and academies they respected. Each college created its own list of approved secondary schools, which usually included at least half of the schools in its state or region. The University of Michigan pioneered this approach in the 1870s in order to boost enrollments, reduce conditional admissions, and align the high school and college curricula as both expanded. Secondary school enrollments, likewise, benefited from admission by certificate. Students had a significant incentive to stay. Why leave early when graduation would eventually yield a wide range of good choices?[23]

Just as important as admission by certificate for coaxing aspiring college students to finish high school was the philanthropy of a very rich businessman. After Andrew Carnegie sold his steel empire for $480 million in 1901 (the equivalent of $14 billion in 2017), he began to give away his fortune. One of his goals was the endowment of pensions for college faculty. To decide who was eligible, his foundation's officers wanted to know what defined a genuine college. In their eyes, a true college had several attributes, including a four-year course of study and admission of graduates from four-year secondary schools. The foundation even spelled out how long a course should meet in a real high school or college (it wasn't the first to make that calculation, to be sure, but the money at stake was unprecedented). Blurring the boundaries between secondary and higher education might let individuals get through faster, but the result was the survival of too many third-rate institutions. There were exceptions—for instance, Catholic colleges in the 19th century adopted the seven-year span of Jesuit schools in Europe.[24] But on balance, the Carnegie Foundation thought that the best way to connect secondary and higher education was to pry them apart. The frequently used word *articulation* did not mean welding together but rather its other sense—to make clear, to indicate what was what.

A full history of the drive to create a well-defined system of schools takes historians beyond admission policies and Carnegie grants—state governments, national associations, accreditation standards, and other influences moved American schools at all levels closer to a system with more definition and less overlapping of the component parts. The piece of that story that is relevant here is the faith that longer was better. It was defended as good for the institution and good for the individual. The shorter schools usually lagged behind in faculty, endowments, and prestige, whatever their convenience and flexibility. And for the students who shaved a year or more off their education, they risked the best part of campus life—full immersion in a special setting with friends, sports, and clubs. Both institutional strength and individual accomplishment required staying around.

As more and more college students continued their education past the bachelor's degree, the prospect of 15 or 16 years in school worried several educators. If well-prepared freshmen would remain in classrooms until they were in their mid-20s, then maybe college could be shorter. Looking at the full span of education for the motivated and talented students—the group best equipped to persevere and flourish over a long haul—prompted several calls on their behalf to find a year that could be saved. As we will see, the case for saving time was persuasively argued, advanced with less hype than the culture and correspondence school vendors used. Without strenuous marketing to drum up recruits, most of the students eligible for the time-saver shortcuts did not pursue them.

BEFORE AND AFTER—LAW AND MEDICINE

The best use of time was a lively issue in the universities that emerged after the Civil War. Their hallmark was a commitment to advanced work—research by the faculty, specialization by the students, and a range of graduate and professional programs. That spirit of investigation and concentration began to alter the undergraduate curriculum, especially in the creation of majors. Once juniors and seniors directed their energies to one subject, the first two years might be recast. Should they be a lower division? Junior college? Dropped entirely? Absorbed by high schools? Many different ideas were put forth by those who thought that the ideal university should have as little introductory work as possible or, if it remained, dignify general education with its own degree and reserve the specialized work for graduate and professional degrees.[25]

Lopping two years from college rarely took hold; the loss of tuition would have been painful, and the social life memorialized by Bagg would have wilted.[26] But trim one year? That was the goal of Harvard's president in the late 19th and early 20th centuries. For Charles Eliot, a shorter but more strenuous education was a better education. Too many American youth wasted time. Eliot thought that a Harvard undergraduate could devote 60 hours each week to his courses without sacrificing food, friends, or sleep. Summer vacation? Five weeks was enough. Acceleration wasn't just for the superstars. Any student willing to work diligently could do it, including future President Franklin Roosevelt, a C+ student who took six courses each term.[27]

Eliot also justified his position by emphasizing what came before and after the undergraduate years. Tougher entrance requirements had raised the average age of incoming freshmen—it took longer to prepare for the increasingly rigorous Harvard exams. If Eliot had magically found himself running America's schools, he would have transformed elementary schools. Eliot said that the French both enriched and condensed the early years (e.g., foreign languages at age eight). The American pace was too slow, the curriculum too boring and too repetitive, and the parents too fretful about pressure on young children. But Eliot had no control over what the lower grades did, and there was no "lab school" connected to Harvard where he could demonstrate his ideas.

What he could influence was the length of graduate and professional education. Eliot had no doubt that longer was better. In 1876, he supported the extension of his law school from 18 months to three years. Enrollment initially fell (as late as 1890, only seven of the country's 61 law schools had a three-year requirement, and a majority of lawyers had never attended law school at all), but the numbers soon rose, reinforcing Eliot's conviction that Harvard Law could become not only the best but also the largest law school, as it did. Entrance requirements increased. In 1875, the faculty recommended but did not require a bachelor's degree, waiving the entrance exams for those who had it. Expectations rose in the 1880s and 1890s—for instance, graduates from only certain colleges escaped the entrance exams, and the students admitted by examination had to maintain a high grade-point average to earn the degree.[28]

At no time did the faculty consider a popular shortcut used elsewhere: evening courses. Night schools proliferated in the late 19th and early 20th centuries. By 1920, there were as many part-time as full-time law students. Some places were for-profit: at Denver's Blackstone Law School, the faculty owned the library books and split the tuition to pay themselves.[29] Others were not affiliated with universities; the YMCA had 10 law schools by the 1920s.[30] Tougher accreditation standards eventually undermined the part-time law schools and also made the profession more homogeneous—there would be fewer immigrant and working-class recruits, such as post office clerks, streetcar conductors, store clerks, and other "poor and worthy" night students praised by one dean in 1924.[31]

The Harvard Medical School followed a similar path in the late 19th century. Before the 1870s, most medical schools supplied only part of the education necessary to be a competent physician. The typical curriculum had one year of courses in six to eight subjects. The instruction was didactic. A lecturer occasionally demonstrated procedures for the class to watch, but few instructors let the pupils carry out the tasks. Students spent little if any time in laboratories or with patients. Learning by doing required finding an apprenticeship, summer schooling, European study, or private instruction. What the medical schools offered was a series of lectures from faculty who usually owned the school, concentrated on their private practices, and saw research and writing as optional.[32]

The final examinations at the Harvard Medical School before Eliot's presidency reflected the modest expectations. At the end of the second four-month term, nine professors sat at nine tables, quizzing a student each, with a bell ringing every five minutes cuing the students to switch tables. One graduate from the mid-1850s recalled the superficiality of one of his brief interrogations: "Well, White, what would you do for a wart?" To a student who did well on his first question, one professor replied, "If you know *that*, you know everything. Now tell me all about your family and the news at home." After the 45-minute promenade, each instructor raised a white card if he felt the student passed; with five white cards, the man had his diploma.[33]

In contrast, medical education in France and Germany was more rigorous. In those countries, medicine was an experimental science mastered through laboratory exercises and service on the hospital wards. In exchange for free care, impoverished patients filled hospitals where faculty carried on research and taught students. A year or two of European study capped the education of many ambitious American doctors, and they brought home the conviction that their colleagues should emulate the standards of the great medical centers of Paris, Berlin, and Vienna.[34]

The ensuing transformation of American medical schools in the late 19th and early 20th centuries was a remarkable achievement in the history of education, and the main contours of that story are well known: better laboratories, full-time clinical faculty, closer connections with teaching hospitals, the end of for-profit schools, tougher state licensing laws, philanthropic grants, and (last but certainly not least) major advances in medical knowledge. There were many reasons for the revolution, and all have been carefully studied by historians. So the comments here will focus on time.

The best American schools extended the course of study to three years by the 1880s and then four years (starting with Johns Hopkins in the 1890s) of full-time study, with tougher entrance requirements not far behind. Starting medical school without college—in 1890 no more than 20 percent of medical and law school students had a bachelor's degree—gave way to one or two years of college, and by the 1930s more than half of the first-year students had a bachelor's degree. Students probed for loopholes—could Yale's Sheffield Scientific graduates opt out of some courses? Could hospital work take the place of classes? Could a student transfer from a weaker to a stronger school? Those maneuvers and exceptions became harder to find as more and more medical schools insisted on the full four years.

The arguments in favor of the eight-year commitment echoed what legal educators said. There was much more to learn as each field expanded dramatically in the late 19th and early 20th centuries. Both professions aspired to be sciences, not trades.[35] Exploring principles and their ramifications took longer than memorizing facts and routines. As respected professionals, doctors and lawyers should have admirable personal traits that put them beyond reproach—trustworthiness, diligence, idealism, and other signs of maturity supposedly jeopardized by starting too soon.

So the Harvard undergraduate who entered at age 18, graduated at 22, and then continued his education would be 25 or 26 before he finished. It would take another few years to start earning a decent income and then—and only then since Harvard graduates without inherited wealth should be prudent—get married. Domestic happiness could begin a year earlier if college were only three years. That was the reward at the end of the time line that Eliot envisioned.

Eliot's time line could have been shortened if only two years of college sufficed to prepare for medical or law school, a compromise he opposed at Harvard. Not until the late 1920s did the majority of law and medical schools require more than that, and even then a popular time-saver remained common—let the first year of law or medical school count as the senior year of college. The future president of the University of Chicago, Robert Hutchins, made that choice at Yale. As a senior, he had to take only one class at Yale College because he spent the rest of his time in the law school, which Hutchins praised for teaching him not just law but also the skills of careful reading, accurate summaries, critical reasoning, and good writing—the habits of mind a Yale undergraduate had begun to acquire. At the same time, Hutchins did not forfeit the extracurricular activities cherished by Yale students. Journalist, debater, actor, and secret society member, Hutchins was elected class orator for commencement and won the "most likely to succeed" award. Departure after the junior year would have jeopardized those honors and made it less likely that the president would bring him back, two years later, as Yale's secretary.[36]

By the 1940s, the longer-is-better, longer-is-mandatory spirit permeated legal and medical education, but there was a significant difference between the two initiations. The future doctor began training before medical school and continued after graduation. The stipulation of particular courses to take as a "premed" had no counterpart for aspiring law students—what they needed were the generic skills Hutchins admired rather than specific subjects. Studying criminology or constitutional history made less difference on a law school application than taking biology and organic chemistry before medical school.

After graduation, the doctors' training continued—the full-time internship added several years, with additional years required to be a specialist.[37] For law school graduates, the transition to full-time practice was faster. Studying to pass the state bar exam might take a summer or its equivalent. After that, new lawyers rarely seek the equivalent of a young physician's internship. The result is that the legal training is concentrated within law school, whereas medical training begins earlier and extends later. Although some critics called for a two-year law school, most reformers wanted to reshape the third year (with courses and fieldwork closer to the tasks done by practitioners) rather than eliminate it.[38]

Training before, during, and after medical school: educators wondered if that long induction could be shortened. Linking the BA and MD in a six- or seven-year program appealed to some universities, with nonscience undergraduate electives pruned far more than the medical school courses. Usually an option rather than a medical school's only route, the shorter path required the identification of talent early on, a tough assignment when character, personality, commitment, stamina, and other hard-to-gauge but essential traits are still evolving (and are not easy to assess in older applicants).

Approximately one-quarter of American medical schools offered some form of acceleration by the 1970s, but rather than establish a new norm, those programs became less rather than more common. The 20th-century medical school curriculum always seemed overloaded and hard to master in four years, with different departments jockeying to get more, not less, time for their areas. If some graduates felt that the fourth-year electives should be pared, other doctors relished them.[39] The author of the best history of 20th-century medical education noted with regret that the pace of medical care (including teaching hospitals) had become rushed. The time spent with patients dropped, the average hospital stay was shorter, and health maintenance organizations expected faster "throughput." Going faster could vitiate medical care as well as medical education. "Habits of thoroughness, attentiveness to detail, questioning, listening, thinking, and caring were difficult if not impossible to instill when both patient care and teaching were conducted in an eight- or ten-minute office visit."[40] No wonder the book was titled *Time to Heal*.

BEFORE AND AFTER THE PhD

Piled higher and deeper—that was one definition of the degree that on average took the longest to complete throughout the 20th century. By the early 21st century, the average time to completion in the humanities was nine years; in the social sciences, eight; and in the sciences, seven.[41] Before then, new doctoral students usually had spent two years majoring in the same subject as an undergraduate, and after finishing graduate school, most scientists and many social scientists added several more years by taking a postdoctoral fellowship. And if the first six years of teaching—the years without tenure—are seen as a probationary period when the young must once again prove themselves, then the journey to secure employment exceeds a decade.

The PhD might be shorter if it did not include three components—extensive knowledge, teaching ability, and intensive research. Devoting the first two years to seminars in a major field and at least one minor field yields what many master's degrees signify—familiarity with a range of material. Serving as a teaching assistant puts food on the table and helps prepare the rookie for life as an assistant professor. Above all, the seminar papers, independent studies, foreign language or research methods requirement, dissertation proposal, and dissertation equip the graduate student to add something new and useful to the discipline, to put another brick in the wall of knowledge. Producing a large brick can be a major advantage on the job market; a significant reduction of the research expectations could hurt the students' prospects. A four-year PhD might be exceptionally diligent and bright, but what if she has fewer publications and conference presentations than a six-year PhD whose dissertation could soon be a book? It is very rare that someone flies through with the success of Woodrow Wilson at Johns Hopkins in the 1880s, when he wrote a book in his second and third semesters of course work, a book that the faculty accepted in place of a dissertation.[42]

If excellent research is so important, why not disentangle it from the course work and teaching? A few universities tried that. In Massachusetts, Clark University faculty in the 1890s initially did not assign grades or even receive class rosters because courses were entirely optional.[43] At the University of Chicago in 1942, the transcript of future Nobel Prize winner Herbert Simon listed credit for only one course: an elective in boxing.[44] When another Nobel Prize winner, John Nash (featured in the movie *A Beautiful Mind*), was in Princeton's Department of Mathematics in the 1940s, there were courses, "but enrollment was a fiction, as were grades."[45] Graduate students began research immediately, and convincing a professor to direct the thesis mattered far more than doing well in a course. That approach to doctoral work remained rare—it presupposed enormous self-direction and early focus by the students, undercut the traditional calculation of faculty workload (and justification of new positions) based on enrollment in courses, and increased the odds that new faculty would be mediocre teachers.

Why not skip graduate school entirely? Another rare option, but it is what historian Arthur Schlesinger Jr. did. After four distinguished years at Harvard—his senior thesis became a book—he joined the Society of Fellows there. The junior fellows held three-year appointments with stipends comparable to an assistant professor's salary and without any responsibilities aside from Monday dinners with the senior fellows (from the Harvard faculty, who would invite guests like T. S. Eliot or Vladimir Nabokov) and periodic lunches with the other junior fellows.[46] Modeled on the Prize Fellowships at Trinity College in Cambridge (where the bliss lasted for six years), the liberty gave "the rare and independent genius" the time to "open new paths."[47]

The Society of Fellows reflected the beliefs of Abbott Lawrence Lowell, the Harvard president who thought that most graduate students lacked the brilliance or the motivation to make enduring contributions to their field. Accumulating credits and earning grades could gauge their progress, but for the truly gifted, rules and regulations "impair the complete freedom that should be enjoyed at some stage in a true scholar's career."[48] Lowell, who donated the bulk of his fortune to endow the society in 1933, might have been disappointed that the new fellows today must have their PhD or be within one year of defending it, but even if the society became a version of the *postdoc* common in the sciences, it still reflected his desire to unleash remarkable young scholars. And he would have been gratified that the book Schlesinger finished as a fellow won the Pulitzer Prize in 1945.

On the other hand, a doctor of arts (DA) degree for college teachers without research aspirations seemed logical: many colleges before the 1970s did not require young faculty to publish as a condition of tenure and promotion. A traditional PhD program slighted teaching; as one Yale alum recalled, "I was told I would make an extremely good teacher—and not to say 'uh' so much. That was the sum total of the instruction I received about teaching during my graduate education."[49] Why subject everyone to years of painstaking research many graduates would rarely if ever do again? Why not focus a new doctorate on life in classrooms rather than the library or the lab?

Seminars, supervised internships, and a capstone project would take three years, with some programs designed for experienced teachers who could get a sabbatical, devote two summers and one academic year to full-time study on campus, and then finish the requirements after they returned home. Instructors who had assumed that a doctorate in their discipline was out of reach could now afford to enroll without losing their jobs or starving the family, and 22-year-olds who might have reluctantly pursued the PhD could also be admitted. A rigorous master's degree for college teaching attracted some interest, and Yale tried it briefly, but institutional prestige and individual status remained tied to the *terminal degree* (one Yale professor said that a better solution would be the French practice of offering a second doctorate for the best PhDs, who would then teach less, earn more, and supervise graduate students).[50] Even when college enrollments spiked in the 1950s and 1960s, it was hard to find attractive jobs without a doctorate. The major concession then was that good doctoral students with semifinished dissertations could get hired.

The new degree aroused much excitement in the late 1960s. Clark Kerr, the former chancellor of the California state universities, predicted that the DA would soon displace the PhD as the standard credential for college faculty.[51] Alden Dunham, the Carnegie Corporation officer who crusaded for the degree and passed out $4 million in planning grants and fellowships, was sure that the DA degree would be the "Rx for higher education." His statistics seemed convincing—50 large research universities graduated 90 percent of the new PhDs hired as assistant professors, yet half of all American undergraduates attended colleges devoted to teaching. Young instructors there often faced cruel choices—abandon serious research, skimp on teaching, or work endless hours to do both. For Dunham, the mismatch between what the undergraduates needed and the PhDs offered was stark, pervasive, and alarming.[52]

Carnegie Mellon graduated the first DA in 1968, and within five years 20 other universities offered the degree. The national Council of Graduate Schools endorsed it, and the federal National Defense Education Act fellowships were available to full-time students. But expansion stalled from the mid-1970s on: adoption at a few more places was offset by desertion at others. On average, 90 men and women in the 1970s and 1980s earned the DA each year, less than one-third of 1 percent of the PhDs awarded.[53] By the early 21st century, there were fewer DA programs than in the 1970s. What happened?

It was no help that the top-tier research universities remained committed to the PhD as the best preparation for academic careers. Early on, Dartmouth and MIT returned their Carnegie planning grants, Berkeley faculty voted against the program, Brown dropped the DA after five years, and the University of Michigan restricted the program to community college instructors. Of the six Carnegie Mellon departments that signed on, only the Department of History sustained the work. The program there relied on the exceptional commitment of Ted Fenton, a Harvard PhD who had turned his attention from labor history to high school social studies. Curricular reform projects, especially new textbooks, offered DA students seminar and dissertation topics and also gave the program national visibility, large grants, and royalty checks. As one student recalled, "We felt that we were contributing to a revolution, an overhaul of what teenagers across the country would read."[54] By 1974, the Carnegie Corporation considered it the strongest of all the DA programs it had supported. More than 2 million copies of its curricular materials were used in American schools.[55] But at no time did a majority of the department teach or advise DA students; although they did not oppose the DA, they welcomed the creation of a conventional PhD program in 1978. So did the new president. Fenton became interested in other projects, and the external grants to support the students disappeared.[56] Without enough allies and resources, the DA was closed in 1985.

Across the country, the old faith that a discipline cannot be fully understood without making an original contribution to the literature stayed in place. So did the belief that the intelligence, creativity, and stamina necessary to write a publishable dissertation would also equip the graduate for the challenges of the classroom. The conviction that American colleges and universities were the best in the world offered little incentive to divert students to a speedier path to college teaching.

Another serious obstacle was the ambiguity about the knowledge and skills that the DA should acquire. The DA was premised on the conviction that PhD programs neglected teaching, that research skills did not guarantee instructional effectiveness, and that everyone knew brilliant scholars who taught ineptly. The negative examples were not the same as defining the material beyond the master's degree to justify this new doctorate. Most programs borrowed PhD seminars rather than create a string of new courses with clear *pedagogical content knowledge*—for instance, studying 19th-century U.S. history with one eye on how to teach the topics to undergraduates.

Rather than invite departments of education to join in creating and teaching those bifocal classes, the DA programs stayed away from the education schools. Some of the wariness was status anxiety—they knew that the EdD degree was less prestigious than the PhD, a fate the DA hoped to avoid. They also knew that the best studies of curriculum, instruction, and assessment focused on elementary and secondary schools, the destinations for nearly all education school students. The interest of education schools in higher education was modest, and it focused on training administrators. Research on the nature, causes, and consequences of excellent college teaching was sparse. That absence excited Alden Dunham—so little is known that a new field with a new literature will arise, he predicted—but it was a wobbly foundation for a doctoral program that lacked allies in the elite schools and in education schools.[57]

So, apart from a few pedagogical courses, the DA would be in the discipline, even though the point of the program was to train teachers. The burden was therefore on the internship and the dissertation (and most programs used that word) to sharpen the ability to teach well, but those requirements were often not clearly defined. Internships took many different forms (and were sometimes waived for veteran teachers), as did the appraisals of the students' performance. The dissertations also varied, with each faculty on its own to establish the scholarly standards for applied work or to accept a shorter version of the traditional dissertation with a final chapter on its implications for teaching. How the course work, internship, and dissertation connected was another daunting challenge.[58]

Even when the program components could be clarified and aligned, the job market awaiting the graduates was an enduring problem. From 1970 on, the annual supply of new PhDs (which had tripled in the 1960s) exceeded the dwindling number of vacancies. The DAs competed with PhDs who would gladly take a state college job with a heavy teaching load rather than switch careers. Small colleges could hire candidates who in the 1950s and 1960s would have gone elsewhere, and with scores of applicants for a vacancy, search committees could find a PhD with demonstrated teaching ability alongside research skills acquired at a first-rate institution (in contrast, three of the four largest DA programs were at less renown universities—Idaho State, Northern Colorado, and Middle Tennessee).

High school teachers who sought the DA as the path to college teaching often found themselves back in the public schools, perhaps as a curriculum specialist rather than a classroom teacher. Community colleges kept growing rapidly, but the doctoral degree was not as valuable as relevant teaching experience. The young DA with a supervised internship in freshman composition at a major university might lose out to the veteran teacher with a master's degree in remedial reading.[59] For the ambitious community college administrators, an EdD in leadership earned in the evenings and on the weekends was more attractive than the DA. And as fellowship support dried up, the average time to completion rose from 5.3 years (1973–1976) to 7.8 years (1989–1991).[60] Anyone in search of a quick route to college teaching had to think twice before entering a DA program.

For another way to shorten the traditional preparation of college teachers and future scholars, Cornell University launched a six-year BA/PhD in 1966. President James Perkins, who had earned his doctorate in three years, convinced the Ford Foundation to commit $2,217,000 over 10 years to let 50 or so students each year accelerate. As with many new programs, this one seemed to offer several benefits. Exceptional candidates lost to Harvard, Yale, and other rivals might now come to Ithaca (the director had taught at Harvard, where he heard Cornell praised only for its engineering majors and fraternity parties).[61] Other undergraduates could eventually benefit if the six-year program demonstrated the value of its distinctive features: interdisciplinary seminars, mastery of a foreign language in the first year, a summer overseas, and small dormitories where faculty and graduate students lived with the superstars.

In addition, the program might alter the dissertation. An appendix to the grant proposal gave students the option to do the tasks faculty do—publish an article, write a review, give a lecture, create a course syllabus, and so on. The Ford Foundation thought the alternative was part of the program and praised it in the annual report. Indignant faculty said that was a separate proposal to Ford, far less expensive and designed just for the humanities.[62]

The silence about the dissertation typified the reluctance to tell the departments what to do with these students, who didn't have to declare a major or meet distributional requirements as long as they earned 120 credit hours, a hard-and-fast New York state rule. No Cornell graduate program was obligated to accept the students; admission as a freshman did not carry automatic acceptance three years later. Everyone had to apply. Some departments were enthusiastic, others were skeptical, and several refused to participate.[63] Similar variations even marked the faculty who volunteered for the seminars. They wanted to teach very bright students, but a Ford Foundation officer heard "grave doubts about 'hurrying' graduate work. . . . They seemed extremely bound by tradition." He told the president that "it is obvious you have great enthusiasm and high hopes for the project. But as I proceeded down the ranks, it seemed to me that the extent of commitment became less and less."[64]

The commitment of the students was also uneven. Of the 50 freshmen in the first group, 36 returned for a second year. Failure, leaves of absence, transfers, dropouts, and three deaths in a dormitory fire thinned the ranks.[65] The inaugural group had sky-high SAT scores (the average exceeded 1,500 of a possible 1,600), but their emotional stability was less impressive.[66] The Educational Testing Service had warned Cornell that there was no reliable method to identify good graduate students in the senior year of high school, and although several hundred applicants had been interviewed, many were "not so mature as we had hoped," the director admitted.[67] He used words like *odd*, *abrasive*, *moody*, and *cynical* to characterize the immature, one of whom probably ignited the dorm.[68]

In subsequent years, the screening paid more attention to psychological fitness, but another problem soon became apparent: a majority of each cohort never began doctoral studies at Cornell, and those who did often took more than three years. In the first group, the Cornell valedictorian finished his BA in five semesters and then left to teach on an Indian reservation. A brilliant medievalist followed her Cornell adviser to Yale, and 15 of her classmates also decided to pursue graduate or professional studies at other universities. Only 13 of the first 50 stayed at Cornell; the numbers were slightly better in the second cohort, but the pattern was clear. Not many students stayed on track for a six-year PhD. They transferred, took leaves of absence, switched to the four-year BA, went elsewhere for doctoral studies, or pursued a different graduate degree.[69]

After seeing how few students would earn the PhD in six years, the Ford Foundation did not renew the grant. The director bravely took credit for other Cornell innovations in the late 1960s—flexible majors, coed dorms, faculty representation on admission committees, and interdisciplinary courses had supposedly been inspired by the six-year PhD program. All of those changes could be carried out within the traditional time spans; acceleration was a more precarious strategy than adding variety and choice to enrich, not speed up, the years spent on campus.

Apart from occasional experiments and alternatives, the journey to the PhD did not change very much. A graduate student from 1915 would feel at home in the doctoral program of 2015. He might be able to substitute statistics for a second foreign language, find more voluntary workshops on teaching, see greater diversity in his peers, receive more financial aid, and get fewer job offers, but the time to completion would be just as daunting, if not more so. As a Ford Foundation officer said, "Tinkering with Ph.D. requirements is roughly comparable with changing the earth's orbit or modifying New York City's accounting practices."[70]

ACCELERATION FOR STUDENTS WHO ARE NOT BRILLIANT

Many of the options to accelerate discussed so far served the very bright and highly motivated. The options acknowledged that promotion on the basis of credits earned by passing courses put a wide range of abilities and temperaments in the same grade level or classroom. The smart high school sophomore might know as much as the not-so-smart college freshman. She could decide how many AP courses to take and whether to seek a college that would let her skip a semester or year. Or she might try the International Baccalaureate (IB) program, another rigorous option that might open the door to accelerate, even though most AP and IB students use their accomplishments to burnish their college applications rather than jump forward.

If she were a prodigy, odds are that she would be with other prodigies in a special program. For the exceptionally bright, AP or IB is too little too late. Woody Allen's son was admitted to law school at age 16; he was far beyond high school by then. The young genius could race ahead as fast as the parents saw fit. Finding intellectual stimulation would probably be less difficult than social success. As one article put it,

"The trick is to challenge them without sabotaging emotional stability or stealing their goof-off time."[71] Who would enjoy what Ralph Tyler heard in 1917 after he started college at 15? When he asked a girl for a date, "She looked at me and said, 'With a freak like you? What would the girls in the dormitory say?'"[72]

But what if Junior is neither a prodigy nor very bright? Why in the world would he accelerate? In the past 30 years, there are more and more options for students who might not reach college if they don't get a head start. One popular opportunity links high schools and community colleges. More American high schools offer *dual credit* (82 percent) than offer AP or IB (69 percent). Enrollments are slightly lower (2 million as opposed to more than 3 million in AP and IB), with about one-third in career and vocational courses. More often than not, the dual credit course is taught in the high school by a high school teacher, reducing the financial burden of transportation, tuition, and books for courses on a college campus. In the 2010–2011 school year, one or more students earned an AA degree (which usually takes two years of full-time study) through dual credit in 7 percent of American high schools.[73] Dual credit includes some students who are capable of taking honors and AP courses, but it extends beyond the top tier. Dual credit can be a strategy to get students who might otherwise never attend college to try it, see that they can do the work, and then continue.

A more intensive version of dual credit is the *early college* initiative, consciously designed for *at-risk* students, often from poor and minority families. Dual credit is an option; early college is a program. Offering counseling, tutoring, after-school assistance, and summer sessions in addition to classes, early colleges provide more individual attention and long-range planning than most high school students ever receive. The participants are coached on study skills, time management, and the other tools that middle-class youth get from their parents and peers. With enough structure and support, coupled with the incentive of saving money by earning college credits in high school, the programs believe that acceleration is possible for adolescents of average ability—above-average motivation and perseverance along with exceptional support will suffice.[74]

As dual credit and early college programs expanded, another type of head start did not—the residential private college where all incoming freshmen left high school before graduation. It was a twist on an old idea: recast public schools in a 6-4-4 sequence of elementary, secondary, and higher education. First proposed at a time when most teenagers did not finish high school and when junior colleges (as they were called) were rare, the last four years would offer, for free, both vocational and academic work. In the few places where the plan was tried, the graduates left with an associate's degree.

Advocates of 6-4-4 relied on two arguments: late adolescence (roughly ages 16 to 19) was a discrete stage of growth and maturation, and much of the course work of grades 11 through 14 was liberal education, an array of survey courses beyond the basics and before the major. Not everyone accepted those points, and few had the muscle to convince colleges to cede two years to their less prestigious high school and junior college neighbors (who themselves did not always want to marry). As an option, private four-year junior colleges occasionally arose, but they were always a small niche that became even smaller as public two-year community colleges expanded steadily.

The history of Simon's Rock illustrates the challenges in creating and sustaining a school for late adolescents. Elizabeth Hall was blessed with a good education (Radcliffe magna cum laude), leadership experience (head of Concord Academy from 1949 to 1963), and wealthy parents (thanks to Chiclets chewing gum). With several million dollars from the family foundation, she opened a boarding school in 1966 on part of her mother's 900-acre estate near Great Barrington, a small village in western Massachusetts. In her opinion, 16-year-olds were treated like children in most high schools. Student government was a farce, teachers rarely discussed what she called "the urgent world of now," and college entrance requirements narrowed the curriculum. Respect adolescents as young adults, and they will act adult, she believed. The best way to grow up is to be treated as if you already have.[75]

Spend four years in rural isolation, pay as much as Yale charged, and leave with an associate's degree from an unaccredited single-sex school: it was hard to recruit students in the early years. Was it a second chance for girls who were miserable or unsuccessful elsewhere? Was it attracting the alienated and the unstable rather than the intellectually adventuresome? Why did so many applications arrive in the summer? Did every small school—50 or so first-year students—lose a half dozen girls each year because they needed psychotherapy? If Mrs. Hall could flout conventions—driving tractors, whistling through her fingers, climbing into the rafters of new buildings, stirring 50-gallon drums of chicken manure with a two-by-four—why couldn't the students do as they saw fit? And why couldn't the faculty be defiant? Some of the instructors opposed Hall so fiercely—they criticized her as autocratic—that they recruited students to join their dissent. Two of her allies were so shrill that they alienated others. Establishing community governance and disciplinary codes took months of discussion, including many "who decides who decides" quarrels over the nature of authority.[76]

By the end of the first year, she knew that five of the 12 faculty had to go, and she spent more time thereafter recruiting and evaluating candidates. The appraisal of potential students also became more thorough. Student tour guides filled out detailed questionnaires (including a question about the girl's relationship with her parents), and the application's essay topic was "the wise restraints that make men free." Rather than take chances, the school had 50 empty beds in the fall of 1969. A June 1970 report said that Simon's Rock was no longer "the target of the desperate parent looking for a solution to the problems of a child that has been dropped out, flunked out, or kicked out of another school," and coeducation in the fall of 1970 doubled the number of applications.[77] As one professor later said, "It took a long time to figure out which students could thrive here and which ones couldn't."[78]

There was no expectation that the incoming students would be Einsteins—overall, they ranked at the 70th percentile of high school seniors—and the school was willing to accept applicants who had finished 11th grade elsewhere (as 37 percent of the current Simon's Rock students do).[79] "We always had interesting students," one professor recalled; another said, "Some were really brilliant and a little wacky; some were maybe smart, but maybe not."[80] The curriculum was strongest in the humanities and weakest in the sciences; the lack of a gymnasium was another sign of the school's priorities. With the help of grants from Carnegie and the National Science Foundation, Simon's Rock in 1972 decided to offer the bachelor's degree at the end of four years; the AA could be earned after three years. Upperclassmen would pick one of six interdisciplinary majors; the most popular option was art and aesthetics.

The BA was ambitious (the seniors took comprehensive exams, wrote a thesis, and defended their work in front of external examiners) but not pathbreaking—students still took courses, received grades, and graduated on a four-year time line. Small seminars, administrators who taught, student participation in campus governance: those attractive features of the school were hardly revolutionary. The school did not have a new approach to college education to offer the world aside from the faith that younger students could take on the familiar challenges sooner than was customary.

The incentive of earning the BA rapidly did not yield thousands of applications, and the attrition rate remained high: fewer than 20 percent of the freshmen earned the BA from 1976 through 1979. Many transfer students used their time at Simon's Rock strategically—after two years, they enrolled in selective colleges, often as sophomores. Simon's Rock was more attractive as an alternative to high school than a rival to traditional colleges. It was "less tense than prep school," one boy said, but he did not stay because he worried it wasn't seen in the wider world as a true college.[81] For instance, the library in 1973 had only 25,000 books, a small fraction of the resources of nearby Williams College. Enrollments fluctuated from year to year—176, 201, 256, and 212 from 1975 to 1978—never close to the administration's goal of 800 students. The annual budget deficits were covered by the Hall family foundation, which by 1976 had devoted more than $5.5 million to the school (a $15 million endowment campaign raised only $1.7 million).

The market for early college, especially at Ivy League prices in the boondocks, was smaller than Elizabeth Hall had imagined. One survey of high school students who requested information but never applied revealed that they did not want to accelerate (the high cost, remote location, and small size also deterred them).[82] And most parents shared similar doubts. It is not hard to imagine the reactions to the paragraph in the 1974–1975 student handbook that declared, "By the age of 16 most individuals are making their own decisions about sex."[83] Elizabeth Hall's successor as president admitted that early college coincided with the precious time when the "communications between child and parent become genuinely adult," and he recalled one admission interview where the father asked his wife, "Don't you think Robert is ready to handle this?" and she said, "Of course he's ready, but I'm not."[84]

Simon's Rock escaped bankruptcy by joining Bard College in 1978, and as a branch of Bard it remained an enduring contrast to larger colleges that offer variety and choice without a special ethos or clear priorities. In the early 21st century, interdisciplinary courses were still prized, the arts were very important, and the faculty's political commitments lay decidedly left of center. The emphasis on community was strong. Classes were small, everyone called each other by their first names, freshmen saw their adviser each week, the provost met with every senior to discuss the capstone project, and the dean of students occasionally cooked Burmese food for the entire school.[85]

But what was most distinctive was the unwavering commitment to start college early. The fact that no other private residential college had that mission indicated the difficulty of persuading Americans that age 16 begins a new stage of life, a crucial period of social and intellectual development to be nurtured apart from the family. Sixteen might be the time to drive or work part-time, but for the vast majority of teenagers and their parents, it seems too early to start college.

EMERGENCIES

Occasionally, a crisis makes the customary pace of education seem dangerously slow. The urgent need for competent graduates required acceleration. Staying with the traditional requirements would be riskier than gambling on swiftness. The examples in this section reveal that a few experiments took hold, evoked concern, and left in place the pathways established before the crises.

World War II was the only time in the 20th century when acceleration became an expectation rather than an option. The mobilization of millions of men included the training of specialists in many fields, with the academic calendar frequently reconfigured as four 12-week quarters.[86] In medical schools, nearly every university held classes year-round and canceled most electives. Internships and residencies were half as long as they had been. With fewer faculty on campus, the instructors usually curtailed their research to focus on teaching larger classes. The result was the graduation of 25 percent more physicians annually, with 80 percent of those graduates pledged to the armed forces.[87]

For other careers, colleges contracted with the services to teach war-related courses and majors as well as enroll students not in uniform. Yale students graduated in 27 months by taking summer sessions and eliminating *reading periods* before exams. "This is a speed-up but not a short-cut program," more substantial than the quick courses offered in

World War I, President Charles Seymour announced.[88] At the University of Chicago, the war let Robert Hutchins convince the faculty to approve his longstanding proposal to grant the bachelor's degree after the sophomore year; students were encouraged to enter at age 16, but well-prepared high school graduates were welcome because earning the diploma hinged on passing a series of examinations.

Both Yale and the medical schools had second thoughts about acceleration when the Korean War began in 1950. "We tried this [year-round] scheme in the last war and found it a failure. It exhausted the faculty and fed the students['] knowledge faster than they could absorb it."[89] A Yale committee defended the value of breaks and vacations; if summer terms were absolutely necessary, focus on one subject, preferably foreign language. The prospect of universal military service during and after the Korean War would raise the pressure to cut a year from the eight years of high school and college, the committee predicted, and it wanted the savings to come from high schools as much as colleges.

In that spirit, Yale was one of the 12 colleges in the Ford Foundation's Program for Early Admission to College. If 18-year-olds would be drafted, then admit *preinduction scholars* for a year or two of college and let them return after their military service. For the 1,350 students who participated (never more than 5 percent of the incoming class at the 12 colleges), the results were mixed. Their academic achievement surpassed the record of a group of comparable students, but more of the "Fordies" failed or transferred. Nearly three-quarters of the group said that it was difficult to adjust to college life—older students kept their distance, and at one college their dormitory was called "the nursery." Asked if they would advise a friend to enter college early, only 20 percent said yes in contrast to the 68 percent who said "yes, with reservations."[90] After four years and the end of Ford funding, the 12 colleges made early admission an option rather than a well-publicized program.

In the medical schools, several national associations warned against "the rapid production of half trained men" in the Korean War. The World War II experience soured them on the value of moving so quickly. "They were concerned about many things, including hurried teaching, the overuse of lectures, the falling use of the library, and the elimination of elective and research opportunities. Most of all, they were troubled by the loss of time, which made it more difficult for students to reflect, assimilate material, and develop reasoning skills, problem-solving capacity, and independence."[91]

The University of Chicago's experiment survived for 11 years in the face of sharp criticism. Many local high schools feared the loss of their best and brightest. Applicants to graduate schools elsewhere often found themselves taking undergraduate courses to close gaps in their knowledge. The regional accreditation organization threatened to suspend Chicago—accreditors defined college as a four-year curriculum, oriented at first to the continuation of secondary education and then, in the last two years, to specialized work.[92] That longstanding combination exasperated Hutchins. "The B.A. degree loses meaning because it is awarded for a mixture of liberal education and professional study."[93] But his own faculty preferred that mixture, and the two-year bachelor's option disappeared soon after Hutchins left Chicago in 1951.

When the fighting stopped, should veterans receive high school or college credits for what they endured? In World War I, many schools gave *blanket credit* for the time spent in the military. Everyone in the class of 1918 at Columbia, for instance, was promised full credit for courses missed if they enlisted during the 1917–1918 academic year.[94] In World War II, the approach to granting credits was more discriminating. To find the academic equivalents of more than 3,000 military courses, a 1,000-page guide was compiled. For the several million servicemen who took correspondence classes, end-of-course exams were used. Neither was a shortcut—after all, the men and women had finished courses—in contrast to the five *general educational development* (GED) tests, two-hour objective tests to measure not the substance of particular classes but rather the incidental learning acquired in many ways, such as pleasure reading, living abroad, watching movies, skimming magazines, conversation, and so on.

The GED would supposedly measure the "lasting outcomes" acquired by high school graduates—quite a claim in that few education researchers had ever studied the long-term effects of high school. Three tests gauged the interpretation of written materials (in social studies, natural science, and literature), a fourth tested mathematical ability, and a fifth examined "correctness and effectiveness of expression." The recommended cut score was modest—the seventh percentile of the high school seniors who took the test in 1943. It was possible to miss 70 percent of the items and still pass (only nine states set higher cut scores). Random guessing plus a few correct answers would yield high school equivalency degrees. The war ended in 1945, and within a few years every state but two used the GED scores to award those degrees. Only 14 states required some time spent and credits earned in high school in addition to the GED. The result was a generous pathway to a credential that mattered.[95]

Estimates vary, but at least half of the enlisted men in World War II were not high school graduates, with significantly higher percentages for blacks and lower percentages for women. One article reported that 29 percent never went past eighth grade.[96] Without the diploma, they were not eligible for the college tuition and expense benefit in the *GI Bill*. Without the diploma, they lacked a qualification needed for many jobs (and the fear of a postwar depression was acute). As one veteran wrote to the principal of Shortridge High School in Indianapolis, "I cannot begin to tell you how much I appreciate what you have done for me. It will now be possible for me to enter many different fields that have previously been closed to me."[97]

But if the diploma had become more important by the 1940s, it had also become less special. That is, high school enrollments had roughly doubled each decade since the 1890s. At the end of World War I, about 30 percent of 14- to 17-year-olds were in high school; at the start of World War II, nearly 75 percent went there. The expanding curriculum offered endless options for earning credits, often for nonacademic work. For many, the diploma was no longer a badge of academic achievement but rather a sign of good attendance, decent behavior, and occasional work. The veterans taking the GED had missed the bull market in secondary education; they had not persevered in the decades when it had become easier and easier to finish. When a major 1944 report on high schools called for a curriculum based on what people needed to cope with daily life, it was hard to argue against the GED for the veterans.[98] They had coped with tougher conditions than the civilian life the report had in mind.

It is revealing that a similar pathway for a college degree went nowhere. That diploma was still special; a 10-hour test to give veterans a BA or BS seemed like theft. The traditional path through college awaited several million veterans who enrolled after the war. On balance, they did better than their classmates, and their success was widely publicized in the late 1940s.[99] It was an experiment far broader in scope than early admission for bright high school students, and it underscored the value of waiting rather than rushing to get through college. Furthermore, the later history of the GED, when it was open to candidates who never served in the military, is a depressing story of a popular credential that conferred significantly less benefit than a regular high school diploma. The recipients lagged behind high school graduates in employment, earnings, college completion, and a host of personal traits, such as perseverance, self-control, and good health, in which, unlike the World War II veterans, they were on balance already deficient before they took the GED. Dropping out of school could save time—the median GED prep time was 32 hours in 2006—but the better investment for the long haul was devoting more time to finish high school.[100]

Sometimes educators claim that conditions in peacetime are an emergency, a crisis that legitimates the acceleration of the usual pace of established programs or the creation of new ones. For instance, the shortage of new college professors in the 1960s helped justify the DA degree and Cornell's six-year PhD. The best-known fast track to the classroom, Teach for America, argued that there was a crisis in impoverished communities. The students who needed help the most often got the weakest teachers. The organization was created in 1989 to convince talented college graduates to commit two years to teach low-income, primarily nonwhite students in urban and rural schools. By appealing to ideals of service and equity, this national teacher corps expanded rapidly after a shaky start.

The selection criteria emphasized not only academic excellence at top-flight colleges but also certain character and personality traits. By defining teaching as a form of leadership, Teach for America required evidence that the candidates were young leaders with the dispositions that good teachers need—passion, stamina, interpersonal savvy, idealism, and the like. What they accomplished before joining therefore qualified them for the classroom without substantial additional training.[101]

The formal induction was brief and strenuous—a five-week summer institute filled with lesson planning, practice teaching, classroom observations, group discussions, and individual mentoring. Meetings continued after dinner, and getting ready for the next morning filled the evening. In the summer institute, the corps members were eager to work around the clock. A sense of urgency pervaded the days. Carlos, for example, got up each morning at 5:50; it used to be 5:30, but then he started taking his shower and shaving the night before. Thirteen hours later, he sat down for a two-hour meeting.

Another corps member said, "It's like finals week for five straight weeks." He knew the institute would be intense, but "in the back of my mind I thought, right, I can handle it. Then I got here and POW." The Teach for America ethos kept everyone on and up. Overload was a conscious strategy to prepare the rookies for the exertions they should make in the fall. Their predispositions to work hard were reinforced, not created from scratch, by the institute's rapid pace.[102]

Teach for America was not trying to transform the participants in five weeks. They didn't need to be transformed. The notion was that education is the time to take risks, explore new interests, and become a different person—the vision of professional education as transformational is less relevant if the young already have the exceptional skills and dispositions their employers seek. The most important job for Teach for America was selection, not retooling. The painstaking and competitive screening of strong students from good colleges would supposedly identify the natural teachers, even if many of them struggled in the fall when they faced challenges far beyond the scope of a five-week institute or their previous leadership experiences.[103] The work was much harder than most imagined, and many former corps members yearned for a longer induction (so much so that in 2013 Teach for America began to let some recruits begin their preparation as college seniors rather than wait for the summer institute). As Teach for America expanded from the mid-1990s and beyond, the vast majority of aspiring teachers continued to prepare for their careers through four-year undergraduate programs rather than half of one summer.

IGNORE TIME AND BASE GRADUATION ON EXHIBITIONS OF COMPETENCE?

Take courses, earn passing grades, accumulate credits, and get the diploma when the total reaches a specified number—that familiar system is very generous. Showing the connections among the courses or even remembering their content is not obligatory. Easy courses count as much as hard courses. C grades earn as many credits as A grades.

Persistence is rewarded—the dutiful students who show up, listen, behave, and exert some effort are likely to graduate in a predictable span of time.

Educators also benefit. Schools and colleges expanded the curriculum to attract and retain students—chemistry, cooking, commerce, criminal justice, and hundreds of other subjects all yielded credit hours. And the reliance on credits let educators finesse a major challenge of mass public education: how to maximize the graduation of students of modest intellectual ability and academic motivation without setting up standards of achievement that would increase failure and reduce enrollment. Countries less troubled by attrition have been more likely to rely on culminating examinations as the basis for receipt of a diploma or for admission to college.

The University of Chicago was one of the very few colleges that took a different path. In the 1930s and 1940s, comprehensive tests created by a board of examiners were the sole basis for graduation; course credits and grades no longer mattered. A student had to spend at least one year in residence; time served was not entirely abolished, although class attendance was optional.

The new arrangement required an expensive commitment to testing. The eight full-time examiners held joint appointments in various departments and also knew the intricacies of test construction, a relatively new field that promised more objectivity than the exams given by individual professors with their idiosyncratic grading practices. The examiners created multiple versions of the tests so that students who failed could retake them in a few months. To reduce ambiguity and guessing, lists of recommended readings and copies of previous exams were distributed. Because the exams went beyond the recall of facts, the faculty and the examiners had long discussions about the competencies they expected students to acquire and how they would demonstrate those skills on six-hour tests.[104] The system also hinged on the subordination of dozens of departments and hundreds of faculty to the powerful president, who championed the novelty; soon after Robert Hutchins left and the departments reasserted their prerogatives, Chicago reverted to credit hours as the path to the diploma.

Comprehensive exams took hold in many colleges in addition to rather than in place of the "horrid machinery" of credits and grades that Hutchins deplored.[105] Four years on campus remained the norm, and preparing for the comprehensives meant more, not less, time and effort. What it marked was a new way to use time, an innovation that could save time after graduation: skills like the ability to synthesize and analyze would endure. Four coherent years were a better long-term investment than four disjointed years.

Harvard was the pioneer. In his 1909 inaugural address, the new president of Harvard set aside Charles Eliot's campaign for a three-year degree. "The most vital measure for saving the college is not to shorten its duration, but to ensure that it shall be worth saving."[106] Abbott Lawrence Lowell took issue with one of Eliot's major innovations—eliminating requirements to the point that all but two courses were electives. "No doubt every boy ought to learn how to paddle his own canoe," Lowell argued, "but we do not begin the process by tossing him into a canoe, and setting him adrift in deep water, with a caution that he would do well to look for the paddle."[107] All undergraduates, not just the candidates for honors, needed to choose a *concentration*, one field of study where they would take at least six full-year courses. Depth was as important as breadth. Lowell liked the old adage that a cultured man knew a little of everything and everything about something. He used words like *grasp*, *judgment*, and *resourcefulness* to describe the adroitness that the high schools rarely forged and the professional schools took for granted.

Lowell thought that the worst flaw in American education was graduation on the basis of course credits. Decent grades in an assortment of classes did not guarantee the prowess that he admired. After finishing each semester, few students had to use what they had learned. As he told one professor in the medical school, students of anatomy "proceed to forget it—sometimes, I gather, with complete thoroughness."[108] The legacy of most courses was not like money in the bank; for Lowell, a better metaphor was unrefrigerated fruit. Large lecture courses were especially dangerous—"One might as well expect to train a crew by having them listen to the instruction of the coach and watch him row. Every capacity worth having can be developed only by personal effort."[109] He was dismayed that the students at one small college told a professor that they resented assigned reading: "You are paid by the college to read these books and tell us what is in them, and now you make us read them ourselves."[110]

The lack of a comprehensive examination as a graduation requirement was the major problem. Better teaching, tougher assignments, and sterner grading would not change the overemphasis on courses. What happened in the classroom was instruction; at best, it was a means to an end. The upshot was a graduating class with vastly different temperaments. As one foundation president asked a Harvard professor in 1908, "What does an A.B. from Harvard mean in intellectual discipline and development? Sometimes four years of real work under good men, sometimes three years of disconnected courses (partly snap) passed with the aid of a widow [private tutor]."[111] Charles Francis Adams said that his son (Harvard, 1899) admitted that his classmates picked their courses on the basis of convenience, avoiding conflicts with their social and athletic pursuits. Adams had done the same in his years at Harvard. "In college I followed the line of least resistance," and in hindsight an ideal elective would have been chess—at least he would have learned to focus, analyze, and plan.[112] In contrast, a comprehensive exam would require everyone to synthesize different courses, work independently to make those connections, and set a high but realistic standard for all students.

Creating the new exams took special effort. Departments had to agree on what mattered most and how to assess it, and students needed to be coached to get ready (under Lowell, small-group meetings with a tutor, a new rank adapted from British colleges, helped students write and reason more effectively). For any school, reorienting education to competencies and mastery as a graduation requirement required more specificity about outcomes than most instructors ever provided; vague and intangible goals would be hard to assess (or assess fairly), and they would give little direction for the months and years before the culminating exhibition of competence. Results that look specific often require more elaboration.

For example, the president of Simon's Rock proposed graduation from high school at age 16 in exchange for a series of minimum standards. "An informed response to a presidential campaign," "a rudimentary knowledge of statistics and probability," "a fundamental knowledge of the Constitution," "demonstrable command of written and spoken English," and other ambitious goals sounded good, but what they meant was not clear.[113] Must students be able to use and display those skills, or does the knowledge demonstrated through paper-and-pencil tests suffice? What level of proficiency is expected of everyone in a country where the average-ability students have never been scrutinized as carefully as the honors and special education ends of the spectrum? Will passing depend on one single test—if so, who is entitled to create it, and what criteria make it fair rather than biased? And should assessors take effort and stamina into account—doing one's best is an admirable outcome, but how does anyone know for sure if John and Susan worked up to their native abilities?

If a college wants to duck those questions, it can let its students *clep* a few courses. The noun/verb is short for the College Level Examination Program (CLEP, created in 1965), sometimes mistakenly called "credit for life experience" because that was one of its purposes—let adults earn college credits without setting foot inside a classroom. Veterans, correspondence school students, housewives who left college on marriage, workers who learned on the job—the market seemed so large that the head of the College Board envisioned a new national university, chartered by Congress, to grant degrees earned off campus, a proposal that a successor recast as a National Educational Registry, a "credit bank" that would keep track of grades, SAT scores, college transcripts, CLEP work, military training, and so on, accompanied by counseling centers to advise each client.[114]

Local discretion prevailed as each college decided what scores deserved credit and what fraction of a diploma could be earned by CLEP. Some places were more generous than others. Almost half of the Florida community colleges set the cut score at the 25th percentile in the early 1970s, and many unselective four-year colleges used CLEP credits as an incentive to attract students who might otherwise enroll elsewhere.[115] The selective schools, in contrast, stayed away from CLEP. Imagine Northwestern University giving credit for a 90-minute multiple-choice test, a test supposedly tailored for nontraditional learners yet remarkably similar to traditional tests of traditional content. External exams had so little appeal to one group of midwestern universities that they returned a $1.5 million planning grant in the early 1960s.[116] The better bet was the AP program, where the high school student spent a year in class on a rigorous curriculum endorsed by the colleges, and even then many excellent colleges were reluctant to say that work done in high school could ever be the same as their courses.[117]

Earning credits by examination rather than course credits might yield a degree for less time and much less money than Yale or Harvard requires, but the diploma will be from Thomas Edison or Western Governors.[118] The top tier still want youth to savor the years on campus, to learn outside the classroom, and to mature gradually at a particularly critical time of life when most parents have less to offer than a vibrant campus can provide.

"Slow Down," Dean Lewis titled his 2004 letter to incoming Harvard freshmen. Find time for friends, recreation, and solitude; anyone finishing in three years should take a year off before going to graduate or professional school.[119] Lewis shared the point of view expressed a century earlier by Princeton's Woodrow Wilson: "A college, the American college, is not a body of studies. It is a process of development. It takes . . . at least four years. . . . The environment is of the essence of the whole effect. . . . You cannot go to college on a street car."[120]

But when that gracious environment can cost $65,000 a year, will the indebted graduates wish they had chosen less expensive alternatives? What if the day comes when hundreds of good schools can dispense with course credits because they found other ways to certify in convincing detail what their students know and can do?

LINKS

An unhappy Teach for America corps member: http://www.theatlantic.com/education/archive/2013/09/i-quit-teach-for-america/279724
History of the GED: http://www.terpconnect.umd.edu/~ehutt/research.html
Overview of CLEP: https://clep.collegeboard.org
Simon's Rock: https://simons-rock.edu/why-simons-rock
Speech by Teach for America founder Wendy Kopp: https://www.youtube.com/watch?v=pubX6pQfVVU

NOTES

1. Kevin Eagan et al., *The American Freshman: National Norms Fall 2014* (Los Angeles: UCLA Higher Education Research Institute, 2014), 43.

2. Russell H. Chittenden, *History of the Sheffield Scientific School of Yale University, 1846–1922*, vol. 1 (New Haven, CT: Yale University Press, 1928), 53–81. For (favorable) comparisons of Sheffield to several dozen 19th-century

schools of science, see Roger L. Geiger, "The Rise and Fall of Useful Knowledge: Higher Education for Science, Agriculture, and the Mechanic Arts, 1850–1875," in *The American College in the Nineteenth Century* (Nashville, TN: Vanderbilt University Press, 2000), 153–68.

3. Christine Ogren, *The American State Normal School* (New York: Palgrave Macmillan, 2005); James W. Fraser, *Preparing America's Teachers* (New York: Teachers College Press, 2007), chaps. 3, 5, and 7. Students could hopscotch through normal schools. Psychologist Lewis Terman enrolled for a year, left to teach, returned for a second year, taught again, came back a third time, and then served for three years as principal of a rural high school before entering Indiana University as a junior. Carl Muchison, ed., *A History of Psychology in Autobiography*, vol. 2 (Worcester, MA: Clark University Press, 1932), 305.

4. Janice Weiss, "Educating for Clerical Work: The Nineteenth-Century Private Commercial School," *Journal of Social History*, Spring 1981, 410.

5. Ibid., 411. The "rapid transit" appeals of 19th-century commercial colleges are explored in A. J. Angulo, *Diploma Mills: How For-Profit Colleges Stiffed Students, Taxpayers, and the American Dream* (Baltimore: Johns Hopkins University Press, 2016), chap. 1.

6. Robert Twombly, *Louis Sullivan: His Life and Work* (Chicago: University of Chicago Press, 1986), 27–28.

7. Princeton Summer School, 1901 and 1903 catalogs, Historical Subject Files Collection, Box 353, folder 6, Princeton University Archives. Created in 1891, the school in 1917 boasted that only 34 of its 870 students had failed to enter Princeton (1917 catalog, which mentioned three other similar private summer schools in Princeton).

8. A. F. Nightingale, *A Hand-Book of Requirements for Admission to the Colleges of the United States* (New York: D. Appleton and Company, 1879), 14–15.

9. W. Bruce Leslie, *Gentlemen and Scholars: College and Community in the "Age of the University," 1865–1917* (University Park: Pennsylvania State University Press, 1992), 92–95.

10. *Proceedings of the Fourth Annual Convention of the College Association of the Middle States and Maryland* (New York: Holt, 1893), 13.

11. C. F. Smith, "Southern Colleges and Schools," *Atlantic Monthly*, 1884, 542–47. For the weaknesses across the South by 1900, see Amy Thompson McCandless, *The Past in the Present: Women's Higher Education in the Twentieth-Century American South* (Tuscaloosa: University of Alabama Press, 1999), 28–36.

12. Carnegie Foundation for the Advancement of Teaching, *Fourth Annual Report* (New York: Carnegie Foundation for the Advancement of Teaching, 1909), 136.

13. Louis Wright, "I Remember" (unpublished autobiography, Howard University Archives), 3.

14. Scott Gelber, "The Populist Vision for Land-Grant Universities, 1880–1900," in *The Land-Grant Colleges and the Reshaping of American Higher Education*, ed. Roger L. Geiger and Nathan M. Sorber (New Brunswick, NJ: Transaction, 2013), 169–71.

15. Colin Burke, *American Collegiate Populations: A Test of the Traditional View* (New York: New York University Press, 1982), 102.

16. Steven Mintz, *Huck's Raft: A History of American Childhood* (Cambridge, MA: Harvard University Press, 2004), chap. 4.

17. David F. Allmendinger, "The Dangers of Ante-Bellum Student Life," *Journal of Social History*, Fall 1973, 77–78; Steven J. Novak, *The Rights of Youth: American Colleges and Student Revolt, 1798–1815* (Cambridge, MA: Harvard University Press, 1977).

18. Timothy Dwight, *Memories of Yale Life and Men, 1845–1899* (New York: Dodd, Mead and Company, 1903), 5.

19. Lyman Bagg, *Four Years at Yale* (New Haven, CT: C. C. Chatfield, 1871), 687, 689, 695.

20. As the title of his book suggests, Bagg rarely mentioned the three-year Sheffield School at Yale. Apart from a few athletic teams, those students kept to themselves, and their extracurricular activities were less extensive and less valorized.

21. Quoted in George Wilson Pierson, *Yale College: An Educational History, 1871–1921* (New Haven, CT: Yale University Press, 1952), 383–84. Rather than reduce the importance of clubs and sports, Hadley told the Hartford, Connecticut, alumni in 1916 that he wanted to "elevate learning to the dignity of an extra-curricular activity." Hadley Family Papers, Box 2, folder 27, Yale University Archives.

22. Norman White to Gertrude Cary, June 5, 1869; March 5, 1868; and June 5, 1869, in Norman Cary White Papers, Yale University Archives.

23. Joseph L. Henderson, *Admission to College by Certificate* (New York: Teachers College, Columbia, 1912); Marc A. VanOverbeke, *The Standardization of American Schooling: Linking Secondary and Higher Education, 1870–1910* (New York: Palgrave Macmillan, 2008), chaps. 2–3; Harold S. Wechsler, *The Qualified Student* (New Brunswick, NJ: Transaction, 2014), chaps. 1–3; Walter Young, "The High Schools of New England," *School Review*, February 1907, 134–44.

24. Edward J. Power, *Catholic Higher Education in America* (New York: Appleton-Century-Crofts, 1972). The name of the first year at Georgetown, Rudiments, signaled the resemblance to the first year of high school even if the words *freshman*, *sophomore*, *junior*, and *senior* were not used. The Fordham catalog of 1895 said that no one under age 12 would be admitted; Gonzaga drew the line at nine. Boston College in 1865 included students as young as 11 and as old as 26.

25. Jurgen Herbst, "Liberal Education and the Graduate Schools," *History of Education Quarterly*, December 1962, 244–58, is an old but excellent snapshot of what he considered "the principal issue in the higher education of the 1870s, 1880s, and 1890s."

26. Columbia let its undergraduates enter graduate and professional schools after two years, a change that prompted Princeton alumni to sing these lines in 1902: "Now Butler at Columbia/Has cut the course in two/He must have quite forgotten/Both the football team and crew." In James Axtell, ed., *The Educational Legacy of Woodrow Wilson: From College to Nation* (Charlottesville: University of Virginia Press, 2012), 46, n. 110.

27. Charles William Eliot, *Educational Reform* (New York: Century, 1898), 152, 182–83, and *Reports of the President and Treasurer of Harvard College, 1907/08* (Cambridge: Harvard University, 1909); Hugh Hawkins, *Between Harvard and America: The Educational Leadership of Charles W. Eliot* (New York: Oxford University Press, 1972), 117–18, 272–73. Three years was the norm at Cambridge University by the 1890s, with Oxford still in favor of four. Janet Howarth, "The Self-Governing University, 1882–1914," in *The History of the University of Oxford*, vol. 7, ed. M. G. Brock and M. C. Curthoys (Oxford: Clarendon Press, 2000), 614.

28. For the changes at the Harvard Law School, see Bruce A. Kimball, *The Inception of Modern Professional Education: C. C. Langdell, 1826–1906* (Chapel Hill: University of North Carolina Press, 2009), chap. 7. For the slower pace of change at Yale, see John H. Langbein, "Law School in a University: Yale's Distinctive Path in the Later Nineteenth Century," in *History of the Yale Law School*, ed. Anthony T. Kronman (New Haven, CT: Yale University Press, 2004).

29. Robert Stevens, *Law School: Legal Education in America from the 1850s to the 1980s* (Chapel Hill: University of North Carolina Press, 1983), 77.

30. Dorothy E. Finnegan, "Raising and Leveling the Bar: Standards, Access, and the YMCA Evening Law Schools, 1890–1940," *Journal of Legal Education*, March/June 2005, 208–33; Alfred Z. Reed, *Present-Day Law Schools in the United States and Canada* (New York: Carnegie Foundation for the Advancement of Teaching, 1928), 94–99.

31. William R. Johnson, *Schooled Lawyers: A Study in the Clash of Professional Cultures* (New York: New York University Press, 1978), 136.

32. Kenneth Ludmerer, *Learning to Heal: The Development of American Medical Education* (New York: Basic Books, 1986), chap. 1.

33. James Clarke Wright, *Sketches from My Life* (Cambridge, MA: Riverside Press, 1914), 152; Henry James, *Charles W. Eliot*, vol. 1 (Boston: Houghton Mifflin, 1930), 275–76.

34. Thomas Neville Bonner, *Becoming a Physician: Medical Education in Britain, France, Germany and the United States, 1750–1945* (New York: Oxford University Press, 1995), chaps. 7–11.

35. "What kind of science, mathematics, and drawing? Those who, consciously or unconsciously, view medical education as a kind of glorified trade discipline, favor a short cut: they wish that the prospective students of medicine might have learned just the kind and amount of general science that is going to profit him, as a physician, to know." Abraham Flexner, *Medical Education: A Comparative Study* (New York: Macmillan, 1925), 88.

36. Robert Maynard Hutchins, *Education for Freedom* (Baton Rouge: Louisiana State University Press, 1943), 7; Mary Ann Dzuback, *Robert M. Hutchins: Portrait of an Educator* (Chicago: University of Chicago Press, 1991), 30–33. In contrast, Louis Auchincloss, deflated by Scribner's rejection of his first novel, decided to enter law school after three years at Yale, but by 1937 the dual enrollment option Hutchins used was gone. Auchincloss's father was upset—"What's the rush? You'll spend the rest of your life explaining why you didn't graduate from Yale. He was right. I have." Louis Auchincloss, *A Writer's Capital* (Minneapolis: University of Minnesota Press, 1974), 81. Auchincloss went to the University of Virginia for law school.

37. When Hopkins established the four-year medical curriculum, most graduates did not intern, and those who did were rarely paid. To be a specialist before World War I was easy—several weeks at a "graduate school," usually a for-profit enterprise. By the 1930s, specialty boards required at least three years of full-time residency. Charles Rosenberg, *The Care of Strangers: The Rise of America's Hospital System* (New York: Basic Books, 1987), 184; Kenneth Ludmerer, *Let Me Heal: The Opportunity to Preserve Excellence in American Medicine* (New York: Oxford University Press, 2015), 63–64, 117–34.

38. Brian Z. Tamanaha, *Failing Law Schools* (Chicago: University of Chicago Press, 2012), chap. 2. Tamanaha proposes flexibility in place of the American Bar Association mandate that every accredited school span three years. Five states allow aspiring lawyers to prepare as "law office readers" for an attorney, and three more states permit a combination of law school and apprenticeship, but only a handful elect this route—60 of the 83,986 who took

the bar exam in 2013, and of those 60, 28 percent passed, far lower than the 73 percent rate for law school graduates. "The Lincoln Lawyers," *New York Times*, August 3, 2014 (Education Life section), 22–23.

39. See the 50 pages of reactions, posted online, to "N.Y.U. and Other Medical Schools Offer Shorter Course in Training, for Less Tuition," *New York Times*, August 24, 2013, B-3.

40. Kenneth M. Ludmerer, *Time to Heal: American Medical Education from the Turn of the Century to the Era of Managed Care* (New York: Oxford University Press, 1999), 84.

41. National Science Foundation, "Survey of Earned Doctorates," table 31, in *Doctorate Recipients from U.S. Universities* (Washington, DC: National Science Foundation, 2015), 7.

42. And he had the advantage of an adviser who assured him before the written and oral exams that he would "pass that ordeal very easily." Herbert Baxter Adams to Woodrow Wilson, April 7, 1886, in Arthur S. Link, ed., *The Papers of Woodrow Wilson*, vol. 4 (Princeton, NJ: Princeton University Press, 1968), 154–55.

43. Muchison, *A History of Psychology in Autobiography*, 313.

44. Herbert A. Simon, *Models of My Life* (Cambridge, MA: MIT Press, 1996), 84–85.

45. Sylvia Nassar, *A Beautiful Mind* (New York: Simon & Schuster, 1998), 60.

46. "Talk continued until late in the night. . . . Sometimes the excitement was so great that on Monday nights after a dinner, I had trouble sleeping." Donald Hall, *Unpacking the Boxes: A Memoir of a Life in Poetry* (Boston: Houghton Mifflin, 2008), 118. Hall was a junior fellow from 1954 to 1957.

47. Crane Brinton, ed., *The Society of Fellows* (Boston: Little, Brown, 1996), 4.

48. Ibid., 25.

49. Jane Tompkins, *A Life in School: What the Teacher Learned* (Reading, MA: Addison-Wesley, 1996), 86.

50. Edgar S. Furniss, *The Graduate School of Yale: A Brief History* (New Haven, CT: Carl Rollins, 1965), 128–33; Henri Peyre, *Observations of Life, Literature, and Learning in America* (Carbondale: Southern Illinois University Press, 1961), 228–29. In 1929 and 1944, Robert Hutchins proposed two tracks—the PhD for candidates who wanted to teach and a different doctorate for the researchers. Both times the idea went nowhere. John W. Boyer, *The University of Chicago: A History* (Chicago: University of Chicago Press, 2015), 281–85.

51. Judith S. Glazer, *A Teaching Doctorate? The Doctor of Arts, Then and Now* (Washington, DC: American Association for Higher Education, 1993), 5.

52. E. Alden Dunham, "Rx for Higher Education: The Doctor of Arts Degree," *Journal of Higher Education* 61, no. 7 (October 1970): 507–9.

53. Glazer, *A Teaching Doctorate?*, 17–18.

54. Telephone interview, Tony Penna, June 11, 2015. In "The New Social Studies in Perspective," Penna recalled the intense pleasure of working with Fenton and other DA students on the "slow learner" book series. *The Social Studies* 86, no. 5 (1995): 155–61.

55. Alden Dunham, "DA Program" memorandum, July 31, 1974, Box 542, folder 2, Carnegie Corporation Papers, Columbia University Rare Book and Manuscript Library; "A Proposal to the Carnegie Corporation from Carnegie Mellon University for Fellowship and Program Support," October 1974, Box 471, folder 1, Carnegie Corporation Papers.

56. Telephone interviews with Ted Fenton (June 19, 2015), Joel Tarr (June 4, 2015), John Modell (June 29, 2015), and Tony Penna (June 11, 2015); e-mail from Peter Stearns, June 1, 2015. On President Cyert's commitment (1972–1990) to research productivity and external grants, see Edwin Fenton, *Carnegie Mellon: A Centennial History, 1900–2000* (Pittsburgh, PA: Carnegie Mellon University Press, 2000), chap. 12.

57. Alden Dunham to Mrs. John Gordon, February 9, 1971, Box 542, folder 5, Carnegie Corporation Papers.

58. Paul Dressel, "The Present Status of the Doctor of Arts," May 1973, Box 542, folder 6, Carnegie Corporation Papers. Much of this report was included in Paul L. Dressel and Mary M. Thompson, *College Teaching: Improvement by Degrees* (Iowa City, IA: American College Testing Program, 1974).

59. Arthur M. Eastman, ed., *Proceedings of the Wingspread Conference on the Doctor of Arts Degree October 25–27, 1970* (Washington, DC: Council of Graduate Schools, 1971), 12–13.

60. Glazer, *A Teaching Doctorate?*, 32.

61. Stephen Parrish to Mark Barlow, October 19, 1965, Box 1, folder 8, Associate Dean of Students Records, 1931–1978, Division of Rare and Manuscript Collection, Cornell University Library.

62. James Perkins to Frank Bowles, April 12, 1965, Box 8, folder 25, James Perkins Papers, Division of Rare and Manuscript Collections, Cornell University Library; "A Proposal to the Ford Foundation to Establish at Cornell University a Four Year Masters and Six Year PhD Program," Box 1, folder 17, James Perkins Papers.

63. This author's adviser at Cornell (from 1972 to 1978) recalled the program as "from high school to a tenure track job in six years," a phrase that underscored his concern that it moved youth to maturity much too quickly. E-mail from Joel H. Silbey, May 9, 2015.

64. Fred Crossland, "Cornell Six-Year Ph.D. Program," interoffice memorandum, November 10, 1965; Fred Crossland to James A. Perkins, December 2, 1965, Microfilm Reel 1248, Ford Foundation Papers, Rockefeller Archive Center.

65. Glenn C. Altschuler and Isaac Kramnick, *Cornell: A History* (Ithaca, NY: Cornell University Press, 2014), 115, wrote that "eight of these talented students" died—eight students did die, but only three of them were in the six-year PhD program.

66. Annual Report, 1968–69, 5, Microfilm Reel 1248, Ford Foundation Papers, Rockefeller Archive Center.

67. Progress Report #2, September 30, 1966, Microfilm Reel 1248, Ford Foundation Papers, Rockefeller Archive Center.

68. Stephen Parrish to President Perkins, May 29, 1967, Box 8, folder 25, Perkins Papers; "The Cornell Six Year Ph.D. Program, Annual Report, 1968–69," 5, Microfilm Reel 1248, Ford Foundation Papers, Rockefeller Archive Center. For the unsolved mystery of the dorm fire, I relied on e-mails and telephone calls from H. William Fogle Jr. (Cornell, 1970).

69. Marian Chamberlain to Robert Schmid, December 29, 1969; Robert Schmid to David Connor, April 24, 1970, Microfilm Reel 1248, Ford Foundation Papers, Rockefeller Archive Center.

70. Fred E. Crossland, "Final Grant Evaluation—Cornell University," interoffice memorandum, December 18, 1975, Microfilm Reel 1248, Ford Foundation Papers, Rockefeller Archive Center.

71. "Very Young, Smart, and Restless," *New York Times*, January 9, 2000, 28 (Education Life section).

72. Ralph Tyler, "Education: Curriculum Development and Evaluation," oral history conducted by Malca Chall, Bancroft Library, University of California, Berkeley, 1987, 8.

73. National Center for Education Statistics, *Dual Credit and Exam-Based Courses in U.S. Public High Schools: 2010–11* (Washington, DC: National Center for Education Statistics, 2013).

74. Anne Newton and Kristen Vogt, "Ensuring College Success: Scaffolding Experiences for Students and Faculty in an Early College School," Woodrow Wilson National Fellowship Foundation, Princeton, NJ, 2008; Tim Weldon, "Improving Access to Postsecondary Education through Early College High Schools," Council of State Governments, Washington, DC, 2009; Harold S. Wechsler, *Access to the Urban High School: The Middle College Movement* (New York: Teachers College Press, 2001).

75. Elizabeth B. Hall, "The House of Education Needs Overhaul," July 1967, and "Simon's Rock in Great Barrington, Massachusetts, 1964–1972," Elizabeth Hall Papers, Bard College at Simon's Rock Archives.

76. "Annual Report, Simon's Rock 1966–1967," Annual Reports—Box 1, Bard College at Simon's Rock Archives.

77. "Provost's Report (1968) on the 1967 Accreditation Visit"; "Report of the Visiting Committee, October 26–28, 1969"; "June, 1970 annual report to New England Association of Colleges and Secondary Schools," Bard College at Simon's Rock Archives.

78. Eileen Handelman (September 23, 2005), Oral History Collection, Bard College at Simon's Rock Archives.

79. "Annual Report, 1975–76," Annual Reports—Box 3, Bard College at Simon's Rock Archives.

80. Larry Wallach (August 16, 2005) and Bob Snyder (August 15, 2005), Oral History Collection, Bard College at Simon's Rock Archives.

81. *Chronicle of Higher Education*, February 15, 1971.

82. "Annual Report, 1974–75," Annual Reports—Box 3, Bard College at Simon's Rock Archives.

83. The handbook did assert that coed dorms were not an invitation to "easy sex or cohabitation" and that students should always have access to their (shared) rooms. In contrast, Phillips Academy–Andover throughout the 1970s expelled sexually active students, headmaster Theodore Sizer told me in 1981.

84. Baird W. Whitlock, *Don't Hold Them Back: A Critique and Guide to New High School–College Articulation Models* (New York: College Entrance Examination Board, 1978), 41.

85. Nancy Yanoshak, ed., *Educating outside the Lines: Bard College at Simon's Rock on a "New Pedagogy" for the 21st Century* (New York: Peter Lang, 2011).

86. Charles Dorn, *American Education, Democracy, and the Second World War* (New York: Palgrave Macmillan, 2007).

87. Ludmerer, *Time to Heal*, 126–31.

88. "Yale's Job in This War," *Yale Alumni Magazine*, March 6, 1942, 8.

89. "Memorandum on Acceleration," President's Committee on Acceleration, Box 1, folder 2, Yale University Archives.

90. *They Went to College Early* (New York: Fund for the Advancement of Education, 1957), 52, 43, 62.

91. Ludmerer, *Time to Heal*, 130–31.

92. Paul B. Diederich, "The Effects of Comprehensive Examinations," *The School Review*, November 1947, 526–33; Dzuback, *Robert M. Hutchins*, chap. 6; Milton Mayer, *Robert Maynard Hutchins: A Memoir* (Berkeley: University of California Press, 1993), 238–43; Walter M. Murphy and D. J. R. Bruckner, eds., *The Idea of the University of Chicago* (Chicago: University of Chicago Press, 1976), 334–35.

93. Hutchins, *Education for Freedom*, 74.

94. Bennett Cerf, *At Random: The Reminiscences of Bennett Cerf* (New York: Random House, 1977), 15–16. As night editor of the student newspaper, Cerf saw the new policy one day before it was announced. He immediately signed up for so many courses that the dean told him it would take 16 hours a day to do the homework.

95. Ethan Hutt, "Certain Standards: How Efforts to Establish and Enforce Minimum Standards Transformed American Schools (1870–1980)" (unpublished dissertation, Stanford University, 2013), 67–101.

96. Earl J. McGrath, "The Education of the Veteran," *Annals of the American Academy of Political and Social Science*, March 1945, 77.

97. Leonard M. Murchison to J. Dan Hull, June 19, 1945, Shortridge High School Collection, Box 17, folder 1, Indiana Historical Society. Besides GED scores, the principal occasionally used his own judgment (e.g., how to give credits for military experiences with no direct counterpart in the high school curriculum) or asked a veteran to demonstrate his skills to a Shortridge teacher. In other words, the GED was one way—but not the only way—that postwar educators tried to allocate course credit fairly and generously.

98. Educational Policies Commission, *Education for ALL American Youth* (Washington, DC: National Education Association, 1944).

99. Glenn C. Altschuler and Stuart A. Blumin, *The G.I. Bill: A New Deal for Veterans* (New York: Oxford University Press, 2009), chap. 4; Suzanne Mettler, *Soldiers to Citizens: The G.I. Bill and the Making of the Greatest Generation* (New York: Oxford University Press, 2005), 71–72.

100. James J. Heckman, John E. Humphries, and Tim Kautz, eds., *The Myth of Achievement Tests: The GED and the Role of Character in American Life* (Chicago: University of Chicago Press, 2014). The authors emphasize the "character skills" fostered by traditional face-to-face education. "A high school diploma not only represents a certain level of academic success, but more importantly, a degree of discipline" (276).

101. The paragraphs on Teach for America rely on Arthur G. Powell, Barbara S. Powell, and Robert L. Hampel, "Teach for America's 1998 Summer Institute: An Examination," October 1998.

102. The summer institutes' curricular choices were not what set it apart from traditional teacher education. Nearly all of the components used mainstream ideas and practices. The novelty was the compression of so much material into five weeks. Jack Schneider, "Rhetoric and Practice in Pre-Service Teacher Education: The Case of Teach for America," *Journal of Education Policy* 29, no. 4 (2014): 425–42.

103. For the challenges, see Molly Ness, *Lessons to Learn: Voices from the Front Lines of Teach for America* (New York: Routledge Falmer, 2004), chaps. 3–6; Sarah Sentiles, *Taught by America: A Story of Struggle and Hope in*

Compton (Boston: Beacon, 2005); and the more critical anthology by T. Jameson Brewer and Kathleen deMarrais, eds., *Teach for America Counter-Narratives: Alumni Speak Up and Speak Out* (New York: Peter Lang, 2015).

104. Chauncey S. Boucher, *The Chicago College Plan* (Chicago: University of Chicago Press, 1935); William H. McNeill, *Hutchins' University: A Memoir of the University of Chicago* (Chicago: University of Chicago Press, 1991), 142; F. Champion Ward, ed., *The Idea and Practice of General Education: An Account of the College of the University of Chicago* (Chicago: University of Chicago Press, 1950).

105. Harry S. Ashmore, *Unseasonable Truths: The Life of Robert Maynard Hutchins* (Boston: Little, Brown, 1989), 144.

106. A. Lawrence Lowell, *At War with Academic Traditions in America* (Cambridge, MA: Harvard University Press, 1934), 35.

107. Ibid., 43. Lowell often used athletic metaphors. For instance, a major without a comprehensive exam was a football game without goalposts. He knew how hard students worked to excel in sports, and he wanted to see comparable exertion for academic excellence. He fought the stereotype that disparaged intellectual achievement as less masculine than athletic prowess: "Undergraduates are prone to believe that athletic sports are a good measure of red blood while high rank in studies indicates only industrious plodding. They often rate the two occupations much as savages do hunting and husbandry" (239).

108. A. Lawrence Lowell to John Warren, February 25, 1911, Series 1909–1914, folder 1163, Records of the President of Harvard University, Harvard University Archives.

109. Lowell, *At War with Academic Traditions in America*, 193.

110. Ibid., 184.

111. H. S. Pritchett to Hugo Munsterberg, May 26, 1908, quoted in Laurence Veysey, *The Emergence of the American University* (Chicago: University of Chicago Press, 1965), 359.

112. Charles F. Adams to Arthur Hadley, May 4, 1907, Hadley Family Papers, Box 2, folder 18, Yale University Archives.

113. Leon Botstein, *Jefferson's Children: Education and the Promise of American Culture* (New York: Doubleday, 1997), 117–18.

114. Frank Bowles to John Gardner, January 16, 1963, Box 499, folder 6, Carnegie Corporation Papers; Arland F. Christ-Janer to Florence Anderson, n.d., Box 498, folder 2, Carnegie Corporation Papers.

115. Edward Caldwell, "Analysis of an Innovation (CLEP)," *Journal of Higher Education*, December 1973, 699–700; in 1973, 40 percent of the CLEP candidates were under age 22—not the market its creators had in mind but hardly surprising since it was cheaper than tuition and easier than the AP

exams. Fred A. Nelson, "Has the Time Come for an External Degree?," *Journal of Higher Education*, March 1974, 181.

116. E. A. Dunham memorandum, "College Level Examinations," December 13, 1967, Box 499, folder 1, Carnegie Corporation Papers. Dunham noted that 11 candidates turned down the job of overseeing the grant.

117. For a firsthand recollection of the origins of AP and CLEP, see John A. Valentine, *The College Board and the School Curriculum* (New York: College Entrance Examination Board, 1987), chap. 6.

118. For a concise account of the challenges in replacing credit hours with competency-based alternatives, see Elena Silva, Taylor White, and Thomas Toch, "The Carnegie Unit: A Century-Old Standard in a Changing Education Landscape," Carnegie Foundation for the Advancement of Teaching, New York, 2015.

119. "Slow Down: Getting More Out of Harvard by Doing Less," January 9, 2004, http://scholar.harvard.edu/files/harrylewis/files/slowdown2004.pdf.

120. Quoted in Axtell, *The Educational Legacy of Woodrow Wilson*, 34–35, 28.

4

THE ZEAL FOR BREVITY

Simplified Spelling, Shorthand, and Speed-Reading

In "Funky for You," the rapper Common replaced several words with grunts. Dostoyevsky claimed that only one word—*khuy*—was necessary for Russians to express all their feelings. Bell Atlantic telephone operators cut three words to two when they dropped *please* and just asked, "What listing?"[1]

Different people streamline language in many ways, with the recent rise of tweets and text messages encouraging everyone to create distinctive space savers (or consult a handbook like *Wan2tlk? Ltl bk of Txt Msgs* to see what others do). Within the history of American universities, a pre–e-mail shortcut that tempted thousands of graduate students was a quick and painless way to pass the language requirements for the PhD.

For many aspiring scholars, the need to know two foreign languages was not urgent. Months and months of careful preparation seemed pointless. Graduate students at Cornell often took a six-week summer course, did some reading on their own, and then barely passed an exam. "I think this is a disgrace," one professor exclaimed; "they could not possibly have learned enough German in that short time to have a really useful knowledge of it."[2] At the University of Chicago, many students took the exam three times, persevering until they passed. A professor there told President Hutchins that custom would continue unless the faculty started assigning books and articles not written in English.[3] For

John Nash and the other young mathematicians at Princeton, the faculty let students pass who could not understand an excerpt as long as they promised to learn it later.⁴

If individuals and groups work out their own modifications of languages, so too do organizations. Pictures, headlines, and captions in newspapers and magazines convey the gist of a short article. Abstracts in scholarly journals offer brief summaries of long articles. Abridgements of entire books enriched many publishers, not just *Reader's Digest*, and Sony Pictures compressed old television shows like *Charlie's Angels*, *T. J. Hooker*, *Bewitched*, and *The Three Stooges* to five-minute "mini-sodes." Complicated policy issues turned into the one-page "mini-memo" in the Reagan White House, a terse analysis with recommendations. Back when elementary schools taught penmanship, the advocates of the Palmer method prospered when they convinced educators that their letters were easy to learn and use—a "plain and rapid style" well suited for "the rush of business"—unlike the ornate swirls of Spencerian handwriting.⁵

Rather than explore a wide range of innovations concerning brevity, this chapter focuses on three well-organized crusades to convince Americans to change their customary ways of spelling, writing, and reading. The following pages trace the rise and fall of *simplified spelling*, a late 19th- and early 20th-century quest to make the language more logical; turn next to phonetic *shorthand*; and finish with *speed-reading*. Each shortcut required substantial time and effort before the promised results could appear. For most people, the cost of making the changes was too high.

Furthermore, each initiative drew criticism as run by zealots. People of common sense and moderate views should keep their distance, the skeptics warned, as the passionate leaders remained sure of the exceptional merit of what they espoused. And in all three instances, the level of satisfaction with the status quo was so high that the only crusade that spread widely, shorthand, fell short of its ambitious goals when it made its greatest gains among female secretaries rather than the wider world.

SIMPLIFIED SPELLING

Bed and *red* are spelled correctly, but not *hed*. *Head* resembles *bead*, but the two pronunciations differ. *Bead* rhymes with *seed*, which sounds exactly like *cede*. *Bough, cough, tough,* and *dough*: four letters in common, four different pronunciations. The letter *s* at the end of *boys, choices,* and *cats* does not sound the same, and many letters in other words have no sound, so why not write *sissors, iland, crum,* and *gost*? Knowing that *pepper* came from Old English and *leper* derived from French is little comfort to the bewildered six-year-old who wonders why one word has *pp* when the other has only *p*.

What a former president of Harvard called the "absurdities" of English orthography have prompted hundreds of entirely new languages.[6] They range from the bizarre (a language based on chipmunk noises) to the plausible (expressions of women's feelings—for instance, separate words for to menstruate, to menstruate joyfully, to menstruate late, and to menstruate painfully). The alternatives would not necessarily be shorter; one had words ending with a syllable to explain the evidence for the statement: *wa*—I saw it myself; *we*—I saw it in a dream; *wi*—it's obvious; and so on. One tough language—3,000 words have to be memorized—is Klingon, created for the *Star Trek* movies and television shows. Its dictionary sold more than 300,000 copies, and an annual conference lets the most ardent fans speak it with each other.[7]

Spel as u pronounce: a phonetic approach has been the most popular strategy to improve English. Sounds and letters should correspond. If speech and writing aligned, learning how to read and spell would be vastly easier. For instance, Benjamin Franklin told his sister not to apologize for her inaccurate spelling. "In my Opinion as our Alphabet now Stands, the bad Spelling, or what is call'd so, is generally the best, as conforming to the Sound of the Letters and of the Words." He relished the story of a gentleman who could not decipher "yf," although a servant, Betty, knew immediately that the elusive word was *wife*. "Some times the Betys has the Brightest understanding" and admirable "Sagasity," Jane Franklin replied.[8] Franklin's proposal to drop six letters (*c, j, q, w, x,* and *y*) and add six new ones went nowhere. Several decades later, Noah Webster kept the alphabet and made more headway in his popular spelling books and dictionaries. He did not win every battle—*labor, error, jail, music, plow, ax,* and *wagon* endured, but he lost on *tung, nabor, abuv, laf, tuf, fether,* and many other words.⁹

Throughout the 19th century, the interest in spelling reform was unrelenting, marked by occasional breakthroughs for specific groups—a new alphabet for the Cherokee Indians, sign languages for the deaf, and codes for telegraph operators. Phonetic spelling always had its advocates who promoted the cause through niche newspapers, itinerant lectures, and small societies. From the mid-1870s through World War I, the devotion to spelling reform was especially widespread. More than what came before or after, an organized national crusade in those years supplemented scattered individual exertions.

Notwithstanding meager donations and part-time unpaid staff, the reform attracted considerable support. The American Philological Association championed the cause; so did the more specialized Spelling Reform Association. Endorsements by well-known writers (including Mark Twain and William James), educators (the presidents of Cornell, Johns Hopkins, and Stanford), officials (Commissioner of Education William T. Harris), and politicians (especially President Theodore Roosevelt) mobilized more powerful allies than spelling reform had recruited in the early to mid-19th century.

The rise of first-rate American universities and scholarly societies in the 1870s and beyond helps explain the timing of the surge—many of the leaders were professors and administrators—but the reform drew strength from many sources because it spoke directly to contemporary hopes and fears. Foreigners would learn our language more rapidly, and in turn English would spread around the world in step with American trade and the acquisition of overseas territories. By saving a year or more of instruction in the earliest grades, the financial benefits for the constantly expanding school districts would be significant. Publishers would also save money—the cost of printing silent letters, one leader claimed in 1876, was $3 million annually.[10] Pioneers of progressive education, such as Francis Parker and John Dewey, welcomed spelling reform for elevating logic over rote memorization. So did their comrade William Torrey Harris, the federal commissioner of education who, when he ran the St. Louis public schools from 1868 to 1880, introduced a new alphabet that kept the familiar letters but tweaked their shape or added little marks (like a dot inside the letter *o*) to cue the young to the correct pronunciation.[11]

Without the equivalent of the Académie française to mandate change, the reformers sought the endorsements of groups that could sway millions. The National Education Association debated the topic frequently and after two decades of discussion agreed to use 12 simplified spellings in its publications. Local and state teacher associations often expressed more support, usually praising longer lists of reformatted words without abandoning the use of traditional orthography.[12] Newspaper editors, academic journal editors, and commercial publishers were courted; influential individuals in other careers were also wooed. Signing a card vowing to use simplified spelling resembled the temperance pledge, and the reformers hoped enough men of property and standing would sign to overcome the views expressed by the editor of the *Brooklyn Daily Eagle*: "The zeal for brevity is simply vulgar. It suggests a desire to save time. That suggests hurry. Hurry suggests want of leisure, and that is what no gentlemen should suggest."[13]

That point of view was only one of the objections the reformers heard. One line of reasoning was historical—words reveal their etymology and languages evolve on their own. Another complaint focused on the practical problems: Would every book in print have to be rewritten? What would happen to the classics? How could the American Revolution occur without England, where students still lost points on exams if they used "American spelling" for words like *honour*? Several writers raised technical points—they questioned whether the alphabet permitted purely phonetic spelling, noted how regional dialects were a cherished American tradition, and chided the reformers for not always agreeing with each other. Bigots wondered if southern blacks would be able to sidestep literacy requirements designed to prevent them from voting.

Another point was harder to proclaim, but it was clear that the challenges of American orthography were seen as useful markers of intelligence and education, markers within reach of most people. The librarian of Congress thought that only a "few ignoramuses" would benefit from phonetic shortcuts.[14] The enduring popularity of local *spelling bees* underscored the expectation that children would demonstrate their prowess by mastering the difficulties, not avoiding them (and thus the hooting in 1992 when Vice President Quayle moderated a spelling contest and mistakenly said that *potato* ends with an *e*).[15] Anyone who could not grasp the language was suspect, as publisher Henry Holt learned when he sent a letter to a woman who knew his wife. Unaware that Holt used simplified spelling, she exclaimed to her son, "George, Florence has married a man who doesn't know how to spell!"[16]

And the praise of efficiency and rationality could backfire. *Crossed* or *crost*: "Which form is shorter? Quicker? Easier? Truer?" the reformers asked.[17] For many Americans, the clipped words looked cold and stark. The aroma in *bouquet* disappears when it is spelled *boka*, the librarian of Congress protested.[18] "Cropped and tail-less words" discarded the cherished emotions and pleasant memories associated with traditional spellings.[19] Saving time and money wasn't a strong enough reason to discard the familiar language.[20]

The familiar dilemma that reformers face—are we going too fast or too slow?—also hampered the cause. The correspondence of Melvil Dewey, the inventor of the Dewey Decimal System for cataloging library books, reveals his desire to do both. As he began a four-year negotiation with philanthropist Andrew Carnegie for an annual donation to a new Simplified Spelling Board, he told his benefactor that "cranks and extremists have made the cause ridiculous."[21] Adding new letters to the alphabet and inserting diacritical marks would backfire; the Spelling Reform Association had made those mistakes in the late 1870s. Several phonetic changes would fall flat. Substituting *ai* for *y* was jarring and unnecessary. What about *dzh* for *j*? "Can't be thought of for a moment."[22] *C* in place of *k*? "After all these years I think we ought to have learned that it is not wise." *Aks* for *ax*? "A pure waste of time to try it."[23] Geographical landmarks and proper names were off limits; he had changed his own name to Dui but reverted to Dewey in 1883. The old spellings should remain whenever reasonably accurate pronunciation ensued.

Dewey knew what many of his colleagues overlooked—spelling had to appeal to the eyes as well as the ears. "The first great rule," he told a colleague who wanted to add three "beautiful new letters," is to "leave every spelling as it is unless it is clearly necessary to change."[24] Even calling the undertaking a reform was risky, he warned Carnegie.[25]

On the other hand, Dewey often yearned to move more rapidly. He loved the idea of a new typeface joining the letters *t* and *h*, which Dewey hoped the press would eventually use in place of *the* because "no word in the languaj is so scandalously overworkt."[26] When he was the secretary for the New York Board of Regents, he often omitted periods and capital letters, prompting the chancellor to scold him—"The page looks unfinished, naked. As I write on this cool morning, it chills me! I shiver. The page reminds me of a rustic whose trousers and sleeves are too short."[27] At his Lake Placid resort in upstate New York, Dewey used simplified spellings extensively when he knew the patrons had no other choices. His son recalled, "Father assumed that everyone would come in the dining room and eat and would have to use the menu," where one item, Stud Prunes, prompted a guest to ask if they were only for men.[28]

The Simplified Spelling Board would avoid "overzealous" action, Dewey assured Carnegie, but an initial list of 300 shortened words seemed much too drastic when President Theodore Roosevelt in August 1906 ordered their use in all publications from the executive branch of the federal government, even though he had doubts about the wisdom of spelling *through* as *thru*.[29]

Newspapers across the country lampooned his decision, unlike the favorable reactions in 1890, when President Harrison created a commission to be sure that government maps and charts used the same spelling for mountains, rivers, towns, and so on. For instance, a "Kikt Out" cartoon had Roosevelt punting a dictionary from the White House porch, and one headline read, "Rozevult Aksepts Latest Spelling Words . . . Here Are Sum of the Wurds Afekted."[30] A friend of his, Owen Wister, wrote a satire, *How Doth the Simple Spelling Bee*, that included (as did the headlines) dozens of words not among the 300, including *Yurrup* and *surrup*.

The Supreme Court refused to use any modifications, and Congress held hearings after President Roosevelt sent a message to Congress in simplified spelling. Less than four months after the initial order, the president rescinded it. "I could not by fighting have kept the new spelling in," he told a friend, promising to retain it in his private correspondence.[31] The critics had quickly made Roosevelt seem like one of the cranks Dewey wanted to avoid.

Sustained by Carnegie's gifts—nearly $300,000 over 13 years—the Simplified Spelling Board remained active, publishing bulletins, mailing circulars, holding conferences, and steadily expanding the number of words it wanted to alter. In January 1908, 75 more words were unfurled (including *sissors*, *iland*, *crum*, and *gost*) with another batch one year later. By 1920, the full list included several thousand words, and the board admitted that its long-range goal was phonetic spelling. Journalist H. L. Mencken said the roster became "wilder and wilder," and Carnegie's support began to diminish even though many newspapers and periodicals used some of the innovations and dozens of colleges, normal schools, and teacher associations praised the simplifications (e.g., the superintendent of the New York City schools said it was absurd to spell *knee* with a *k* and *gnat* with a *g*, but his board voted 32 to 4 against The List of 300).[32] For Carnegie, a sharper focus on a handful of words would have been a more successful strategy. Without any provision for the board in his will or financial support from his various philanthropies, the board languished in the 1920s.

Some of the short words survived—*program, catalog, hiccup,* and *plow*—and many advertisements felt free to use phonetic spellings to sell TruFit shoes, Az-Nu enamel, and other merchandise.[33] The rise of e-mail encouraged abbreviated spelling, but no organized crusade to recast standard usage ever again arose. The struggle against centuries of traditional orthography had been forceful and carefully reasoned, but the shortcutters could not overcome the satisfaction with the status quo and the defenses marshaled by its advocates. The upheaval of getting from here to there seemed too great, and *there* was not seen as undeniably better than *here*.

But what if a reformer proposed a new way to write that no one could understand apart from the writer and the others who had learned it? Why did that reform—shorthand—take hold more extensively than simplified spelling yet still fall short of its aspirations?

SHORTHAND

Francis Bacon's memorable remark about shortcuts—"Some books are to be tasted; others to be swallowed; and some few to be chewed and digested"—can be written as "Sm bks rtb tstd; os tb swld; & sm fw tb chwd & dgstd." Seneca's warning against shortcuts—"The world was not made in a day, neither can anyone hope to gain wealth by sudden efforts"—could be jotted down as E W w n md I a d-, nei c ny hp t gn wlth b sdn efrt. Andrew Graham, the inventor of *brief longhand*, said his methods would cut in half the time spent taking notes. The savings when writing less truncated sentences to persons unacquainted with brief longhand was only 10 percent, but "all economizers of time and labor should be accepted as blessings."[34]

The truly dramatic gains came from the use of shorthand, which one of his admirers, Woodrow Wilson, learned on his own when he was 16 and 17. During a year at home preparing for the Princeton entrance exams, Wilson told Graham that he was "spending all the time I have to spare and more too I am afraid" studying Graham's manuals and periodicals.[35] In two months, he devoured the 25 lessons in the introductory text—"I regard this book as a perfect gem and would not part with it . . . for anything."[36] He then ordered several harder books from Graham to learn the "reporting" style of shorthand used to capture legislative debates, court proceedings, convention speeches, and the like.

Wilson wanted to move from North Carolina to New York City to spend part of the summer studying with Graham to master the reporting style even though he never envisioned stenography as his career. The skill "will be of great use to me in college but being young I have a great deal to learn about the art of putting a man's words on paper as quickly as he can get rid of them."[37] Graham declined because of poor health, but he assured Wilson that he was making excellent progress. At Princeton and beyond, Wilson used shorthand in many ways—taking notes, keeping diaries, writing lectures, drafting books, and outlining speeches.

Shorthand was a very old skill by the time Wilson learned it. On the eve of colonization, 16th- and 17th-century Englishmen could read dozens of tracts and manuals on the topic. Adept practitioners would record—and often publish—sermons, trials, last words at executions, and other noteworthy public events, including Shakespeare's plays (e.g., the different versions of *King Lear* probably stemmed from varying transcriptions—*mistresse* or *mysteries*? *my rackles* or *miracles*?).[38] Shorthand was also prized for masking religious texts that were illegal or might be in the future if the monarch reverted to Catholicism.

Secrecy was equally valuable for descriptions of political twists and turns; the famous diary of Samuel Pepys is an extraordinary chronicle of the mid- to late 17th century. Its value is enhanced by the vignettes of his turbulent domestic life, including several crushes on young women. In those passages, his shorthand often used other languages to increase the secrecy: "I aime her de todo mi corazon" and "did tocar mi cosa con su mano."[39] More than Pepys, Isaac Newton used his shorthand diary to castigate himself for "uncleane thoughts," "peevishness with my mother," "punching my sister," "making pies on Sunday night," and several dozen other transgressions in 1662.⁴⁰ Stronger guilt marked the anguished 17th-century diary of Reverend Michael Wigglesworth, who lamented his "unnatural filthy lusts" for Harvard students and his erotic "night pollutions."⁴¹ Other colonists who knew shorthand were often ministers (including Samuel Parris, who recorded testimony in shorthand during the Salem witchcraft trials) or well-educated men who had no intentions of making it a career.⁴²

The popularity of the phonetic shorthand developed in the 1830s changed the prospects for the proficient. Shorthand always relied on shortcuts—eliminate vowels, omit articles, overlook punctuation, memorize arbitrary symbols for frequently used words, let some marks represent several words, and so on. Isaac Pitman paid more attention to the sounds of the language than the letters, and to do so he relied on eight curves, four straight lines with different slants, various hooks and dots attached to those marks, and distinctions between light and dark signs. Half-length marks added more options, and placement above, on, or below the lines on a page further extended the scope of *phonography*.⁴³

Pitman claimed that his system increased speed without sacrificing accuracy or legibility.⁴⁴ Now it would be possible for skillful phonographers to follow legislative debates, court cases, state constitutional conventions, or long speeches with fewer errors, omissions, or interpolations than their predecessors made. A scribe might not be able to keep pace with an extremely fast speaker or continue for an entire day, but the goal of verbatim transcription seemed within reach.

In the 1840s and 1850s, phonographers often found work with newspapers, which at the time usually affiliated with a political party and therefore tried to print as much campaign and legislative news as possible. The famous Lincoln–Douglas debates of 1858, for instance, were captured by reporters for Republican and Democratic papers in Chicago, and, not surprisingly, their accounts differed. Each side printed more of their candidate's words than the other side, and parenthetical notes about cheers from the audience lopsidedly favored their man. Each side accused the other of misrepresentations. Did Douglas say *nigger*, as the Republicans claimed, or *negro*? Did Lincoln use "bad rhetoric and horrible jargon," as the Democrats claimed, or did he just speak more rapidly than Douglas?⁴⁵ At least neither party endured the garbled account of a speech by the abolitionist Horace Greeley, who supposedly asked, "Is there no barn in Guilford?" when in fact he said, "Is there no balm in Gilead?"[46]

Employment by the government gradually eclipsed newspaper work as the most prestigious option for shorthand experts. Courts hired more and more phonographers; so did state legislatures. After decades of paying for summaries, Congress secured verbatim records of its debates from the late 1840s on, and several cabinet members had assistants to take dictation. Nearly all of the state constitutional conventions in the 1840s and 1850s and thereafter paid for and published complete transcripts. There were occasional doubts and reservations about spending money on proceedings that were also covered by the press, but the trend was unmistakable—local, state, and federal officials wanted fuller documentation of what transpired. The number of well-paid government positions was small by the 1860s, but all the signs pointed to more jobs in the future. Business employment was another option, but before the invention of reliable typewriters in the 1870s, clerks with good penmanship rarely needed to know shorthand to get their work done.[47]

Because the field was unregulated, newcomers could enter it at will. What mattered was swift accuracy; when, where, and how it was acquired was up to each individual. Most practitioners before the 1880s learned on their own, and the best-known experts usually had at least one other occupation before they devoted themselves to shorthand. Joseph Pulsifer was a teacher, lawyer, postmaster, California gold rush prospector, and army paymaster in addition to his shorthand work in courts and legislatures. Ruel Smith was a teacher, telegraph operator, lawyer, inventor (he patented an eraser), and court reporter.[48] Dan Brown's similar zigzags—wagon maker, teacher, newspaper reporter, court phonographer, railroad manager, and proprietor of the largest private shorthand school in Chicago—were not unusual in an era when the word *career* meant a course of action, not a lifelong pursuit of a particular trade or profession open only to the fully credentialed.[49] The hard work and self-discipline necessary to acquire this arcane skill reinforced the reputation of phonographers as industrious and ambitious.[50]

The phonographic pioneers of the 1840s and 1850s were also ambitious to improve the world by way of other crusades. Spelling was, not surprisingly, a favorite reform, with many journals and manuals including sections written phonetically, sometimes with new letters. Mrs. Eliza Burns publicized her commitment by changing her last name to Burnz one year after her husband died. Several eminent phonographers campaigned for abolition, and the most ardent abolitionist, William Lloyd Garrison, occasionally lectured on behalf of phonography.[51] More controversial causes—women's rights, vegetarianism, spiritualism, hydrotherapy, phrenology, and socialism—attracted Isaac Pitman, Andrew Graham, and other well-known rapid writers.

Those commitments help explain the "crank" reputation of spelling reform that Melvil Dewey lamented, with one man in particular, Stephen Andrews, tainting the cause. An Amherst College student who dropped out to teach school with his sister in Louisiana, Andrews switched to law, moved to Texas, and started to advocate for compensated emancipation. After a mob expelled him from Galveston, he went to England to raise money to free the slaves and instead discovered Pitman's manuals. Andrews marveled at what he read and immediately devoted himself to spreading the good news in Boston and New York in the mid- to late 1840s through lectures, short courses, books, magazines, and public exhibitions of illiterates who had learned to read shorthand. He hoped that shorthand would replace longhand and lead to a universal language.

The flurry of activity was expensive, and as his debts approached $10,000, Andrews began to espouse radical solutions for the world's problems. He started a utopian community on Long Island that revamped capitalism—currency took the form of notes pledging either one hour of labor or 12 pounds of corn—and set aside monogamy. After the venture collapsed, he returned to New York City and renamed himself Andrusius, leader of a new society, the Pentarch, devoted to anarchism, free love, and women's rights. He created Alwato, a language for every nation to adopt, and chartered the Normal University of the Pentarchy with "planetary purposes" for the "grand mutual reconciliation of humanity." He had several dozen students and admirers, but most people thought he was mad. Near death, he wanted to announce that he was Christ reincarnate, but the woman who took his dictation dissuaded him.[52]

The reputation of the leaders also suffered from their constant bickering with one another. The path to prominence typically entailed small modifications of Pitman's system, publication of the changes in manuals and books, opening a school, selling supplies, and editing a monthly journal to explain and promote the novelties. The pages of those journals usually included letters from grateful students who often criticized the rivals, and the editors also felt free to mock their competitors.

Woodrow Wilson's mentor, Andrew Graham, was especially combative. He called one of his counterparts "beneath contempt," sued another for allegedly stealing his ideas, and took a third to court for slander (and that man, after he was cleared, said that Graham "doesn't live a day without telling a lie to cover up a lie").[53] In turn, Graham was sued for slander by James Munson, who, according to Graham, did not use the system he had created.[54] Benn Pitman, who moved to America to disseminate Isaac's breakthrough, did not speak to his brother for 25 years after they differed on whether Isaac's 10th revision in 20 years—a new way to designate vowels—was necessary.

The fragmentation and competition can be quantified thanks to two national surveys of shorthand teachers. In 1884 and 1893, the federal Bureau of Education revealed the wide range of choices in front of an aspiring student. The bulk of the instruction took place outside the public schools. Of the 287 names in the inventory for 1882 and 1883, 27 percent were private instructors.[55] Most of them taught a handful of pupils—only 19 of the 78 teachers had 20 or more students. Just as numerous were business colleges, which ranged from very small outfits named for the teacher to national chains like Bryant and Stratton. Shorthand institutes, shorthand schools, and a few shorthand colleges: those specialists accounted for another 13 percent of the vendors, and an additional 2 percent included typewriting in their names. In the cities, nine YMCAs taught shorthand; so did six urban high schools, where the subject was usually scheduled in the evening, often after a local phonographer had petitioned the board to offer it. Normal schools, universities and colleges, academies, and rural high schools accounted for 40 more entries in the tabulation. For the beginners who did not want or could not find face-to-face instruction, one-third of the 287 vendors offered lessons through the mail.

Outside the South, the range of options was extensive, especially in the cities, and growing rapidly—in the "date of introduction of study" column, 86 percent said it started in the last five years, coinciding with the production of reliable typewriters, an invention that spurred the demand for office workers who could take dictation, type, and carry out other clerical and secretarial tasks without aspiring to the more demanding, better-paid, and male-dominated careers as newspaper, court, and legislative reporters.

The growth accelerated throughout the 1880s. The Bureau of Education's census of shorthand instruction for July 1890 through June 1891 had 1,310 entries, more than four times the total in 1882–1883.[56] The number of correspondence students more than tripled, with the classroom population rising nearly fivefold from 10,197 to 50,130. Slightly more than half (52.6 percent) of the pupils were female, a significant change from the 32.5 percent in the 1882–1883 tally. The number of female instructors also rose sharply, almost doubling from 11.9 to 23 percent, with nearly one-third of those women listed as "Mrs." The array of choices remained vast, with business colleges (25 percent), private instructors (22 percent), and shorthand institutes (14 percent) still dominating the field. Several other niches outside the educational mainstream also welcomed stenography—YMCAs, normal schools, and Catholic academies and colleges. There were even shorthand classes in orphanages, on Indian reservations, and in two prisons.

The public schools and nonsectarian colleges, in contrast, did not account for much of the growth in the 1880s. Only 31 public high schools offered it in the 1890–1891 academic year. The leading colleges and universities showed no interest—of the 39 colleges where shorthand was taught, 18 were Catholic, and most of the rest were small rural outposts. Four of the five first-rate colleges that offered the subject in 1882 no longer did so in 1890–1891, when the most prestigious college with shorthand, Antioch, reported only four rapid writers. Just one of the land grant colleges, places where practical course work was encouraged, offered shorthand.

The surging interest in shorthand, in other words, happened outside the educational mainstream in the decade when the demand for secretaries soared. As shorthand became seen as a useful skill for ambitious youth bound for college and the professions, the size of that potential market would increase rapidly in the early 20th century. But before then, shorthand had been tagged as secretarial work done by women.

Another form of choice—the particular shorthand to learn—expanded in the 1880s. Few places taught more than one method—only 5.4 percent did so in 1882–1883 and 6.6 percent in 1890–1891. The five most popular techniques had 81.3 percent of the single-system vendors, with the next four representing 14.0 percent, followed by 14 other options taught by one or two instructors. Of those 14, nine teachers used their own name for the method. That was how their larger rivals got started; why not try to get a share of a burgeoning field? The profusion of small systems increased by the early 1890s. The top five held 71.8 percent of the market, the next four had 13.0 percent, and 31 other options vied for the remaining students, with 15 of those 31 methods taught by the person who created it.

There was no copyright protection on shorthand (only on the books expounding it), so the entrepreneurs who wrote manuals, published magazines, sold supplies, and taught in the evening and through the mail had a chance to find a foothold in this rapidly expanding market. Although Graham often called his methods the Standard and the American shorthand, there was no consensus on his behalf to justify those words. In 1891, one man boasted that "for over 20 years I have intended to publish my own 'system,' entitled GRAFONY— AMERICAN SHORTHAND. You will soon see that it is 'a new thing under the sun.'"[57] Those ambitions never panned out, but John Gregg in that same decade introduced his version of phonography that soon became widely adopted for its simplicity and its resemblance to cursive handwriting.

As the competitors jostled for students, they often cast shorthand as a fast track to white-collar employment. The average course listed in the 1890–1891 survey took six months—less time than Woodrow Wilson needed to become proficient—yet many places offered three-month terms, and occasional promises along the lines of "ten easy lessons" appeared. The titles of many manuals and books proclaimed the fast and easy acquisition of a skill that required diligent practice and extensive memorization—Simplified Shorthand, Shorthand Made Easy, Ten Days Shorthand Complete, The So Short Phonic Shorthand, Shorthand Shortened, and the boastful Stenography reduced to certain and fixed principles—whereby the acquisition of that once-tedious, dry and difficult science may be readily acquired and easily retained.

Competent court and newspaper reporters could never be trained so fast; the inflated claims in the 1880s and later from "scab schools" and "loud sounding so-called Colleges" played on the dreams of finding respectable office work as quickly as possible.[58] What had been valued as a tool for a few well-educated men in Tudor–Stuart England and colonial America became a vocational skill for female secretaries.

Learning shorthand to take notes and appreciate the language? That was one shortcut that, if more widely adopted, might have benefited millions. But that long-range strategy required a large short-term investment of time and energy that most people were unwilling to make.

SPEED-READING

Dismissing shorthand as a hoax was not the criticism that its advocates faced; they quarreled with each other about the relative merits of different methods, not about the legitimacy of the entire enterprise. In like fashion, the simplified spellers did not have to prove that phonetic spelling was possible. The issue was that it should be done, not that it could be done.

For speed-reading, there were always doubts that it could be done. Modest acceleration, yes, but flying along at three times the normal rate of 300 words per minute without a significant drop in comprehension? Researchers have always been skeptical. At supersonic speed, reading becomes skimming, and the subtleties of the text vanish.[59] One skeptic said that the Gettysburg Address would be nothing more than "here's again in on of what should consecrate would to we the living who to be from which resolved God people time."[60] The focus of reading specialists has been the diagnosis and treatment of slow reading, not the acceleration of the proficient.

"IT SOUNDS INCREDIBLE but Evelyn Wood graduates can read *The Godfather* in 64 minutes"—477 pages in little more than one hour. At that rate, college students could save 630 hours on their annual assignments "without any drop in comprehension!" Why not come to a free introductory lesson? "You'll increase your reading speed 50 to 100% on the spot!"[61]

The best-known rapid reader of the 20th century, Utah high school teacher Evelyn Wood, answered the skeptics by claiming that rapid reading could be very rapid. In the late 1950s, she interviewed dozens of speed readers who had developed their exceptional prowess without special training. Figuring out what they had in common became the basis for her Dynamic Reading courses. Two bad habits had to stop—silently saying the words (*subvocalizing*) and going backward to reread (*regression*). A new habit had to be learned—rather than look at individual words, take in phrases. She reminded students that they saw more than the details when they drove a car, watched an animal, or admired a mosaic. How could that be done with print? Never read line by line. Use a finger to trace new patterns for the eyes to follow. If attention wanders, put red nail polish or a red Band-Aid on the finger:

- *Half and half*: Read the first half of the first line and the second half of the second line.
- *Zig*: Read diagonally—from the first word of the first line to the last word of the third line.
- *Zigzag*: The same but going left to right after each right to left.
- *Roll-away*: Spiral motions down the page.
- *Lazy L*: Resembles the symbol for the British pound; repeat several times on each page.
- *Big E*: Capitalized E but backward, with loops instead of straight lines.
- *S, X, and Z*: Just as they look.
- *The middle sweep*: Finger under the middle third of each line.
- *Beeline*: Finger moves straight down the center (best for narrow pages).

How could anyone retain ideas when sailing through the pages? To get anything valuable from a text required a sense of the entire work, just as a city can be glimpsed from an airplane. Let the words pour in until the "total concept" of the text emerges. With a few "magnet ideas," the smaller points can be retrieved. Those magnets were often visceral—Wood wanted readers to feel the tone and mood that the writer established. But the reader's reactions, not the writer's intentions, mattered most. "Meaning is inside people, not in words," she liked to say.

The script for one lesson put the point this way: "Your mind does not register what's in front of your eyes; it is your eyes that register what is in the back of your mind."[62] Wood never explained how "the back of your mind" initially took shape and changed over time, nor did she address the question of whether interpretation was entirely subjective. She preferred metaphors ("the eyes are to the mind what the feelers are to the insect") over close analysis of how the brain works.

What she clearly conveyed was faith in the capacity of ordinary people. Anyone of average ability who had the motivation, stamina, and

$150 to take her 30-hour course and do one hour of daily homework for 12 weeks could make dramatic gains. When she heard one student worry that she would never improve, Wood told her, "Young lady, if there is any doubt in your mind about ultimate success, I promise you that you will fail. You must have perfect confidence in yourself."[63] In a teacher's manual, she stressed the importance of optimism. The calm and cheerful person "will reach his goals if he has clear purpose, faith, and persistence." Wood said that instructors might therefore want to read inspirational books such as *Wake Up and Live* or *Think and Grow Rich*, both of which extolled the importance of belief.[64] For her own uplift, the devout Mormon collected short "thoughts for the day," little quotes on diligence and warnings against fear and doubt—"Let CAN DO be your servant," "An idle life is death anticipated," and "We must believe in ourselves."[65]

Another way to dispel doubt featured the spectacular accomplishments of a few superstars. Wood arranged demonstrations, often as part of a free lesson, of the prowess of exceptionally swift former students. She could have done those herself—her own rate of 6,000 words per minute let her finish the Old Testament in one afternoon—but she hired younger talent (approximately three-quarters of the people who took her course were age 25 or younger, and about two-thirds were enrolled in school or college).[66]

For instance, high school senior Robert Darling of Wilmington, Delaware, could rip through a biography of Mozart (he'd never seen it before) at four seconds per page, hand it to an audience, and answer their questions. He later recalled that his average rate was 1,500 to 2,000 words per minute, and even that could be a stretch—1,000 to 1,200 words per minute was ideal. Reaching peak speed required intense concentration. "I was in a trance, and after a few minutes my eyes hurt."[67] Newspaper headlines, however, proclaimed his fastest pace—15,000 words per minute—and marveled at the 4,000 books he had read in one year.[68] Television shows also focused on peak performance. Darling was a guest on the *Art Linkletter Show*, and another Delaware prodigy, Louise Mahru, appeared on *I've Got a Secret*, holding a copy of *Gone with the Wind*. The panelists failed to guess her secret—she had read the book in one hour.[69]

Dynamic reading also gained legitimacy from other superstars: famous people took the course and praised it. Several U.S. senators raved about the results. Herman Talmadge of Georgia wanted schools across the country to adopt it, and Wisconsin's Senator William Proxmire appeared in advertisements for Dynamic Reading ("he reads a book in 40 minutes"). Wood gave her course to 10 White House staff members in 1962. "They weren't very good students because they were always travelling somewhere," she said in 1970, but the publicity was priceless.[70] Later, her colleagues taught speed-reading to a dozen of President Nixon's aides, and in the late 1970s, Jimmy Carter and his family enlisted. In Denmark, Queen Ingrid, after personal tutoring by Wood in the Royal Palace, finished *Moby Dick* in three hours.

Not surprisingly, Wood herself became famous. In print and on television, she looked reassuringly normal, a close resemblance to Mamie Eisenhower. Her talks were precise and well organized. "She spoke in sentences and paragraphs. I could hear the punctuation marks," Robert Darling said. She spent most of 1961 and 1962 on the road giving speeches and visiting several dozen local branches of Reading Dynamics.

Wood tried to connect her controversial methods with the technological revolution that was transforming many aspects of contemporary America. Acceleration was the mark of computers, jet airplanes, space travel, and laser beams. Wood's parents owned a horse and buggy— "Little did I think I would live to see the time when a man would circle the earth three times in four hours!"[71] If Americans could split the atom, track satellites millions of miles away, and build missiles, why shouldn't reading methods also make spectacular advances? Just as shorthand experts compared their craft to the marvels of the telegraph and steam printing press, Wood linked rapid reading with other awe-inspiring forms of previously unimaginable speed that Americans respected.

The national marketing was no guarantee of financial success. Four similar companies were already in business when she moved to Washington, D.C., to take her approach nationwide in 1960. Her rivals did more than teach small classes; they also had corporate clients and worked with school districts (often Catholic schools) and colleges, frequently offering remedial reading courses.[72] Wood quickly won contracts with large corporations (GE, Lockheed, IBM, Xerox, CBS, United Air Lines, Shell Oil, and a half dozen others) and a handful of colleges and school districts, but the heart of her company was in the speed-reading classes taught by her 25 local "institutes" across the country. District supervisors oversaw five institutes, with a "promotional assistant" to drum up enough new business to open more institutes. It was an expensive structure—each institute was projected to spend at least $40,000 annually, and the total district overhead exceeded $200,000.[73]

It might have worked if the expansion had not been so fast, with all 25 centers opened within one month, and if Wood's husband, Doug, had not been the president. His previous job was selling commercial ironing machines in Utah, where his territory was split in half when his performance lagged.[74] On tour with his wife, they flew first class, stayed in fine hotels, ate at the best restaurants, and asked one of their high school student-demonstrators, "Are you sure we are paying you enough?"[75] In 1962, the tottering company had to reorganize under new management, with Evelyn Wood concentrating on instructional methods and public relations.

The Woods' federal tax returns reveal that they did well but never got rich. From 1967 through 1971, their annual income ranged from $53,383 to $68,949. In 1965, the Woods returned to Salt Lake City, where they held the Utah and Idaho franchise (with no franchise fees to the parent company, which paid her as a consultant for up to 60 days a year). The sale of the company for $3.7 million to the Famous Artists Schools in 1967 was not a windfall for her; the Woods' 1971 tax return reported only $4,506 in dividends and interest. When the Famous schools went bankrupt in 1972, her $20,000 annual retainer ended; in 1973, the Utah–Idaho revenues plummeted, and 1974 was even worse.[76] Doug Wood retired, and Evelyn kept working for the new owners of the national chain, but their bank accounts never reflected the national reputation Dynamic Reading achieved by the early 1960s. Creating a novel and attractive shortcut was no guarantee that it would be lucrative or even profitable.

Staying solvent, a challenge faced by the advocates of all three reforms discussed in this chapter, might not have been so difficult if simplified spelling, shorthand, and speed-reading had found homes in the nonprofit sector. Promoted as research, affiliated with a university, endorsed by scholarly societies, funded by the government: those options were the paths not taken. Simplified spelling came closest to those paths, but as with shorthand and speed-reading, the messianic leaders saw little need for further exploration of the intricacies of language.

The intensity of a Melvil Dewey or Evelyn Wood found its outlet in the marketplace rather than the seminar room—they took their wares directly to the public. Notwithstanding occasional efforts to convince educators to mandate their methods, they had better luck selling their remedies as a choice, an option that anyone could try. Asking people to devote time and money and effort and exertion to a shortcut that might pay dividends in the future: the market was there, but it was smaller than the Deweys and the Woods imagined.

LINKS

A parody of Evelyn Wood (with Dan Aykroyd, Bill Murray, and Ray Charles): www.nbc.com/saturday-night-live/video/evelyn-woodski-slow-reading-course/3007522?snl=1
The 1920 Handbook of Simplified Spelling: https://archive.org/details/handbooksimplifooboargoog
Samples of shorthand: http://www.omniglot.com/writing/shorthand.htm

NOTES

1. *New York Times*, December 26, 2002, B-2; Victor Erofeyev, "Dirty Words," *New Yorker*, September 15, 2003, 42; James Gleick, *Faster: The Acceleration of Just about Everything* (New York: Pantheon Books, 1999), 206.

2. William Moulton to Norman A. McQuown, March 5, 1951, Dean of the College Papers, Box 17, folder 1, University of Chicago Archives.

3. Ralph Tyler to Robert Hutchins, January 19, 1942, President's Papers, 1925–1945, Box 79, folder 7, University of Chicago Archives.

4. Sylvia Nassar, *A Beautiful Mind* (New York: Simon & Schuster, 1998), 60.

5. Tamara Plakins Thornton, *Handwriting in America: A Cultural History* (New Haven, CT: Yale University Press, 1996), 67.

6. Rev. Thomas Hill, *The True Order of Studies* (New York: G. P. Putnam's Sons, 1876), 107.

7. Akira Okrent, *In the Land of Invented Languages* (New York: Spiegel & Grau, 2009), 288, 243, 246–47, 273–78.

8. Jill Lepore, *Book of Ages: The Life and Opinions of Jane Franklin* (New York: Knopf, 2013), 212–13.

9. Jill Lepore, *A Is for American: Letters and Other Characters in the Newly United States* (New York: Knopf, 2002), 15–41.

10. E. O. Vaile, *Our Accursed Spelling: What to Do with It* (Oak Park, 1901), reprint of F. A. Marsh's 1876 speech.

11. Paul D. Travers and Wallace Z. Ramsey, "Initial Teaching Alphabet a Hundred Years Ago?," *Elementary School Journal* 74, no. 5 (February 1974): 274–79.

12. Chris Ogren, "Complexities of Efficiency Reform: The Case of Simplified Spelling, 1876–1921," *History of Education Quarterly* 57, no. 3 (August, 2017): 333–70.

13. Editor, *Brooklyn Daily Eagle* to Melvil Dewey, February 1, 1898, Box 39, "Miscellaneous Correspondence" folder, Melvil Dewey Papers.

14. A. R. Spofford, *American Anthropologist*, April 1893, 153.

15. James Maguire, *American Bee: The National Spelling Bee and the Culture of Word Nerds* (Emmaus, PA: Rodale, 2006), 89.

16. Simplified Spelling Board Circular #10 (December 1906), Box 23, folder 136, David Todd Papers, Yale University Archives. To avoid that reaction, Eliza Burnz's stationery had a paragraph stating that she used *f* in place of *ph* and also dropped the final *e* unless the preceding vowel was long. Eliza Burnz to Julius Ensign Rockwell, November 26, 1889, Box 1, folder 3, Rockwell Collection, New York Public Library.

17. From a Simplified Spelling Board card in the Todd Papers.

18. Spofford, *American Anthropologist*, 153.

19. M. M. Hawes to "Friende Deweye," December 5, 1874, Box 83, "A–Z" folder, Dewey Papers.

20. For the doubts about the early 20th-century gospel of efficiency, see Jonathan Zimmerman, "Simplified Spelling and the Cult of Efficiency in the 'Progressiv' Era," *Journal of the Gilded Age and the Progressive Era* 9, no. 3 (July 2010): 365–94.

21. Dewey to Andrew Carnegie, February 18, 1902, Box 84, "January–June 1902, A–I" folder, Melvil Dewey Papers, Columbia University Rare Book and Manuscript Library. In the spirit of simplification, Dewey often abbreviated the date of his letters: in this case, 18 F 02.

22. Melvil Dewey to Calvin Thomas, March 25, 1904, Box 85, "January–June 1904, A–M" folder, Dewey Papers.

23. Dewey to O. C. Blackmer, February 6, 1903, Box 84, "January–March 1903, A–L" folder, Dewey Papers.

24. Dewey to O. C. Blackmer, May 20, 1903, Box 84, "April–June 1903, A–I" folder, Dewey Papers.

25. Dewey to Carnegie, February 18, 1902. As the treasurer of the Simplified Spelling Board said in 1906, it was easier to oppose reform than to say, "I'm against simplification." *New York Times*, March 13, 1906.

26. Dewey to R. W. Mason, January 6, 1905, Box 85, "January–June 1905, A–Z" folder; Dewey to Editor, Book Hill, March 23, 1928, Box 39, "Efficiency Correspondence from Melvil Dewey" folder, Dewey Papers.

27. Anson Upson to Melvil Dewey, July 1896, Box 39, "M to Z" folder, Dewey Papers.

28. "The Reminiscences of Godfrey Dewey," p. 18 in Oral History Research Office, 1972, Columbia University Archives; Wayne A. Wiegand, *Irrepressible Reformer: A Biography of Melvil Dewey* (Chicago: American Library Association, 1996), 327.

29. Theodore Roosevelt to Thomas Lounsbury, April 30, 1907, Box 18, folder 389, Lounsbury Papers, Yale University Archives.

30. For the opposition to Roosevelt's order, see Zimmerman, "Simplified Spelling and the Cult of Efficiency in the 'Progressiv' Era," 372–74, and also Mark Sullivan, *Our Times: 1900–1925*, vol. 3 (New York: Charles Scribner's Sons, 1936), 176–90.

31. Theodore Roosevelt to Brander Matthews, December 16, 1906, in *The Letters of Theodore Roosevelt and Brander Matthews*, ed. Lawrence J. Oliver (Knoxville: University of Tennessee Press, 1995), 294–95.

32. H. L. Mencken, *The American Language: Supplement II* (New York: Knopf, 1961), 311; *Simplified Spelling Bulletin* 8, no. 1 (April 1919); *New York Times*, November 29, 1906.

33. Richard L. Venezky, *The American Way of Spelling: The Structure and Origins of American English* (New York: Guilford Press, 1999), 36, 40.

34. Andrew J. Graham, *Brief Longhand* (New York: A. J. Graham, 1857), ix.

35. Woodrow Wilson to Andrew Jackson Graham, April 24, 1875, in Arthur S. Link, ed., *The Papers of Woodrow Wilson* (Princeton: Princeton University, 1966), vol. 1, 62.

36. July 17, 1874, notebook entry, *The Papers of Woodrow Wilson*, 57.

37. Woodrow Wilson to Andrew Jackson Graham, April 24, 1875, *The Papers of Woodrow Wilson*.

38. Adele Davidson, *Shakespeare in Shorthand: The Textual Mystery of King Lear* (Newark: University of Delaware Press, 2009), 23.

39. Claire Tomlin, *Samuel Pepys: The Unequalled Self* (New York: Knopf, 2002), 208, 206. For the shorthand Pepys used and the difficulty of transcribing it, see Robert Latham and William Matthews, eds., *The Diary of Samuel Pepys*, vol. 1 (Berkeley: University of California Press, 1970), xlix–lxvii.

40. Richard S. Westfall, "Short-Writing and the State of Newton's Conscience, 1662," *Notes and Records of the Royal Society of London* 18, no. 1 (June 1963): 13–14.

41. Edmund S. Morgan, ed., *The Diary of Michael Wigglesworth, 1653–1657: The Conscience of a Puritan* (New York: Harper and Row, 1965), 3, 36.

42. E-mail correspondence with Professor Mary Beth Norton (Department of History, Cornell University), December 2, 2014.

43. I use the words *phonography*, *stenography*, and *shorthand* interchangeably in these pages; most 19th-century publications also did so.

44. Alfred Baker, *The Life of Sir Isaac Pitman* (London: Sir Isaac Pitman and Sons, 1913). Dissertations on the history of shorthand are less valuable than the late 19th-century shorthand journals and magazines, but there are useful tidbits in Woodrow W. Baldwin, "History of Shorthand Instruction in Schools of the United States" (unpublished EdD dissertation, University of California, Los Angeles, 1952); Edna Lyndall Gregg, "The Teaching of Shorthand prior to 1900" (unpublished EdD dissertation, Indiana University, 1955); and Roger Landroth, "The History and Development of Pitmanic Shorthand in the United States, 1843–1976" (unpublished EdD dissertation, New York University, 1977).

45. Michael Burlingame, *Abraham Lincoln: A Life* (Baltimore: Johns Hopkins University Press, 2008), 489; Walter B. Stevens, *A Reporter's Lincoln*, ed. Michael Burlingame (Lincoln: University of Nebraska Press, 1998), 70; Rodney O. Davis and Douglas L. Wilson, *The Lincoln-Douglas Debates* (Galesburg, IL: Knox College Lincoln Studies Center, 2008), xxxiii–xliii.

46. *Proceedings of the New York State Stenographers Association* (Albany, NY: Weed-Parsons, 1899), 154. Another gaffe was the rendition of Greeley's quote from Shakespeare: "tis true tis pity; and pity tis, tis true" came out as "tis two, tis fifty; tis fifty, tis fifty two."

47. Sharon H. Strom, *Beyond the Typewriter: Gender, Class, and the Origins of Modern American Office Work, 1900–1930* (Urbana: University of Illinois Press, 1992). The 1870 federal census listed only 154 stenographers and typists, according to Ileen A. DeVault, *Sons and Daughters of Labor: Class and Clerical Work in Turn-of-the-Century Pittsburgh* (Ithaca, NY: Cornell University Press, 1990), 16.

48. For Pulsifer and Smith, see the January and April 1878 issues of *Browne's Phonographic Monthly*. I found 12 more autobiographies in *Illustrated Phonographic World* (1894), *The Phonographic Magazine* (1894), and the 1877 issues of *Browne's Phonographic Monthly*. Only one of the 12 (Edward Murphy) devoted his entire career to stenography (but even he studied law when Congress recessed). I also read comments by and about pioneering ste-

nographers in *The American Journal of Stenography* (1872–1875), *The Exponent* (1884–1885), *The Phonetic Advocate* (1871), *Rapid Writer* (1875–1876), *The Shorthand Writer* (1886), and *The Student's Journal* (1883–1886).

49. *The Phonographic Magazine*, May 1, 1894; *Brown and Holland Shorthand News*, November 1882. For doctor–editor–teacher–phonographer Isabel Barrows and her phonographer–minister–congressman–prison reformer–author husband Samuel, see Isabel Barrows, *A Sunny Life: The Biography of Samuel June Barrows* (Boston: Little, Brown, 1913).

50. For insightful comments on independence, ambition, and many other aspects of 19th-century stenography, see Carole Srole, *Transcribing Class and Gender: Masculinity and Femininity in Nineteenth-Century Courts and Offices* (Ann Arbor: University of Michigan Press, 2010), 35–42, 106–7.

51. Walter M. Merrill, *Against Wind and Tide: A Biography of Wm. Lloyd Garrison* (Cambridge, MA: Harvard University Press, 1963), 234.

52. Madeleine B. Stern, *The Pentarch: A Biography of Stephen Pearl Andrews* (Austin: University of Texas Press, 1968).

53. *The Standard-Phonographic Visitor*, October 1866; *Browne's Phonographic Monthly*, August 1877.

54. *The Phonographic Quarterly*, July 1871.

55. Julius Ensign Rockwell, *The Teaching, Practice, and Literature of Shorthand*, Circular of Information No. 2 (Washington, DC: Bureau of Education, 1884). Of the instructors, 5.6 percent were ministers (in 1891, the percentage rose to 6.9 percent as more and more Catholic schools taught shorthand).

56. Julius Ensign Rockwell, *Shorthand Instruction and Practice*, Circular of Information No. 1 (Washington, DC: Bureau of Education, 1893). Many of the entries on the 1882–1883 tally disappeared by 1891—for instance, only eight of the 42 listings for Illinois and Massachusetts reappeared. The pace of change continued in the 1890s—Rockwell later said that publication in 1893 meant that the statistics were already out of date. Julius Rockwell to C. C. Beale, December 15, 1901, Box 2, folder 3, David O'Keefe Collection, New York Public Library.

57. W. H. Grigsby to J. B. Howard, March 23, 1891, Box 1, folder 1, James B. Howard Papers, New York Public Library.

58. Lisa M. Fine, *The Souls of the Skyscraper: Female Clerical Workers in Chicago, 1870–1930* (Philadelphia: Temple University Press, 1990), 15.

59. For a recent review, see Keith Rayner et al., "So Much to Read, So Little Time," *Psychological Science in the Public Interest* 17, no. 1 (May 2016): 4–34. For earlier criticisms, see "Speed Reading," in Marcel Adam Just and Patricia Carpenter, *The Psychology of Reading and Language Comprehension* (Boston: Allyn and Bacon, 1987), 425–52. They said that the speed readers with decent comprehension used their prior knowledge of a subject to infer

connections among different parts of a text. In the early 1960s, Columbia University professor Eugene Ehrlich gave speed readers a text in which lines from another book had been interspersed throughout. They did not notice. "Speed Reading Is the Bunk," *Saturday Evening Post*, June 9, 1962.

60. Clifford Owsley, "Confessions of the World's Fastest Reader," *Saturday Review*, June 9, 1962.

61. Undated advertisement, Box 19, folder 24, Evelyn Wood Papers, Utah State Historical Society, Salt Lake City.

62. The quotes in this paragraph are from "Student Manual," lessons 3, 4, and 9, Box 3, folder 2, Evelyn Wood Papers. A Japanese writer had a simpler explanation—because she had two eyes, she read two lines simultaneously. Robert Lyons Danly, *In the Shade of Spring Leaves: The Life and Writings of Higuchi Ichiyo, a Woman of Letters in Meiji Japan* (New Haven, CT: Yale University Press, 1981), 12.

63. Quoted in Jeffrey Alexander, "Evelyn Wood: Most Just Waste the Money," *The Harvard Crimson*, May 3, 1967.

64. "Teacher's Manual, 1962," Box 8, folder 3, Evelyn Wood Papers.

65. "Thoughts for the Day," Box 9, folder 1, Evelyn Wood Papers.

66. "Statistical Report" for 1969 and 1970, Box 17, folder 7; "Statistical Report" for 1971, Box 17, folder 8, Evelyn Wood Papers. With so many students enrolled, Wood's speed-reading courses included tips and advice on how to study. The statistical reports also reveal that 78 percent of the students were male.

67. Telephone interview, July 21, 2015.

68. "Boy Reads 15,000 Words a Minute Using New Technique" and "Students Learn How to Read Books About as Fast as They Turn Pages," Box 19, folders 28 and 27, Evelyn Wood Papers.

69. "Brandywine High Graduate Baffles TV Panel Show with Speed Reading," *Wilmington Evening Journal*, June 24, 1961.

70. Peter Kump to Evelyn Wood, May 14, 1970, Box 15, folder 5, Evelyn Wood Papers.

71. "Annual Education and Reading Conference, University of Delaware, March 3, 1962," typescript, Box 18, folder 14, Evelyn Wood Papers.

72. "Competition," Box 26, folder 11, Evelyn Wood Papers. Readak, Dan Ro, Baldridge Reading, and Reading Laboratory never claimed that their students would reach extraordinary speeds.

73. "Instructional Units—Field" and "Administrative Units—Field," Box 24, folder 17, Evelyn Wood Papers.

74. R. J. Anderson to Doug Wood, August 23, 1957, Box 29, folder 1, Evelyn Wood Papers. The Woods were two of the five partners in a local institute, and a balance sheet for the first half of 1962 reveals income of $28,312 and

expenses of $84,669. "Institute Operating Statement," Box 24, folder 20, Evelyn Wood Papers. The Wood Papers contain very little information on the national organization; the collection is strongest on the instructional materials she created and the Utah–Idaho franchise she and her husband managed.

75. Interview of Robert Darling, July 21, 2015.

76. Federal tax returns for 1956, 1959, 1965, and 1971 are in Box 27, folder 1 (the "income averaging" used in 1971 provided the figures from 1967 through 1971). Box 23, folders 5–10, trace the Utah–Idaho franchise revenues, advertising expenses (from 15 to 25 percent of annual revenue), bad debts (very few), and annual profits (30 percent of annual revenue in 1967–1969, the best years) from 1966 through 1973.

EPILOGUE

The Enduring Appeal of Shortcuts

Why do Americans still seek shortcuts? The history of educational sprints has been so mixed that one might predict less and less interest in the fast lane. The faster-easier shortcuts to success and culture (sketched in chapters 1 and 2) abounded, but most people who tried them never finished, and those who did persevere rarely secured the ambitious goals they sought. The faster-harder shortcuts (profiled in chapters 3 and 4) also abounded, but they recruited far fewer volunteers. Furthermore, many of the shortcuts evoked doubts and criticisms even if their advocates' efficiency and ambition were praised.

Yet most Americans see education as an investment rather than an intrinsic pleasure to prolong, so getting it for a good price is a priority. People are prone to calculate the value of education outcomes and then decide what they will pay in time, effort, and cash. A favorable cost/benefit ratio is immensely important for everyone who sees schooling as a means to an end. If more education yields more status and more money (and that has not changed in recent years—if anything, it has intensified), then the entrepreneurs who promise the consumers an economical way to reap those rewards will stay in business. For instance, summer *bridge programs* for liberal arts college graduates offer fast introductions to accounting, finance, and other subjects learned by business majors, and the crash courses are sometimes called *boot camps* to suggest the no-nonsense intensity of the first two months of military training.[1]

Moreover, most Americans know that learning is usually full of challenges, fun moments notwithstanding. The teacher might be aloof or inept and the textbooks dull or difficult. Even with talented instructors and the liveliest materials, most students will stumble. They will fail on many first tries and thus need the grit to try again and again. They will have to unlearn their old preconceptions of a topic, an uprooting that can be harder than learning new ideas and methods. It is thus not surprising that many people want education to be less onerous—if not easy, then easier than it would otherwise be, and if not fast, then faster. Too easy and too fast might be worthless—foreign language tapes under the pillow at night, for instance—or even ruinous if cheating and plagiarism are detected. The lazy and the corrupt want to avoid any exertion, but most people in search of more education are anxious and a bit naive rather than slothful or dishonest. They want advice, encouragement, and as little pain as possible as they pursue their dreams.

What can convince the marketplace today that a shortcut is worthwhile? Aren't consumers more savvy, and isn't the government more vigilant? Hasn't an award-winning teacher written *There Are No Shortcuts* to underscore the importance of long hours and hard work?[2] In recent years, several shortcuts have gained credibility as something other than common sense by linking themselves to popular and well-respected academic fields. Psychology and computer science have been drafted frequently on behalf of shortcuts.

Thousands of *self-help* books have borrowed the ideas, language, and prestige of psychology. A paperback on *codependent relationships* or *toxic parents* lets the reader spend an afternoon on problems that might consume months of face-to-face therapy. Dale Carnegie's blockbuster self-help book *How to Win Friends and Influence People* promised on the first page to "make the principles of psychology easy for you to apply in your daily contacts."[3] Some books exonerate the reader—you are a victim, so it's not your fault—and others take the opposite approach—you alone have the power to transform your life. In either case, the emphasis is on what to do next. "Growth is hot, diagnosis is not. . . . I don't care what got me to where I am, just help me get to where I want to be."[4]

EPILOGUE

Catchy book titles offer straightforward answers—for instance, the best seller *All I Really Need to Know I Learned in Kindergarten*—and often count the small number of changes to make: Deepak Chopra's *The 7 Spiritual Laws of Success*, Suze Orman's *The 9 Steps to Financial Freedom*, Stephen Covey's *7 Habits of Highly Effective People* (three huge best sellers), and Dale Carnegie's chapter "Six Ways to Make People Like You." Diagrams also simplify the issues—for instance, the spiritual adviser to Oprah Winfrey and Lady Gaga drew a triangle with health, wealth, and love as the three points, with a circle in the center for purpose, to show MBA students at Columbia University what gives meaning to life.[5] The old correspondence school tactic of unveiling secrets from the experts—in simple folksy prose so that everyone can understand—appears in titles like *The Rules: Time-Tested Secrets of Capturing the Heart of Mr. Right*.

If reading a book is too onerous, it's possible to attend seminars, hear a speech, buy a DVD, call for advice at $1.99 a minute, or turn on the television to see Dr. Laura or Dr. Phil, who, along with other popular gurus, make a fortune from their "do this, get that, be happy" exhortations.

Linking a shortcut with the newest technology is another common association. Correspondence schools capitalized on the late 19th-century expansion of cheap and reliable postal service, but recent innovations seem more spectacular. Before the invention of computers, there were high hopes that radio, motion pictures, and television would make learning more efficient by sending the best instruction directly to millions of students, bypassing their less adept teachers. In the 1960s, teaching machines let students work at their own pace, moving ahead when they mastered small slices of the curriculum.[6]

The dawn of the PC brought CD-ROMs with snazzy titles like *Reader Rabbit* and *JumpStart*, and soon thereafter the Internet called into question the merits of the traditional classroom. With *online learning*, the obligation to go to campus at fixed times could be eliminated by virtue of well-designed multimedia instruction consumed whenever and wherever the students chose to log on. The traditional diplomas might soon be rivaled by *nanodegrees*—certificates for the completion of bundles of rigorous online courses finished, on average, in five months for $500.[7]

And, of course, technology made it easier to access information; the term paper that previously required days in the library stacks could now be done on a laptop, and the morning newspaper turned into online summaries from the *information concierges* at companies like Trimit and theSkimm. A tape-recorded lecture can be replayed at twice the original speed with no loss of comprehension thanks to modern software, or the professor can be bypassed with an online tutorial from Khan Academy, created by a man who, as an undergraduate at MIT, skipped most lectures in large classes.[8] And technology has given the language a new word for shortcuts—*lifehack* covers everything that saves time, simplifies work, and solves problems.

Sounds too good to be true? The weak spots in the self-help and the high-tech shortcuts have not escaped notice. *How to Lose Friends and Alienate People* mocked Dale Carnegie as manipulative and insincere.[9] Covey's *7 Habits* became *The 7 Habits of Highly Defective People: And Other Bestsellers That Won't Go Away*, while *Who Moved the Cheese?*'s career advice was parodied as *Who Cut the Cheese?* A serious critique of the self-improvement genre blasted "one-dimensional answers to complex, heavily nuanced questions" and concluded with these lines: "We all want so badly to believe in miracles. That's what makes us vulnerable. And that's what makes them rich."[10]

And for technology, the warnings are less satirical than cautionary—don't get addicted to the quick jolts of dopamine from opening e-mails, checking Facebook, or sending tweets. Being busy isn't the same as being productive. Checking a portfolio every hour is rarely useful; as one journalist said, "The stock doesn't know you own it."[11] Beware of multitasking. Talking on the phone while reading the morning news rapidly (thanks to the text-streaming Spritz software) might seem efficient—spare everyone the work of finding what journalists call the *nut graf*, the paragraph with the basic points—but a Stanford University study found that multitaskers often lack focus, get distracted, and organize poorly. Daydreaming and procrastination should not be scorned—"You're more likely to let your mind wander. That gives you a better chance of stumbling onto the unusual and spotting unexpected patterns."[12]

Another connection between shortcuts and reputable academics has so far generated less criticism. Brain research that uses sophisticated diagnostic tools is revealing a variety of methods to improve our minds.

Some are common sense, others are counterintuitive, and they are all garnering respectful attention along with some hype. The next section explores what seems to be the latest chapter in the quest to find ways to be alert without returning to school or slogging through difficult books.

BRAIN POWER: AEROBICS, NEUROBICS, AND NOOTROPICS

If athletes usually enjoy the intrinsic pleasures of sports, most people exercise so that they will feel better and live longer. The short- and long-term extrinsic rewards vary from person to person, but on balance the physiological benefits are substantial. The payoff includes what we get (energy, stamina, and strength) and what we avoid (all sorts of medical ailments).

More and more evidence links fitness to mental agility. If people exert some effort for the sake of fitness, they can often reap the side effect of a sharper mind. "A Brain Tonic for Children" reported that active eight- and nine-year-olds outscored their peers.[13] At the other end of life, aerobic exertion lets older brains work more efficiently, using fewer areas of the prefrontal cortex to answer questions and solve problems.[14] Middle age has not been neglected by researchers; for instance, one study of female twins compared leg power and thinking skills. After 10 years, the twins with the strongest legs at the start outperformed their sisters.[15]

And for people who don't like to sweat, less vigorous exercise also enhances the mind. Newspapers often spotlight the good news with breathless enthusiasm. Dancing keeps the neurons nimble, as one septuagenarian scholar put it.[16] Yoga "brings creativity to the table," according to the *Wall Street Journal*.[17] Fidgeting in class helps schoolchildren with attention deficit/hyperactivity disorder (ADHD)—replacing a chair seat with an exercise ball, for instance, can do the job. "If they move their bodies while they're working it doesn't disturb anybody but it fills their own neurological need for motion and activity."[18] The office worker who might seem to be goofing off by squeezing a ball, clicking a pen, or playing with the pebbles in a $45 "Executive Sandbox" is in fact raising the odds of clear and creative thinking. Active hands can also benefit students—taking lecture notes with a pen is usually preferable to typing them on a laptop.[19] And an involuntary motion, a yawn, helps cool an overheated brain: "Reaction times slow and memory wanes when the brain's temperature varies even less than a degree from the ideal 98.6 Fahrenheit."[20]

A strategy more direct than exercise is *neurobics*, cognitive calisthenics to keep the mind fit. Games, puzzles, and other fun tasks promise to help young and old alike see patterns, recall words, solve problems, and so on. Mastering a particular subject or preparing for a high-stakes test is not the goal; neurobics will sharpen generic skills like concentration and speed. The market for brain training is growing rapidly, with the materials offered online, in books, or in franchised outlets of national chains. One estimate put annual sales at $1.3 billion in 2014.[21] Even the well-developed minds in New Haven, Connecticut, could have seen a "Who's Smarter Than You?" sign in the Yale Campus Bookstore, where a special display table in July 2013 featured *Brain Power*, *The Brain Workout*, *Achieving Optimal Memory*, *Make Your Brain Smarter*, *Brain Games for Word Nerds*, and, for a somewhat different slant, *The Sociopath Next Door*.

As the interest spread, so did the hype. Although the names of many vendors appealed to science—Cogmed, Neuronix, and Learning Rx—there was little rigorous evidence of enduring gains from the exertions, and Lumos Labs was fined $2 million by the Federal Trade Commission for unsubstantiated promises in its ads. Performance on the brain-training tasks usually rose, not surprisingly, without necessarily transferring to other tasks. Better benefits might be gained from traditional pursuits; for instance, learning to play a musical instrument often improves the novice's ability to plan, organize, and solve problems.[22]

Why bother with physical or mental exercise if swallowing will do the job? The shortest shortcuts could be *nootropics*—food, drink, or pills. The advantages begin before birth, not in the form of playing music for the fetus but in weight: "The chunkier the baby, the better it does on average. . . . All else equal, a 10 pound baby will score an average of 80 points higher on the 1,600 point SAT than a six pound baby."[23] And in the first year, "babies breast-fed less than a month had a mean I.Q. of 99 [as adults] compared with an average of 106 among infants breast-fed seven to nine months."[24] In the school lunchroom, too much fast food, which is low in iron and high in sugar, correlates with lower reading, math, and science scores.[25] A "Mediterranean diet" of fish, fruits, vegetables, beans, unrefined grains, and wine can slow the effects of aging. Adding a handful of nuts and a tablespoon of olive oil increases the benefits.

Most people struggle with diets—as Warren Buffet said about investing, it's simple but it's not easy.[26] The lack of self-discipline to follow a few rules over months and years dooms most resolutions to eat and drink prudently, thus the appeal of dietary supplements such as antioxidants, dark chocolate, ginkgo, and fish oil. The evidence for dietary supplements is weak; there is more consensus on what to avoid—cigarettes, hard liquor, and a slipshod diet that elevates blood sugar and hypertension. But what if a pill would work the miracle?

The breakthrough drugs for impotence, HIV, cholesterol, and dozens of other ailments raised hopes for the equivalent of Viagra for the brain. Strong coffee might be fine for extra alertness, but many students think Adderall and Ritalin are better. "I don't want to be at a disadvantage to everyone else. My grades weren't that great this year, and I could do with a bump," in the words of a college student who said her friends broke the law to find prescription drugs.[27] Over-the-counter vitamins and herbs packaged for the student market such as Cerebral Success or Smart X have done well.[28]

Older men and women yearn for comparable pills that would slow or prevent dementia, but in the meantime there is growing interest in what one doctor called cosmetic neurology—using drugs designed for specific medical problems (like attention deficit disorder) for healthy people who want a competitive edge. If plastic surgery can improve the looks of ordinary people, why not let doctors sculpt the minds of millions of men and women who can afford it?

That's one issue with all the brain boosters—who can afford them? Will the rich get richer because they can buy exercise classes, tutoring at Learning Rx, and a shelf of expensive drugs? Or are they within reach of everyone because the largest cost is time rather than money? As with many shortcuts, the brain boosters are sold in a lightly regulated marketplace, and the issue isn't just who can make a purchase but whether or not the merchandise is fraudulent.

Spam e-mail from a "Harvard Study" to fight brain bacteria, revive dead cells, and restore memory with a 10-second trick: that sounds completely bogus, and what about a *New York Times* advertisement for a brain oxygen–boosting miracle that removes "brain fog" and "erases

15 years of lost memory power"? Call toll free. Satisfaction guaranteed! Free rapid detox gifts for the first 500 callers! Who would fall for that?[29]

But because the ad carried a snapshot of two brain scans, the readers might not dismiss it. Recent research often features MRI brain scans before, during, and after an intervention. Reputable scientific journals convey the results of many studies, faculty at first-rate universities contribute to the literature, and President Trump's secretary of education owns part of Neurocore, where clients are likely to have sensors on their scalps and earlobes to monitor their emotional ups and downs.[30] Summaries of the findings appear frequently in serious newspapers. It's not as if a quack doctor is injecting goat glands to cure impotence, as John Brinkley did in the 1920s. The wonders of modern medicine and 21st-century science promise to do more than prove what common sense tells us should be true—fit body, fit brain. Maybe a few pills in the future will be able to clear away brain fog.

Until that time, there is another contemporary trend that is already established: thinking about thinking. Unlike the self-help platitudes, a series of excellent books have translated peer-reviewed research into clear prose for a large audience. Each book sketches the limits of shortcuts. Even the best seller *Blink: The Power of Thinking without Thinking* is more complicated than its subtitle lets on. Journalist Malcolm Gladwell celebrates snap judgments and first impressions in his charming descriptions of speed dating, improvisational comedy, forgery detection, marriage counseling, and more. Quick decisions "can be every bit as good as decisions made cautiously and deliberately," Gladwell claims early in the book. But it soon becomes clear that what he calls "thin slicing"—focusing on the most relevant information—works best after many years of experience, and he acknowledges in the final chapter that "we are often careless with our powers of rapid cognition" thanks to racial and gender stereotypes.[31]

So the title of Gladwell's page-turner could have been *Thinking, Fast and Slow*, which is what psychologist and Nobel laureate Daniel Kahneman called his longer and more nuanced book. Fast thinking (automatic reactions, intuitions, habits, and gut feelings) is usually reliable but stumbles on various biases and illusions, especially overconfidence. Slow thinking, marked by analysis, skepticism, self-control, and other effortful reasoning, can monitor and correct the impulsive fast thinking. Vigilance should keep watch on shortcuts.[32] In a more specialized book, *How Doctors Think*, Jerome Groopman made the same point. Fast-and-frugal diagnosis can let a doctor size up a patient in less than one minute, but it can also overlook alternative explanations. The urge to act can be too strong—as one of Groopman's mentors had to remind him: "Don't just do something, stand there." "Good thinking takes time," Groopman concludes.[33]

For the student in search of advice, several other popular books make the case against shortcuts. Don't trust the obvious—"the most effective learning strategies are not intuitive." Rereading a chapter, for instance, is less effective than taking a quiz; even better is taking a quiz before as well as after reading the chapter.[34] A well-written text can be a trap—"you can get the idea that it is actually pretty simple and perhaps even that you knew it all along."[35]

Better to undertake *desirable difficulty*, challenges that force the mind to shift gears, such as *interleaved practice*—for instance, on the putting green, alternate short, long, downhill, and uphill putts (and add some chip shots) rather than rely on *massed practice*, devoting 10 minutes to short putts, then 10 minutes to the long ones, then 10 minutes going uphill, and so on. An *effort mind-set* can dispel the notion that achievement requires innate ability, and *grit* helps students bounce back from failures that might otherwise be totally demoralizing.[36]

The how-we-think literature needs to reach far and wide, not just reaffirm what a few people already know. It's encouraging to see how well the books are selling, and it's also heartening that the world's most popular online course is called "Learning How to Learn."[37] In the past, many shortcuts oversimplified the complexities of learning, and as a result too many ambitious people gave up rather than persevered.

NOTES

1. *Wall Street Journal*, March 7, 2013; *New York Times*, May 31, 2013.
2. Rafe Esquith, *There Are No Shortcuts* (New York: Pantheon, 2003). Inspired by Esquith, the founders of the KIPP (Knowledge Is Power Program) schools adopted *there are no shortcuts* as a motto.
3. The 1936 book eventually sold more than 30 million copies, according to Steven Watts, *Self-Help Messiah: Dale Carnegie and Success in Modern America* (New York: Other Press, 2013), 3.

4. Steve Salerno, *SHAM: How the Self-Help Movement Made America Helpless* (New York: Crown, 2005), 113. For the growing impatience with long-term psychiatric treatment, see T. M. Luhrmann, *Of Two Minds: An Anthropologist Looks at American Psychiatry* (New York: Random House, 2000).

5. *Wall Street Journal*, February 3, 2016, B-5.

6. Bill Ferster, *Teaching Machines: Learning from the Intersection of Education and Technology* (Baltimore: Johns Hopkins University Press, 2014); David Tyack and Larry Cuban, *Tinkering toward Utopia: A Century of Public School Reform* (Cambridge, MA: Harvard University Press, 1995), chap. 5.

7. *New York Times*, September 17, 2015, B-7. As with correspondence schools, the majority of Udacity students who start do not finish, even with the significant incentive (never offered by correspondence schools) of recouping at graduation half of the tuition, which is paid month by month for Udacity courses in specific high-tech skills like Web development.

8. Salman Khan, *The One World Schoolhouse* (London: Hodder & Stoughton, 2012), 186–87.

9. Watts, *Self-Help Messiah*, chap. 12.

10. Salerno, *SHAM*, 104, 251.

11. Adam Smith, *The Money Game* (New York: Random House, 1968), 81.

12. *New York Times*, January 17, 2016 (Sunday Review), 1, 6.

13. *New York Times*, October 14, 2014, D-4.

14. *New York Times*, December 15, 2015, D-8.

15. *New York Times*, November 24, 2015, D-6.

16. Judith L. Hanna, "Need Smarts? Just Dance," *Teachers College Record* (online), October 30, 2015.

17. *Wall Street Journal*, May 12, 2015, D-3.

18. *Wall Street Journal*, June 23, 2015, D-1.

19. *Wall Street Journal*, March 3, 2015, D-1, D-4.

20. *Wall Street Journal*, August 19, 2014, D-1.

21. *New York Times*, October 26, 2014 (Magazine), 60.

22. *Wall Street Journal*, October 11–12, 2014, C-3.

23. *New York Times*, October 12, 2014 (Sunday Review), 9.

24. *Wall Street Journal*, May 8, 2002, D-2.

25. WebMD, May 2015, 12. For a fascinating history of the school lunch (including the fierce debates over what counts as nutritious, such as President Reagan's claim that ketchup was a vegetable), see Susan Levine, *School Lunch Politics: The Surprising History of America's Favorite Welfare Program* (Princeton, NJ: Princeton University Press, 2008).

26. CNBC television interview, June 14, 2002.

27. *New Yorker*, April 27, 2009, 34. For a good history of writers' fondness for coffee, liquor, marijuana, and other drugs, see Marcus Boon, *The Road of Excess: A History of Writers on Drugs* (Cambridge, MA: Harvard University Press, 2014). One shortcut attraction was the possibility that writing might become automatic, with the words dictated "by some unknown agency, without conscious effort" (Boon, *The Road of Excess*, 35).

28. Cerebral Success is well known to the audience of the *Shark Tank* television show. The entrepreneur who pitched the $69-per-bottle product in April 2014 heard objections from four of the five panelists: "There's too much competition," "There's no credible research to prove your product works," "You aren't famous," "It's unethical to give desperate students an edge over their hardworking peers." The fifth panelist, in contrast, said she knew there was a market for this product, including her ADHD husband who benefited from over-the-counter herbs and vitamins. Thanks to her connections, GNC stores sold it, with the clever new name Smart X. *Shark Tank*, season 5, episode 26, April 25, 2014.

29. *New York Times*, April 8, 2009, A-14.

30. For a skeptical account of Neurocore, see *New York Times*, January 31, 2017, A-1.

31. Malcolm Gladwell, *Blink: The Power of Thinking without Thinking* (New York: Little, Brown, 2005), 14, 252.

32. Daniel Kahneman, *Thinking, Fast and Slow* (New York: Farrar, Straus and Giroux, 2011).

33. Jerome Groopman, *How Doctors Think* (Boston: Houghton Mifflin, 2007), 34, 169, 268. At Groopman's Harvard and elsewhere, students spend time in museums where they must examine paintings carefully in order to sharpen their observational skills. "We are trying to slow down the students. . . . They have an urge to come up with a diagnosis immediately." *Wall Street Journal*, June 2, 2012, C-12.

34. Benedict Carey, *How We Learn: The Surprising Truth about When, Where, and Why It Happens* (New York: Random House, 2014), chap. 5.

35. Peter C. Brown, Henry L. Roediger III, and Mark A. McDaniel, *Make It Stick: The Science of Successful Learning* (Cambridge, MA: Harvard University Press, 2014), 116.

36. Carol S. Dweck, *Mindset: The New Psychology of Success* (New York: Ballantine Books, 2006); Angela Duckworth, *Grit: The Power of Passion and Perseverance* (New York: Scribner's, 2016). For a journalist's summary of the research on *deliberate practice*—focusing on particular skills in the presence of a coach—see Geoff Colin, *Talent Is Overrated: What Really Separates World-Class Performers from Everybody Else* (New York: Penguin, 2008), chap. 5. What has not yet reached the mass market is the power of *backward transfer*—

learning a new subject often enhances our understanding of a topic or skill previously learned. For an example of research on this overlooked shortcut, see Charles Hohensee, "Backward Transfer: An Investigation of the Influence of Quadratic Functions Instruction on Students' Prior Ways of Reasoning about Linear Functions," *Mathematical Thinking and Learning* 16, no. 2 (2014): 135–74.

37. *New York Times*, January 4, 2016, B-4.

RECOMMENDED READING

For the centuries not covered in this book, Ann Blair, *Too Much to Know* (Yale University Press, 2010), brilliantly explores medieval and early modern anthologies, abridgements, reference books, bibliographies, note taking, and other ways to cope with the *information overload* we mistakenly assume began in the 20th century.

Shortcutters knew how to sell, so the history of advertising is essential reading. The best book is still Roland Marchand's *Advertising the American Dream* (University of California Press, 1985). Beautifully illustrated and exhaustively researched, Marchand's book spotlights the fantasies of a better life (not just ownership of good products) that permeated sales and marketing. Another excellent history of advertising is Charles F. McGovern's *Sold American* (University of North Carolina Press, 2006), which stresses the point that "resources and privileges once enjoyed only by elites were now available to all" (98), a recurring promise made by shortcutters. For autobiographies by two advertising men affiliated with correspondence schools, see G. Lynn Sumner, *How I Learned the Secrets of Success in Advertising* (Prentice Hall, 1952), and John Caples, *Making Ads Pay* (Harper and Brothers, 1957).

The scholar-promoters who hawked great (and not-so-great) literature to the masses are skillfully examined by Joan Shelley Rubin, *The Making of Middlebrow Culture* (University of North Carolina Press, 1992), and Janice Radway, *A Feeling for Books* (University of North Carolina Press, 1997). Radway is more sympathetic than Rubin to the quest for pleasurable, entertaining, and useful books; Rubin is harsher on the entrepreneurs who assured their audiences that they could be sophisticated (or at least appear so) without much effort. Less well known is John C. Burnham's *How Superstition Won and Science Lost* (Rutgers University Press, 1988), a thorough history of the rise of easy-to-read summaries and condensations of scientific research in the early 20th century.

The title of Joseph Kett's insightful *The Pursuit of Knowledge under Difficulties* (Stanford University Press, 1994) points to the 18th- and 19th-century conviction that "to choose a course of mental improvement was to embark upon an ambitious enterprise that involved self-denial, persistence, and resilience" (xiii). Over time, adult education (Kett's topic) lost its early faith in strenuous intellectual exertion; for a rare defense of arduous study in middle age, see David Denby, *Great Books* (Simon & Schuster, 1996), the story of his year in two humanities seminars at Columbia University, and his recent *Lit Up* (Henry Holt, 2015), for his late-in-life rediscovery of great books alongside high school students. For more justifications of difficulty, see the valuable collection edited by Jonathan Culler and Kevin Lamb, *Just Being Difficult? Academic Writing in the Public Arena* (Stanford University Press, 2003), and David Mikic's superb *Slow Reading in a Hurried Age* (Harvard University Press, 2013).

Edwin Battistella's *Do You Make These Mistakes in English?* (Oxford University Press, 2009) is the only biography (of Sherwin Cody) in the meager scholarship on correspondence schools, where primary sources are hard to find (Battistella had to rely entirely on published material). A. J. Angulo, *Diploma Mills* (Johns Hopkins University Press, 2016), provides a concise and devastating history of for-profit colleges and universities.

Should higher education be shorter? Charles Eliot's 1897–1908 annual reports as president of Harvard University set forth his views (they are available online: search for "Harvard/Radcliffe Annual Reports" at http://pds.lib.harvard.edu). His successor, A. Lawrence Lowell, collected his essays and speeches in *At War with Academic Traditions in America* (Harvard University Press, 1934). Hugh Hawkins's analysis of Eliot, *Between Harvard and America* (Oxford University Press, 1972), has held up well, but we need a new biography of Lowell, who is too easily dismissed as a snob and a bigot rather than celebrated for his defense of intellectually coherent undergraduate education. For the

University of Chicago and Robert Hutchins's quest to substitute comprehensive exams for course credits, see the anthology edited by F. Champion Ward, *The Idea and Practice of General Education* (University of Chicago Press, 1950), and the meticulous biography by Mary Ann Dzuback, *Robert A. Hutchins: Portrait of an Educator* (University of Chicago Press, 1991).

In this book, I have emphasized the Ivy League and several other top-tier colleges; for the full range of American higher education, start with Roger Geiger's first-rate anthology, *The American College in the 19th Century* (Vanderbilt University Press, 2000), and then tackle Geiger's magnum opus, *The History of American Higher Education* (Princeton University Press, 2014), as well as the admirably focused overview by Charles Dorn, *For the Common Good* (Cornell University Press, 2017). For professional schools, Kenneth Ludmerer's books on the history of medical schools (*Time to Learn* and *Time to Heal*) and residencies (*Let Me Heal*) are exemplary. James Fraser, *Preparing America's Teachers* (Teachers College Press, 2006), traces the rise of the longer-is-better view of teacher education. Brian Tamahana, *Failing Law Schools* (University of Chicago Press, 2012), questions why each and every law school must span three years.

Don't take a shortcut because other people your age rarely move ahead quickly: the belief that "growth depended on a natural schedule that must be guarded and nurtured lest external pressures impair it" (88) is examined in Howard P. Chudacoff's *How Old Are You? Age Consciousness in America* (Princeton University Press, 1989), a book I would have used more fully if my chapters had paid more attention to children and teenagers. A related belief—some people are "late bloomers"—is a neglected topic that awaits its historian.

For readers less interested in history than the current views on whether there are legitimate shortcuts to learning, Nobel Prize winner Daniel Kahneman, *Thinking, Fast and Slow* (Farrar, Straus and Giroux, 2011), provides a "Yes, sometimes" answer that is more convincing than the praise of "the power of thinking without thinking," the subtitle of journalist Malcolm Gladwell's best seller *Blink* (Little, Brown, 2005). Most psychologists agree that it is more fruitful to think in terms of efficient strategies—knowing how to read, study, and prepare for tests—that take time and effort but in the long run save time and effort by eliminating the need to search for other ways to think. For a good summary, see Peter C. Brown, Henry L. Roediger III, and Mark A. McDaniel, *Make It Stick* (Harvard University Press, 2014).

Shortcuts abound when learning is less important than getting one or more valuable credentials. The ratio between investment (time and effort in school) and payoff (the extra income generated by having a diploma) is the crucial consideration for many students. That matters far more than personal growth, close friends, liberal education, or the intrinsic pleasures of reading, writing, and thinking. The books by historian David Labaree develop that point, especially his aptly titled *How to Succeed in School without Really Learning* (Yale University Press, 1997).

Several books take a different approach to shortcuts: they look (sympathetically) at the reaction against speed and hard work. Billy Ehn and Orvar Lofgren's *The Secret World of Doing Nothing* (University of California Press, 2010) is a graceful study of waiting, daydreams, and routines. Tom Lutz's *Doing Nothing* (Farrar, Straus and Giroux, 2006) is, to quote the subtitle, "a history of loafers, loungers, slackers, and bums in America," which unfortunately has nothing about schools or colleges. Like Lutz, journalist Carl Honore, *In Praise of Slowness* (HarperCollins, 2006), ranges widely. Food, medicine, sex, cities, work, and leisure—only the chapter on children brings us to education, but before then we learn about a Sloth Club in Japan, tantric orgasms, Super Slow weight lifting, the Italian origins of Slow Food, and a piece of music by John Cage that will take 639 years to finish.

INDEX

abridgements, 58, 63, 64, 126, 165
Adler, Mortimer, 47–49
Alexander Hamilton Institute, 7–8
Allen, Woody, 98
American School, 16, 22
AP (*Advanced Placement*), 77, 79, 112
Art Instruction School, 19
Atlas, Charles, 18, 39n49

backward transfer, 163n36
Bagg, Lyman, 82–83
Baldwin, Faith, 9
Butler, Nicholas Murray, 23, 116n26
Bryne, Robert, 28–29

Caples, John, 7, 31
Carnegie, Andrew, 84, 130, 131
Carnegie, Dale, 154, 155, 156
Catholic colleges, 19th century, 84, 116n24
Cerf, Bennett, 9, 27–28, 31, 122n94
Chautauqua Literary and Scientific Circle, 13–14
Classic Comics (Classics Illustrated), 53–55
CLEP (*College Level Examination Program*), 112
CliffsNotes: advertisements for, 59; Bluffer's Guides, 60; Cram Cast, 64; criticisms of, 62–63; origins of, 58–59; revenues, 60, 70n60; students' use of, 61, 71n64, 71n65; teachers' use of, 62, 71n70
colleges : early enrollment in 19th century, 81–82, 83; admissions requirements, 79–80, 83
Columbia University correspondence courses, 22–24
commercial schools, 78
Cornell University, 96–97
correspondence schools: dropouts' obligation to pay, 12, 17–18, 23, 39n49; enrollments, 1, 15, 18, 20, 22; hyperbolic claims, 3, 16, 21, 22–23; in research universities (1890s–1930s), 20–24; self-regulation, 16; zealous salesmen, 17
culture: criticism of shortcuts to, 56–57; liberal culture, 45–46; outline books, 50–52. *See also* Adler, Mortimer; Eliot, Charles W.; Warhol, Andy

Darling, Robert (speed reader), 142, 143
Denby, David, 51
desirable difficulty, 161
Dewey, John, 128
Dewey, Melvil, 130–131
Doctor of Arts degree: at Carnegie Mellon, 93; obstacles, 94–96; origins of, 93; requirements for, 92, 94–95
Dorne, Albert, 5, 6, 12, 19–20, 25
dual credit, 89, 99

Durant, Will, 50–52

early college programs, 99, 104
Eliot, Charles W. : *Harvard Classics* , 46–47; Harvard law school, 86; three year bachelors degree, 85, 88
Evans, Bergen, 9, 70n56
exercise, 157

Famous Artists School: advertisements, 10; expansion (1960s), 25, 26, 41n77; graduation rates, 11; instructors, 34n4; origins of, 5–6; profits and losses, 12, 26, 31–32, 36n26, 43n100; salesmen, 10, 27, 34n8
Famous Writers School: admission to, 10, 27, 35n15; advertisements, 8–9, 30; attacked by Jessica Mitford, 27–29; graduation rates, 11, 27; instructional methods, 11, 29, 30; market for freelance work, 28; origins of, 6; salesmen, 29, 30
Fawcett, Robert, 27
Federal Trade Commission, 16, 29–30, 38n43, 48, 158
Ford Foundation, 96, 104
Franklin, Benjamin, 127

Garrison, William Lloyd, 135
GED *(general educational development)* test, 105–106, 122n97
G.I. Bill, 106
Gladwell, Malcolm, 160
Goldberg, Rube, 6, 33n3
Graham, Andrew, 132–133, 137, 139
Great Books of the Western World, 47–49

Hall, Elizabeth, 100–101
Harper, William Rainey, 20–21
Harris, William Torrey, 128
Harvard University: comprehensive exams, 110–111; law school, 86; medical school, 87; Society of Fellows, 92. *See also* Eliot, Charles W.; Lowell, Abbott Lawrence
Harvard Classics , 46–47
Hicks, Granville, 34n6
Hillegass, Clifton, 58, 62, 63, 70n60

Hutchins, Robert M. : alliance with Mortimer Adler, 47, 49; early admission to law school, 89. *See also* University of Chicago

International Correspondence Schools: advertisements for, 14, 37n36; expansion (1960s), 26

Kahneman, Daniel, xvii, 160

La Salle Extension, 16, 17–18, 22
law schools: 19th century, 86; 20th century, 88–89, 117n38; evening courses, 86
Little Blue Books (1920s), 52–53
Lowell, Abbott Lawrence, 92, 110, 123n107

McGinley, Phyllis, 28
medical schools: 19th century, 87–88; 20th century, 85–88, 89–90; World War 2, 103, 104
Mitford, Jessica, 27–29, 42n91

Nash, John, 91, 125
National Home Study Council, 15–16
neurobics (brain training), 158
nootropics (food, diet,drugs), 158–160, 163n28
normal schools, 78–90

paint-by-numbers, 55–56
PhD (Doctor of Philosophy): foreign language requirements, 125; job market (1970s), 95; requirements for, 91, 98; six year BA/PhD, 96; time to complete, 90–91

Rockwell, Norman : Famous Artists guiding faculty, 5, 10, 25; financial gains and losses, 12, 32
Roosevelt, Franklin, 50
Roosevelt, Theodore, 131

Sarducci, Guido, 73
Schlesinger, Arthur Jr., 92
Schulz, Charles, 19
Scranton, William, 26, 41n81

INDEX

Serling, Rod, 2, 9, 30
Shahn, Ben, 19
Shakespeare, editions of, 62, 63
shorthand : before 19th century, 133; best-known experts, 135–137, 139; Lincoln-Douglas debates, 134; phonetic, 134; rivalries, 136–137, 138–139; teachers of, 137–138
Shmoop, 64–65
Simon's Rock : curriculum, 101; faculty, 100, 101; origins of, 100; students, 100–102
simplified spelling: objections to, 129–130, 131; origins of, 128; support for, 128, 129, 131
Society to Encourage Studies at Home, 13
Spark Notes, 61
speed-reading: criticisms of, 140, 149n59; methods of, 140–141; politicians' endorsements, 142; students' testimonials, 142
Stahl, Ben, 32
study strategies, 161

Teach for America, 107–108
Thug Notes, 65
Trump, Donald, 32
Tyler, Ralph, 98

University of Chicago: comprehensive examinations, 109; correspondence courses, 21–22; Mortimer Adler's seminars, 48; 6-4-4 bachelors degree experiment, 103, 105
University of Wisconsin, 24

van Loon, Hendrik, 50–51

Warhol, Andy, 57
Welk, Lawrence, 18
Wilson, Woodrow: dissertation by, 91; learns shorthand, 133; prefers 4 year bachelors degree, 113
Wood, Evelyn: *Dynamic Reading* course, 140–141; financial ups and downs, 144, 150n74; praise of modern technology, 143; reading speed, 6000 words per minute, 142; temperament, 141, 143
World War I, 105
World War II, 103–106

Yale University: acceleration during World War II, 103; Sheffield Scientific School, 78, 88; undergraduate life c. 1870, 82–83

ABOUT THE AUTHOR

Robert L. Hampel graduated with honors from Yale University and received his PhD in history from Cornell University. In 1981, his research shifted from 19th-century American politics to 20th-century education when he joined Theodore Sizer's "A Study of High Schools," a four-year appraisal of American secondary education. For the project, he wrote *The Last Little Citadel: American High Schools since 1940* (1986). In addition to several dozen articles, he was the coauthor of *Kids and School Reform* (1997), a study of 150 students in the Coalition of Essential Schools. More recently, he edited *Paul Diederich and the Progressive American High School* (2014), an annotated anthology one reviewer called "a terrific lens to see the ebb and flow of the history of progressive education" from the 1930s through the 1960s.

Since 1985, Hampel has taught education history, policy, and program evaluation at the University of Delaware, where he won three awards for outstanding teaching and twice served as interim director of the School of Education. In Delaware, Hampel has been a public service fellow for the governor, a trustee of the Sanford School, and a consultant to the Delaware Department of Education. Outside Delaware, he served from 2002 to 2011 as the secretary/treasurer of the national History of Education Society.

www.ingramcontent.com/pod-product-compliance
Lightning Source LLC
Chambersburg PA
CBHW020830020526
44115CB00029B/95